流畅美语会话系列

Fluent American English for Daily Communication

生活流畅美语

邱立志 编著
张道真 审订

北京大学出版社
PEKING UNIVERSITY PRESS

图书在版编目(CIP)数据

生活流畅美语 / 邱立志编著. —北京:北京大学出版社,2008.12
(流畅美语会话系列)
ISBN 978-7-301-14568-5

Ⅰ.生… Ⅱ.邱… Ⅲ.英语—口语—美国 Ⅳ.H319.9

中国版本图书馆 CIP 数据核字(2008)第 176237 号

书　　　名:生活流畅美语
著作责任者:邱立志　编著
责 任 编 辑:徐万丽
标 准 书 号:ISBN 978-7-301-14568-5/H·2144
出 版 发 行:北京大学出版社
地　　　址:北京市海淀区成府路 205 号　100871
网　　　址:http://www.pup.cn
电　　　话:邮购部 62752015　发行部 62750672　编辑部 62765014
　　　　　　出版部 62754962
电 子 邮 箱:xuwanli50@yahoo.com.cn
印 刷 者:北京汇林印务有限公司
经 销 者:新华书店
　　　　　　650毫米×980毫米　16 开本　18 印张　293 千字
　　　　　　2008 年 12 月第 1 版　2010 年 5 月第 2 次印刷
定　　　价:36.00 元(配有光盘)

未经许可,不得以任何方式复制或抄袭本书之部分或全部内容。
版权所有,侵权必究　举报电话:010-62752024
　　　　　　　　　　电子邮箱:fd@pup.pku.edu.cn

Preface（前言）

　　说起来真是惭愧，教英语二十余年却教出了很多不会说英语的"哑巴"学生，他们会读会写，就是听不懂，说不出。有人将此归咎于学生的不勤奋和考试制度的弊病，对此，我觉得这只怪我们做老师的懒惰，惰在没有把英语这门外语当作一种交际技能和工具教给学生，而过分强调了考试和考试的成绩。语言是一种交际工具，学习一门外语就是要学会用这种语言去跟别人开展交际活动，对学生来说就是一种技能了。阅读和写作是书面的交际技能，而听说则是口头的交际技能。

　　检讨以往的过失，不能仍然停留在原来的状态，那是不思进取的表现。所以，笔者觉得要做一些事情，不为别的，就是为了使得有觉悟的英语学习者真正把英语当作一项全面的技能去培养，听、说、读、写四项技能同步发展。鉴于目前仍有相当多的读者在英语听说方面存在障碍，本套书编写重在口头交际技能的培养和训练。当然，市场上关于英语口语训练方面的书籍种类繁多，但是水平也良莠不齐，存在着这样或那样的问题，最明显的一点是落后于时代步伐，很多口语书使用的材料过于陈旧，说法也已经过时。而英语是有生命力的，随着时代的前进，英语也在发展、变化，口语表达习惯更是与时俱进、不断变化的。还有就是许多书中并没有能够反映英语口语的客观实际，一些编写者对英语日常交流用语并不是很了解，所谓的"典型句型"并不是人们经常使用的，而很多常用的表达方式却没有反映出来。因此学习者只学到了皮毛，在肤浅的框架式英语结构中原地踏步，不能贴切或正确地运用到交流中去。

　　读者的选择往往是多方面的，不同的读者群有不同的偏好和需要，本系列力图覆盖以下几个方面。

　　出国之旅：出国的梦想是令人激动的，之所以激动是因为走出国门可以开阔眼界、感受异域风情；但是手续的繁杂、文化的差异，尤其是语言的障碍让很多人或者望而却步，或者倍感艰难，从而使许多人的出国梦想不得不搁浅。所以，这一专题细致入微地呈现了签证、登机等场景所需的习惯表达方式，让你从容踏上出国之旅。

　　日常交往：异域生活是新鲜的，同时也是琐碎的。我们每天都要面对：衣食住行、购物买菜、朋友聚会、生日宴会、乔迁之喜、结婚晚宴，以至生病住院等各个生活场景,这些都是在海外生活的每个人必须亲历的。而作为一个新的参与者,要想生活惬意,能够无障碍地交流,避免文化冲突,你就必须做一个有准备的人。

校园生活:海外求学是很多有志青年追求的人生目标。海外校园生活是丰富多彩的,许多情况与国内迥然不同,如果你不了解,感到茫然是不可避免的,从申请入学、注册、选课、咨询教授、学分等级、奖学金到校内打工等具体问题是无法从教科书中得到答案的。

旅游参观:在今天,到国外旅游已是人们尤其是越来越多时尚年轻人假期的主题活动。入住酒店、景点参观、客房服务、餐厅服务、通讯服务等既是旅游六要素"行、住、食、购、娱、游"的具体表现,又是旅游中不可或缺的环节,此专题让你在旅游中克服语言的不便,充分享受游玩的乐趣。

求职工作:不管是在境外公司,或是在中国外资企业的蓝领、白领甚至金领,还是到外资公司跃跃欲试的求职者,你都必须跟"老外"打交道。在车间、办公室、会议等各个场景你想躲都躲不掉,不能够灵活地沟通交流,将会给工作带来极大的障碍。

本系列可读性强,语言地道,内容权威,因为书中70%的语言材料来自于笔者本人在美国生活、学习的语言记录,并加以整理和提炼,生动而不失规范;30%的语言材料来自于已经出版的书籍、文献和网络等媒体,并根据本系列书的需要而采取了改编、吸收和融合等手段,以采众家之所长;张道真教授多年以来对笔者关怀备至,对本系列书稿进行了审订,修改了不少错讹和疏漏之处,并把自己在美国生活十多年的感受和经验融合其中。

口头交际技能的培养,不能只是学会英语句子,学习者还必须了解英语国家的政治经济制度、文化习俗、教育体系、消费习惯、历史传统等多个方面的内容,才能把已经学到的句子应用到真实的交际环境中去。正是基于如上的考虑,本系列各书的主题框架设计的如下:

话题导言(Topic Introduction)和背景知识(Background)是会话主题所在的文化氛围。一句话说出来是否得体,是要以其所在的文化背景来判断的。我们把这称作"交际的得体性(Communication Appropriateness)"。一句话说出来不得体,还不如不说,因为不得体的话轻则会让听者不知所云,或者会得罪人,或者会丧失生意机会,从而达不到交际的目的甚至起到相反的作用;重则可能影响国家之间的关系,造成不可挽回的损失或恶果。所以,得体性意识的培养是口头交际训练中不能缺少的一个环节。

Preface

前言

情景对话(Situational Dialogs)和典型句型(Typical Sentences)是语言的具体运用。任何一个句子只有存在于一定的语言环境(contexts)中才有确定的实际的交际意义。把话题置于情景和大的文化背景之下，就是想尽可能地展现语言的实际应用状态，让学习者在一定的实际状态下学习真实的交际技能。

难点注释(Notes)对情景对话和典型句型中的词语用法、特殊的语法现象、特别的含义以及理解困难的语句进行注解。

大道理谁都明白，归结到一点：掌握一种外语的口头交际技能，得体地有效地开展交际活动，最好的方式就是开口说出来！找到一切可能的机会与说英语的人保持交流！这样才能给书上死的句子赋予生命力！

邱立志

2008年5月5日

Contents (目录)

1. Greetings and Addressing ············· 1
   问候与称呼
2. Introduction ························· 9
   介绍
3. Making Compliments ··················· 15
   称赞与夸奖
4. Congratulations and Wishes ··········· 22
   祝贺与祝愿
5. Thanks and Responses ················· 29
   致谢与答谢
6. Apologies and Excuses ················ 35
   道歉与原谅
7. Weather and Time ····················· 41
   天气和时间
8. Parting and Farewell ················· 48
   道别与告辞
9. Renting an Apartment ················· 55
   租房
10. Applying for SSN ···················· 62
    申请社会安全号
11. Driver's License ···················· 68
    考驾驶执照
12. Buying a Used Car ··················· 74
    购买二手车
13. At the Supermarket ·················· 79
    超市购物
14. Buying at Farmer's Market ··········· 84
    逛农民市场
15. Going Yard-Sale ····················· 88
    逛庭院售卖

16. At an Electric Appliance Shop 94
    在电器商店

17. At the Barber's 101
    在男美发厅

18. At the Beauty Salon 107
    在女美发美容厅

19. Eating at a Restaurant 112
    餐馆就餐

20. Spending Holidays 119
    过节日

21. Chinese Festivals 126
    中国节日

22. Going to a Dinner Party 131
    参加宴会

23. At a Birthday Party 138
    生日晚会

24. Going to a Wedding 143
    参加婚礼

25. At a Potluck Party 148
    家常聚餐会

26. At a Public Library 155
    在公共图书馆

27. Arranging Children to School 160
    安排子女上学

28. At the Post Office 166
    在邮局

29. Phone Service I 172
    电话服务 1

30. Phone Service II 179
    电话服务 2

31. Mobile Phone Service 185
    移动电话服务

32. Network Service 190
    网络服务

33. Opening an Account 195
    开设账户

34. Depositing and Cashing 201
    存款和取款

35. Remitting Money 206
    汇款

36. Credit Card and Checks 211
    信用卡与支票

37. Renting a Car 217
    租车

38. Laundry Service 222
    洗衣服务

39. Making Appointments with Doctors 228
    预约看病

40. A Narrative of Sickness 233
    叙述病情

41. With a Dentist 241
    看牙科医生

42. With an Oculist 246
    看眼科医生

43. In Hospital 251
    生病住院

44. At the Pharmacy 256
    在药店买药

45. Getting Directions 261
    迷路问路

46. Something Wrong at Home 266
    家什故障

47. A Traffic Accident 272
    交通意外

Acknowledgements（致谢）............ 277

Greetings and Addressing
问候与称呼

Topic Introduction
话题导言

人们见面都要相互问候,这是人们相互交往的礼貌原则,古今中外,少有例外。但在问候的方式方法和内容上,不同国家与地区的人们因为文化上的差异,反映出不同的问候方式。中国与英美等西方国家远隔千山万水,历史发展进程也不同,积淀起来的文化差异更大,了解这种差异,对于我们出国留学、定居、旅游、访问以及和到中国来的外国人交朋友,非常有用。

问候的同时,还要称呼对方,如何称呼又是一门大学问,先生、小姐、太太、教授、博士、总统、主席、阁下等等,枚不胜举。称呼不当,容易获罪于人,也可能带来意想不到的后果。

和熟人见面总是要打招呼,也要互相问候。李康(Li Kang)刚去美国不久,交了新朋友,也偶遇老朋友。

Dialog 1

Li Kang: Hello, Mrs. Smith. How are you?
史密斯夫人,你好吗?

Mrs. Smith: Pretty good, thank you. How are you?
很好,谢谢。你呢?

Li Kang: Not bad, thanks.
不错,谢谢。

Dialog 2

Mrs. Smith: It's so nice to see you again, Prof. Li.
李教授,又见到你了,真高兴。

Li Kang: It's been a long time since last time, hasn't it?
从上次见面到现在好长时间没见了,是吗?

Mrs. Smith: You said it. How have you been getting along?
对极了,你还好吗?

Li Kang: Quite good. And what about you and your family?
我很好,你和你家人都好吗?

Mrs. Smith: All are pretty good, thank you. How was your vacation?
谢谢,全家都很好。假期过得还好吗?

Li Kang: Terrific. I went to Atlantic City with my wife and had a very good time there.
好极了。我同太太去了大西洋城,我们在那儿玩得真开心。

Dialog 3

Mary: Hi! Is that you, Li Kang?
嘿,是李康吗?

Li Kang: Hi, Mary. It's fancy meeting you here in Seattle. How are you?
哟,玛丽,想不到在西雅图见到你。你好吗?

Mary: Very well, thank you. And you?
很好,谢谢。你呢?

Li Kang: I'm very good. I got here yesterday for my vacation. My parents live near in Seattle, you know.
我很好。我是来这儿度假的。你知道的,我父母住在西雅图附近。

Greetings and Addressing

Mary:	How wonderful you are! I'm attending a scientific conference on marine resources.
	你太有福气了。我来参加一个海洋资源的学术会议。
Li Kang:	So you'll stay here a couple of[①] days, will you?
	这么说,你在这儿还会住几天,是吗?
Mary:	Yes. I'll stay here until this weekend.
	是的,我在这儿呆到周末。
Li Kang:	Great. Do you think we should have a get-together before you go back to New York?
	太好了。你看在你回纽约前咱们能否聚一下?
Mary:	Good point.[②] Our meeting ends Friday morning. How about Friday evening, at six o'clock?.
	好主意。我们的会议星期五上午结束。星期五晚上6点怎么样?
Li Kang:	Wonderful. Friday evening is all right for me. I'll pick you up then.
	很好。星期五晚上很合适,我到时来接你。

典型句型

1) How are you doing?
    你过得好吗?
2) How's it going?
    你好吗?
3) How are you today?
    你今天好吗?
4) How have you been?
    你近来好吗?
5) What's happening?
    有什么事吗?
6) What's up?
    什么事?

7) What's new?
什么新鲜事？

8) Long time no see.
好久不见。

9) I haven't seen you for a long time.
我很长时间没看到你了。

10) Long time no talk.
好久没和你通话了。

11) How are things going?
事情进展得怎么样？

12) How are you getting on?
你过得如何？

13) How are things with you?
你的事情进展得怎么样？

14) How are things?
情况如何？

15) How is everything?
一切如何？

16) How is life?
生活如何？

17) Very well, thank you. And you?
很好，谢谢。你怎么样？

18) Quite well, thank you. What about you?
很好，谢谢。你怎么样？

19) Wonderful, thank you. How about you?
好极了，谢谢。你呢？

20) Fine, thanks. And you?
好，谢谢。你呢？

21) Ok, thanks. And how are you?
还好，谢谢。你呢？

22) Not too good, I'm afraid. Actually, it's going from bad to worse. What about you?
我觉得情况不是很妙，实际上是每况愈下。你怎么样？

23) You can call me Bill.
你可以叫我Bill。

24) Just call me Bill.

叫我 Bill 好了。

25) Don't honey me.

不要心肝宝贝这样叫我。

背景知识

问候的表达：在正式场合,中国人见面常说"您好!",被问候的人也回答"您好!"。这同英语中的正式问候是一样的:How are you? 回答:Fine, thank you. And you? 而在非正式场合,差别就比较大了,中国人常问候"吃饭了没有?/你上哪儿去?/上班去呀?"回答的人则多半不会正面针对问题回答"没呢,你呢?/去买报纸,你呢?/是啊,你去买早餐呀?"而英语中非正式场合与正式场合基本一致: How are you doing? / Good morning, etc., 回答:Fine, thank you. And you? / Good morning, etc. 不难看出,正式场合下的问候方式,二者基本相同,主要因为我们的"您好"实际上是泊来品。在非正式场合,差异就大了。中国人的这种可谓奇特的问候语言,对于不谙汉文化的西方人来讲,简直是不可思议的。据专家研究,西方人对此的反应是,客气一点的人想:"你们为什么老问我吃了饭没有?我有钱。"更多时候则会认为:"It's none of your business!"(不关你事!)

Good morning(早晨好),用于早晨起床后至午饭前这段时间。Good afternoon(下午好)时间限定在午饭后至下午6点钟之前这段时间里。晚上6点钟之后,英语国家的人们相见则用 Good evening(晚上好)互相致意。Hello, Hey 和 Hi 是英语中的非正式用语,中文一般译为哈罗、嘿、嗨等词,有祝好的含义。Hello 一词英国、美国及其他英语国家均用。但 Hey 是英国英语,而 Hi 则是美国英语。在人们用以上套语互致问候时,常常伴有 How are you?或 How are you doing?比如,Good morning. How are you?(早晨好!你身体怎么样?)Hello. How are you doing?(你好!工作怎么样?)How are you?一语询问的是对方的身体状况,比较正式。而 How are you doing?则询问对方的工作状况,比较随便。

在英语国家,不太熟悉的人们,常常以谈天气来打招呼,比如 It's a fine day today, isn't it?(今天天气真不错,是吧?) It's a terrible weather today.(今天的天气真糟)。

称呼问题:英美国家的普遍称呼是"先生"(Mr.—mister)、"太太"(Mrs.—mistress)、"小姐"(Miss),但在这些之外,还有很多。

(1) 先生(Mr.):"先生"是称呼一般人士的呼语,Mr.多用于对无职称者或不了解其职称者的称呼,语气正式,关系不密切。如 Mr. John Smith 或 Mr. Smith(约翰·史密斯先生或史密斯先生)。而对于教授或博士应称其为"博士"(Dr.)或"教授"(Prof.)。Mr.也可以和职务连用,如 Mr. President(总统先生)、Mr. Chairman(主席先生)等。也可以和某些地名或国名、运动或职业名称连用,如 Mr. America(美国先生,男子健美赛冠军)、Mr. Baseball(棒球先生,用于表现出色而被评选出的最佳棒球运动员)。Mr.如果不与姓名连用,需要写做 mister,仍然是一个敬称语。mister 单用时,相当于 sir 的非正式形式,英、美英语中均有此类情形。如 Hey, mister, you dropped your wallet.(先生,你的钱包掉了。)

(2) 夫人(Mrs.):Mrs.主要用于对已婚妇女的称谓,和其丈夫的姓氏或婚礼后的姓名连用,如 Mrs. Jones(琼斯太太)、Mrs. Mary Jones(玛丽·琼斯太太)。Mrs.和 Mr.一样,也可以和地名、运动或职业名称连用,如 Mrs. America(美国太太,已婚妇女的选美冠军)、Mrs. 1988 In her Modern Kitchen(1988 年现代化厨房主妇)。如果 Mrs.单用,则需写作 missis,一般前面加定冠词 the,指一个人的妻子或家庭主妇。

(3) 女士(Ms.):Ms.(女士)是英语中近年来出现的一个女性敬称词。实际上,它是 Mrs.(太太)和 Miss(小姐)合成而来的,是妇女争取平等的产物,和妇女本人的姓名或姓连用,不与婚姻状况相联系。

(4) 小姐(Miss):是对未婚女子的称谓语。一般情况下,小姐一词要与姓氏或姓名连用。它也可以和地名或某一活动连用,代表某一地区或活动的妇女,如 Miss England, 1978(1978 年英格兰选美冠军)。美国南部的习惯 Miss 可以和名连用,如 Miss Lillian(莉莲小姐)。小姐一语也可以单用,比如,商店的售货员对年轻的女顾客可以以小姐称呼。

(5) 先生、阁下(Sir)和夫人、女士、太太、小姐(Madam)：是一组男女对应的敬称语，一般不与姓氏连用，它们表达的人际关系不亲密。具体说，Sir 是下级对上级、晚辈对长辈、士兵对长官、老百姓对警察、学童对老师、商店店员对男顾客的通用称谓语。美国社会上陌生人相见时，不少人以 Sir 相称。Madam 是对陌生女性的尊称，多见于商店店员对女顾客称呼使用。Sir 可以和姓名或教名连用，但不能和姓氏连用。当它和姓名或教名连用时，而表示此人有爵位。如 Sir John White 或 Sir John(约翰·怀特爵士或约翰爵士)。Madam 以前可以和教名连用，但现在主要和姓氏或职称连用，如 Madam Smith(史密斯夫人)、Madam President(总统女士或总统阁下)、Madam Chairman(主席女士)、Madam Ambassador(大使女士)等。

(6) 女士(Lady)：另一个用于女士的称谓语。我们经常听到人们在开会时说：Ladies and Gentlemen(先生们、女士们)。此外，Lady 常用来称呼贵夫人，如 Lady Smith(史密斯夫人)。Lady 也可以和职称连用，如 Lady President(总统女士)。其单、复数形式可以单独使用。比如，"Good morning, Ladies!"(女士们，早晨好。) "You dropped your handkerchief, Lady!"(小姐，你手帕掉了。)

(7) 职务称谓：和中文一样，英语中也有职务称谓，即用职务或职称来称呼他人。一般做法是：职称＋姓氏，如 Dr. Davis(戴维斯博士)、Professor Brown(布朗教授)或者 Doc. King(金医生或金大夫)等。有职称的人宁愿别人用"职称＋姓氏"来称呼，而不愿意接受"先生＋姓氏"的形式。对于学术界人士来说，用"先生"而不用职称称呼别人，有故意贬低被称呼者的意思。有博士学位的教授也可以用 Dr.＋last name(博士＋姓)的形式相称。只有对那些获得医学博士学位(MD)的大夫或医生才能单用 doctor 一词。而没有这一学位的医生只能用"大夫＋姓"的形式来称呼，可见 doctor 单独使用其敬意更深。英语中另一类职务称谓或衔称多见于对皇族、政府官员、军界、宗教界或法律界人士的称呼，如 Your Honor(先生或阁下)。而如下这些称呼，像 waiter(男侍者、男服务员)、boy(旅馆、餐厅的男服务员、男勤杂人员或家庭男仆)、conductor(汽车售票员)、usher(剧院领座员)等是存在的，但听起来不很礼貌，带有一种低下卑微的含义。

(8) 姓名称谓：在正式场合，或在陌生人之间，单独称名是不礼

貌的。可以称姓，但姓前必须冠以恰当的称谓语，如先生、太太、小姐、教授、博士之类。在熟悉的人们之间，包括亲友和同事，直接称名是很普遍的，用得最为普遍的是首名或教名的昵称。

Notes 注 释

① a couple of 意为"几个人，几件食物"，如：
She jogs a couple of miles every morning. （她每天早上要慢跑几公里。）

② Good point. 的意思是"有道理"，类似意思的表达还有：You got a point there. / You made a point there. / You got a good point there. / Good idea. / Good thinking. 等等。

Introduction
介绍

Topic Introduction
话题导言

　　初次见面离不开介绍,要么由别人来介绍,要么就自我介绍,如果没有介绍,就没有交谈的开始。别人介绍自己,要礼貌回应;自己介绍别人,要讲究方法;自己介绍自己,就要掌握谈话的主动权。中国人特别注重介绍,介绍朋友、介绍对象、介绍工作、介绍同学、介绍老师等等,有时是口头的,有时是书面的。读完硕士、博士找工作,最重要的就是要有导师的推荐信。同样,出国留学,对方也要求至少要有两位以上教授的推荐信。因此,懂得介绍,学会介绍,实在是一项立足于社会之技巧,不可等闲视之。

　　到了英美国家,或者接待外国朋友,介绍是少不了的。怎么用英语介绍自己和朋友,什么样的语言是礼貌的说法,如何回应别人的介绍,以及先介绍谁和后介绍谁等等,都是值得注意的问题。

Situational Dialogs
情景对话

　　刘杭(Liu Hang)和丁唐(Ding Tang)初次和别人见面,怎么自我介绍,怎么被介绍,都是需要注意的。

Dialog 1

Liu Hang: I don't believe we've met before. My name is Liu Hang.
我们是第一次见面吧,我叫刘杭。

Brian: It's nice to meet you, Liu Hang. I'm Brian.
很高兴见到您,刘杭。我是布赖恩。

Liu Hang: Nice to meet you, too, Brian.
见到您我也很高兴,布赖恩。

Brian: Are you working for① the University?
您在这个大学工作吗?

Liu Hang: No, I'm just studying here. Are you a graduate student?
不是,我只是在这里学习。您是这里的研究生吗?

Brian: Yes. My major is outdoor recreation and tourism.
是的。我的专业是户外消遣和旅游。

Liu Hang: Nice talking with you.② I've got to go. See you later.
很高兴和您交谈,我得走了。以后见。

Brian: See you.
再见。

Dialog 2

Brian: Mrs. Liu, I'd like you to meet Dr. Edward Smith.
刘女士,我想给您介绍一下爱德华·史密斯博士。

Liu Hang: How do you do, Dr. Smith?
您好,史密斯博士。

Dr. Smith: How do you do, Mrs. Liu?
您好,刘女士。

Brian: Dr. Smith is an anthropologist. He's just finished writing a book on the difference of breast-feeding behavior between different nationalities.
史密斯博士是位人类学家,他刚写完一部关于不同民族哺乳行为差异的书。

Liu Hang: That sounds very interesting. Do you work at a university?
那听起来很是有趣。您是否在一所大学工作?

Dr. Smith: Yes, I teach at Washington State University.
是的,我在华盛顿州立大学教书。

Introduction 2
介绍

Liu Hang: So we are neighbors. I'm a student at the University of Idaho. We could have a dinner some day③.
这样,我们是邻居了,我是爱达荷大学的学生。哪一天我们可以在一起吃顿饭。

Dr. Smith: I'd love to.
我愿意。

Dialog 3

Ding Tang: Hello. Are you here for the conference?
您好！你们是来参加会议的吗?

Diana: Yes, we are. And you?
是的,您呢?

Ding Tang: Me too. I'm Ding Tang form China.
我也是。我是中国来的丁唐。

Diana: I'm Diana Collins, and this is Emily, Emily Bronte.
我叫戴安娜·柯林斯,她叫爱米丽,爱米丽·勃朗特。

Emily: It's very nice to meet you.
见到您真高兴。

Ding Tang: Hello, I'm pleased to meet you. Here's my card.
您好,很高兴见到您。这是我的名片。

Typical Sentences
典型句型

1) May I present / introduce Mr. Wilkins?
我可以向你介绍威尔金森先生吗?

2) Allow me to introduce Mr. Wilkins.
请允许我向你介绍威尔金森先生。

3) I'd like you to meet Mr. Wilkins.
我向你介绍威尔金森先生。

4) This is Mr. Wilkins.
这是威尔金森先生。

5) President Johnson, may I present Mr. Henry Green? Mr. Green, this is President Johnson.
约翰逊校长,我可以向您引见亨利·格林先生吗?格林先生,这是约翰逊校长。

6) Dr. Smith, I'd like you to meet Mr. Richard Wilson. Richard, this is my adviser Dr. Henry Smith.
史密斯博士,我想向您介绍理查德·威尔逊先生。理查德,这是我的导师亨利·威尔逊博士。

7) I'm delighted to meet you, Dr. Smith.
史密斯博士,见到您很高兴。

8) I'm delighted / pleased / glad to meet you.
很高兴见到你。

9) It's a pleasure to meet you.
见到你很荣幸。

10) I'm pleased to meet you, too.
我也很高兴见到你。

11) Hi, Bob, this is Andy, my friend.
你好,鲍勃。这是安迪,我的朋友。

背景知识

关于介绍:一种是自我介绍。中国人在传统上是崇尚"自谦"的,正所谓"满招损,谦受益",谦虚被视为一种美德。谈到自己或与自己密切的事物时,使用谦辞为一大传统,如"鄙人、鄙姓、愚见、寒舍、陋室、鄙校",即使著名学者也要自谦为"才疏学浅,孤陋寡闻",否则就会被视为"傲慢"或"无礼"或者"没有教养"。西方人自我介绍时,一般是男方向女方先作自我介绍。力求尽可能将个人好的素质及优秀面展现出来,有一说一,有二说二,既不夸大,更不缩小,让对方充分了解自己,获得赏识。不了解这一点,就会引起误解。中国常有人在作学术报告时说"本人只是做了一些肤浅的研究,肯定有不足和不对之处，恳望各位专家学者批评指正。"(I have just made some shallow research, and I think there must be something incomplete and incorrect. I do hope that experts present can point them out and criticize me.)这样的话要是在国际会议上说出来，定会产生误解。英美等西方国家的专家会认为"既然研究不够，还有错误的，为什么还在此报告？我们也没有资格批评你"。造成这种误解的原因是双方都不太了解对方的文化。

　　一种是介绍他人。这方面的差异没有自我介绍时那么大，双方注重的基本一样，即尽量拣被介绍者好的方面讲，方式上有些细微差异。中国人"尊老"，一般是将年长者、位尊者介绍给年轻者、位卑者。西方人一般是先将年轻者、位卑者介绍给年长者、位尊者。如果是年轻的位尊者，则按社会地位的高低来介绍，即将年长位低者介绍给年轻位高者。男女都有的时候，西方人一般是将男方先介绍给女方，而中国人似乎还是习惯按年龄大小去介绍。在女士之间，西方人先向已婚的介绍未婚的；先向年龄大的未婚者介绍年龄小的已婚者。在一般的社交场合，如家庭宴会，先向主人引见客人。赴宴的客人有先来后到之分，一般应先向先到的客人介绍后到的客人。

　　在正式场合，无论自我介绍还是介绍他人，都应该说出全名、头衔、目前所从事的工作及担任的职务，尽量求全，以示郑重。例如：Allow me to introduce myself. My name is Zhang Zhiqiang. I'm an engineer at Simpson Paper Plant in Canada. Thank you.(请允许我介绍一下我自己。我叫张志强，是加拿大辛普森造纸厂的工程师。谢谢！)而在非正式场合，要适合轻松的气氛，一般给出名字(first name)、身份及与介绍者的关系就可以了。例如：I'm a graduate student from China and my name is Liu Hang, and my major is business administration.(我是来自于中国的研究生，我叫刘杭，我的专业是工商企业管理。)介绍完毕，就是握手。握手也有讲究，西方是年轻者、位卑者、男士等候年长者、位高者、女士伸出手来。如果对方没有伸手，可以微微颔首表示礼貌。如果戴着手套，要先摘除手套。握手时不可握得太紧太长，这一点也与我们不同。

① 注意 work 和不同介词的搭配,如:work as (+job),work for (+company),work in (+place)

② Nice talking with you. 是结束交谈的用语,不同于开始交谈时的用语:It's nice to meet / to know you 等。

③ some 用于单数普通名词前表示"某一个(人,物,时间)",如:He went to some place in Africa. (他到非洲一个地方去了。)

Making Compliments
称赞与夸奖

Topic Introduction
话题导言

当有人称赞你出席宴会穿的衣服漂亮时，作为中国人多半的回答是"哪里哪里，一般一般，是件便宜货。"而英美等国的西方人受到同样的称赞(What an attractive new blouse!)时的回答就不同：I appreciate the compliment.(谢谢你的称赞)。称赞用语在英语国家使用的频率很高，到处都可以听到赞美声。西方人对人喜欢说恭维的话，这是他们讲究礼貌的一种表现方式，当面赞美女士的长相、才气、衣着等被认为是有教养的表现。

称赞的方法依场合不同而有所不同，同等地位之间或上对下可以使用称赞用语；下对上则要小心使用称赞用语，以防被认为是在拍马屁；逼着别人称赞你也不是礼貌的事情(fish for compliments)，如 How do you like my new dress?(你喜欢我的新衣服吗？)称赞别人是一种客气，但客气也有一定的程度，称赞过度也会令人生气或讨厌。

Situational Dialogs
情景对话

赞美是一种美德，不管是被赞美的人还是自己都会觉得高兴，何乐而不为呢？看看刘杭(Liu Hang)、丁唐(Ding Tang)和朋友之间是怎样赞美和被赞美的。

Dialog 1

Dr. Johnson: Good morning, Ding Tang.
丁唐,早上好!

Ding Tang: Good morning, Dr. Johnson.
约翰逊博士,早上好!

Dr. Johnson: Ding Tang. This is Dr. Parker. He is also a professor in our department.
丁唐!这是帕克博士。他也是我们系的教授。

Ding Tang: It's nice to know you, Dr. Parker.
很高兴认识您,帕克教授。

Dr. Parker: Me, too, Ding Tang. You speak very good English.
我也是,丁唐,您的英语讲得很好。

Ding Tang: It's very kind of you to say. I began to learn English at the age of eight.
谢谢您这么说,我八岁就开始学英语了。

Dr. Parker: Where did you learn it?
您在什么地方学的英语?

Ding Tang: At school, in China. This is the first time for me to be abroad.
在中国的学校。这是我第一次走出国门。

Dr. Parker: It's amazing.
这太使我吃惊了。

Dialog 2

Liu Hang: Hi, Dr. Smith. How are you?
嗨,史密斯博士,您好吗?

Dr. Smith: Very well. Thank you. Oh, Liu Hang, you look beautiful today. Your dress is perfect. Everything matches perfectly.
很好,谢谢。哇,刘杭,你今天好漂亮呀!你的衣服真是完美无缺,一切都搭配得很好。

Liu Hang: Thank you. Today is special for me, you remember?
谢谢!今天对我来说有特别的意义,您忘记了吗?

Dr. Smith: Oh, yes. You're going to give us a presentation about open China.
哦,对了。你要向我们展示开放的中国。

Making Compliments 3

……

Dr. Smith: Congratulations! You've made an excellent presentation. I'm deeply impressed.
恭喜你！一个精彩的演示会,我深受感动。

Liu Hang: Thank you. I hope I did.
谢谢,我希望我成功了。

Dr. Smith: Sure. Your talk was informative. We learned a lot about today's open China.
当然做到了。你的报告信息量大,我们获得了很多有关今日开放之中国的情况。

Dialog 3

Liu Hang: Bill, you do have a very beautiful house.
比尔,你确实有一个漂亮的房子。

Bill: Yeah, we've spent all our money on it①.
是啊,我们把所有的钱都花在这上面了。

Liu Hang: The garden is also big and lovely. You have all kinds of flowers planted in it.
花园又大又可爱。花园里种有各种各样的花。

Bill: You see, different flowers bloom in different seasons. So, you can see flowers all the year round②.
你看,不同的花在不同的季节开放。所以,一年到头你都可以看到花了。

Liu Hang: It's indeed a lovely home.
确实是一个可爱的家。

Bill: It's very kind of you to say so.③
谢谢。

Typical Sentences
典型句型

1) That's marvelous!
   真了不起！
2) It's a lovely picture!
   多好看的照片！
3) You have a beautiful smile!
   你的笑真美。
4) You have a good sense of humor.
   你很有幽默感的。
5) You did a beautiful job.
   你干得不错。
6) Well done.
   干得好。
7) I appreciate the compliment.
   谢谢你的称赞。
8) It's nice of you to say so.
   很高兴你能这么说。
9) Thank you for saying so.
   谢谢你这么说。
10) I'm glad you like it.
    很高兴你喜欢它。
11) You handled that lesson superbly.
    你这一课上得好极了。
12) That was outstanding.
    好极了。
13) This is good. I like the way you are handling this.
    不错，我喜欢你这种处理办法。
14) Well, don't you look cute today?
    呀，您今天可真漂亮。
15) Thank you. I have had this for a while.
    谢谢。这衣服我已经穿了一阵子了。

16) Your wife is beautiful. You're very lucky to have such a pretty wife.

你的太太很漂亮。你真好运,有这么一个漂亮的太太。

17) What a big house!

好大的房子呵!

18) The garden is nice with the green lawn and the trees around it. They are just so beautiful.

你的花园也相当漂亮。绿色的草坪及周围的树,实在太美了。

19) The floor is splendid.

这地板漂亮极了。

20) My wife is very good at cooking, and perhaps we can bring some Chinese food then.

我太太做菜很在行,到时我们可能会带上几个中国菜。

背景知识

　　称赞习俗:西方文化把称赞与夸奖看成是人类生活的必需品。所以,当一个人得到另一个人的称赞时,就像得到一件有用的物品,人们通常的反应是感谢。莎士比亚说:Our praises are our wages.(给我们赞扬就是给我们俸禄。)马克·吐温说:I can live for two months on a good compliment.(一句恰到好处的赞语,可以使我活两个月。)美国前国务卿基辛格博士是外交谈判的能手,也是恭维他人的专家。

　　孩子对家长的赞扬非常重视,远远超过来自同学或朋友的赞扬。老师对学生也常常使用赞扬和夸奖的言辞,尤其是以此鼓励那些后进学生。

　　一般地说,你可以称赞任何人,甚至完全陌生的人也可以得到你的称赞。就称赞内容来说,话题多集中在人们的才学、技能、业绩、外表、衣饰、房屋、家具、汽车等个人的优秀品质或器物上。美国人尤其擅长称赞他人,包括称赞他人的孩子、妻子或丈夫、父母甚至他们的朋友。

cute（漂亮）和divine（好极了）用于称赞女性,而great（棒,了不起,好极了）和terrific（好极了,了不起）称赞男性。使用称赞语时还应记住:要尽量做到自然、真诚、得体。过分夸张的恭维话会使听者感到不自在,甚至起到相反的作用。

称赞答语：社会规范要求人们对他人的称赞语做出反应或回答。英语国家的人们对称赞语的一般回应是表示感谢。表示感谢就是接受称赞。回答别人的称赞可以分为两种,即接受称赞和拒绝称赞。

接受称赞的情况即Agreement（同意称赞）,听到称赞后一律用Thanks（谢谢）、Thank you（谢谢你）或微笑来回答,有如下几种情况:(1)Comment Acceptance（表示赞同性意见）。(2)Praise upgrade（使称赞升级）。接受称赞,但认为称赞程度不够,还要自我称赞。(3)Comment history（说明器物来历）。(4)Reassignment（转移称赞）。接受称赞,但又将它转移到第三者或者物品上去。(5)Return（回敬称赞）。接受称赞的同时再称赞对方。

拒绝称赞的情况即Disagreement（不同意称赞）,有如下几种情况:(1)Scale Down（弱化称赞）。不同意对自己的称赞,指出被表扬的物品的缺陷, 或表明称赞过分。(2)Question（质疑称赞）。(3)Disagreement（否定称赞）。(4)Qualification（限定称赞）。常用but, although之类的连词,接近完全否定,但程度要弱一些。(5)No acknowledgement（对称赞不表态）。(6)Request interpretation（把称赞理解为请求）。

注 释

① spend money on something 是"花钱买什么"的意思,如:
She spent one million dollars on the house.（他花了一百万买了这座房

子。)

注意 spend time (in) doing something 是"花时间做什么事情"的意思,如:

She spent three years making her small shop into a big factory. (她花了三年时间把一个小店铺变成了大工厂。)

② all the year round 是 "一年到头" 的意思, 还可以说 all the year long 等。当然,其他表示时间的词语也可以套用,如 all the day long(整日)、all the month round(整月)等。

③ 这是一句表示感谢的话,其句型结构比较特殊,相当于说 You are very kind to say so. 而不同于其他的 it 作形式主语的句子(如 It's important to attend the meeting.)。

Congratulations and Wishes
祝贺与祝愿

Topic Introduction
话题导言

　　当你在某项工作上取得了成绩、获得了某项重要的奖励、学术上获得了成就,抑或是买了新房子、晋升了职务、庆祝节日、新婚大喜、生了孩子、过生日等等,都希望得到人们的祝贺。祝贺的方法也多种多样,至亲密友往往送来礼物,普通朋友也会从语言上给以良好祝愿的表达。英语表示祝贺和祝愿的语句简单有力,强烈地表达祝贺人的主观愿望,大量地使用虚拟语气。受到了别人的祝贺,回应祝贺是很有必要的,一般是对祝贺表示感谢,如"谢谢你的祝贺!"(Thank you very much for saying so!)或"你真好,谢谢!"(It's very kind of you to say that!)

　　值得注意的是,英语对结婚的祝贺跟我们是不同的,不说"Happy marriage!"(婚姻幸福!)和"Happy wedding!"(婚礼快乐!)对新郎和新娘的祝贺是不同的,尽管都是表达"恭贺新婚!",对男方要说:"Congratulations!"(恭喜!)对女方要说:"Wish you happy!"(祝你幸福!)此外,对于不是基督徒的人也最好不要祝贺他"圣诞快乐!"(Merry Christmas!)

Congratulations and Wishes 4
祝贺与祝愿

Situational Dialogs
情景对话

韩力刚(Ligang)刚刚获得了博士学位并在技能比赛中获得第一名,他的老师斯科特博士(Dr. Scott)最近也搬进了新居,这都是些值得祝贺的事情。

Dialog 1

Dr. Scott: You have just obtained a Ph.D. Degree. Congratulations!
你刚获得博士学位,恭喜你!

Ligang: Thank you very much, Dr. Scott. I appreciate① your help and teachings for all these years.
非常谢谢,斯科特博士。感谢您这些年来对我的帮助和教诲。

Dr. Scott: The pleasure was all mine.② I'm proud of you. I've never expected you could get your Ph.D. Degree in such a short time.
别这样说。我为你感到骄傲,我从未想到你能在这么短的时间里就拿到学位。

Ligang: I have to, you know. My homeland is expecting me to work for her.
你知道的,我必须这样。祖国期待着我为她工作。

Dialog 2

Dr. Scott: You won the first place. Please accept my congratulations.
你获得了第一名,请接受我的祝贺。

Ligang: Thank you for saying so.
谢谢你的祝贺。

Dr. Scott: Your skills are terrific!
你的技巧真是太了不起了!

Ligang:	I've been trained for several years. I hope I did what I could. 我接受培训好几年了,我希望我做了我能做的。
Dr. Scott:	Yes, you did. We are all proud of you.③ 你做到了,我们为你骄傲。

Dialog 3

Ligang:	Let me congratulate you on buying a new house! 恭喜你买了新房子!
Dr. Scott:	It's very kind of you to say so. 谢谢你这么说。
Ligang:	I've never seen any people who work so hard like you and your husband. 我从来没见到有人像你和你丈夫这么努力地工作。
Dr. Scott:	We have to. We have four daughters and two sons. My eldest son has just graduated from Rice University. 我们必须如此,我们有四个女儿,两个儿子。大儿子刚从赖斯大学毕业。
Ligang:	Congratulations on getting his degree! 祝贺他获得学位。
Dr. Scott:	Thank you very much. He also works hard at college, and has just got a job with IBM. 非常感谢。他在大学学习也很努力,找到了 IBM 公司的工作。
Ligang:	Allow me to congratulate you once more on his job. 让我再次祝贺你,祝贺你儿子找到了工作。
Dr. Scott:	So many happy things. Please come to my home and have a drink tonight. 这么多高兴的事情,今晚到我家来喝一杯吧。

Typical Sentences
典型句型

1) Congratulations!
   恭喜!
2) Congratulations on your promotion!
   恭喜你晋升!
3) Allow me to offer my congratulations on your promotion.
   我诚心恭贺你晋升。
4) I hear you have just obtained a Ph.D. Degree. Congratulations!
   听说你刚获得博士学位,恭喜你!
5) I was really happy to hear about your new position.
   你晋升到新的职位,我真高兴。
6) I'd like to congratulate you on your promotion!
   恭喜你被提拔!
7) Let me congratulate you on buying a new car!
   恭喜你买了新车!
8) Please accept my congratulations.
   请接受我的祝贺。
9) That's great / fantastic / terrific!
   真是太了不起了!
10) You won the first place. Congratulations!
    你获得了第一名,恭喜你!
11) Best wishes to you for the New Year!
    祝你新年快乐!
12) Happy birthday!
    生日快乐!
13) Congratulations on getting married!
    新婚愉快!
14) Merry Christmas!
    圣诞快乐!
15) A very merry Christmas to you!
    圣诞快乐!

16) Happy New Year!

    新年快乐!

17) Thank you. Same to you!

    谢谢。你也快乐!

18) Thank you very much, and more of the same to you!

    非常感谢,你也是!

19) Thank you very much for saying so.

    谢谢你的祝贺。

20) It's kind of you to say that.

    你真好,谢谢。

21) How kind of you to say so.

    谢谢你诚心的祝福。

背景知识

送礼习俗:作为关系比较密切的亲戚或朋友,遇到可喜可贺的事情,除了言辞上表示恭喜之外,还要送些礼物,就是节日也可以送些礼品以示祝愿。有时人们并不清楚在诸如圣诞节、生日庆典、结婚典礼等场合送什么礼物好,于是便询问受礼者想要什么。不同的时候和场合,所送的礼品应该有所选择。

(1) 祝贺生日:送给十五六岁女孩可以是带有小饰物的手镯、耳环、女孩喜欢的书籍、刻有孩子名字的文具、香水、头巾、腰带、墙画或者女孩子的卧室饰品等;送给十几岁的男孩可以是衣服、体育器材、音乐唱片、电影DVD或者摇滚乐队的录音带、墙画、游戏机软盘、电脑游戏软件等;送给妻子或丈夫的礼物最好是对方十分想要,但由于价格太贵或别的什么原因而没有买的东西;送给老年夫妇可以是商店礼品卷、盆花、他们感兴趣的书籍等或者为他们订一份报纸,甚至给他们提供旅行机票都是可以选择的礼品;给朋友送礼很难说送什么好,没有固定的选择模式,以双方关系的亲密程度或感情的浓厚程度而定。

（2）恭贺新婚：可以送蜜月旅行的行李用品、女用内衣、床上用品、浴室毛巾、厨用毛巾、桌布或餐巾、瓷制塑像、绢花等。赠送的礼物要求实用、得体、新颖。传统上这些礼品都是手制的，直到今天仍被视为是最理想的馈赠物品。礼品必须当面赠与，不能让商店转交；礼物上应附有一张贺卡以让受礼人知道是谁人所送；礼物应当面打开并当场向馈赠者表示感谢。

（3）乔迁之喜：应邀参加某人的乔迁喜宴，客人总要带点小礼品，如烟灰缸、毛巾、带框的墙画、壁炉毛刷等，以耐用物品为好，或者是记事簿、集邮簿、当地的地图、交通时刻表、旅游说明书等，以助主人开始新的生活。

（4）祝贺毕业：可以送的礼品主要有钟表或收音机、电视机、个人电脑、台灯，以及与该学生专业有关的书籍或参考书、照像机、体育用品、手表或戒指之类的首饰、商品礼券、钱、股票，等等。

（5）祝贺节日：节日期间，如果被邀请做客或参加私人宴请，通常送的礼物有鲜花、水果、糖果、书籍等物。送书时要了解主人的爱好和需要。也可以先送一些一般的礼物，如一瓶酒、自己种的西红柿或一瓶特制的果酱。了解到主人的具体需要时，可以再补送一份礼物。如果事先征得主人的同意，也可以带牛扒或其他半成品的菜肴，到时热或简单炒一下就可食用。

注 释

① appreciate 是一个多义词,在这里的意思是"感激,感谢",亦可以指"欣赏,赏识",如：appreciate good food（欣赏美味）；或者可以指"体会,了解",如：appreciate the difficulties of the situation（意识到局势困难）。

② 回答感谢的话语很多,不要总是用 You're welcome. 这样一句话回

答，应当根据情况选用 My pleasure. / The pleasure was all mine. / Don't mention it. / Any time. / Think nothing of it. 等等。

③ be proud of 的意思是"为……感到自豪"，如：
We are proud of being students of this university.（我们为是这所大学的学生而感到骄傲。）

Thanks and Responses
致谢与答谢

Topic Introduction
话题导言

生活在不同文化背景下的每个人对于是否应该感谢别人都有自己的判断标准,这是不同价值取向的结果。比较而言,中国人说"谢谢您"的时候要比西方人少得多。在英美等西方国家,别人为自己做了事、帮了忙,说声"Thank you."是礼貌的表现。而受到的别人的称赞、祝愿、夸奖、邀请等等也要表示感谢。即使在家里也是如此:丈夫为妻子倒了一杯茶、孩子为父母开了门、兄弟之间传递了学习用具等等,都要说一声"Thank you."。

英语老师教给我们说感谢的语句是"Thank you.",但其实表达感谢的说法很多,有些比较随意,如 Thanks. / Thanks a lot.;有的属于一般用语,如 Thank you. / I appreciate it.;还有的则属于正式的用语,如 Thank you very much. / I would like to thank you. / I appreciate what you did.等。音调也是表达客气与否的一个手段,如对服务人员可以用降调,但想要表达得客气一些可以将语调上扬。选择适当的语句和声调要看场合而定,如对于老师的感谢,只说 Thank you, and I appreciate your time.(谢谢您,谢谢您花了时间。)就可以了。不要照搬中国式的说法,如说浪费了时间(I'm sorry to waste your time.),别人听了会以为他做了一件没有意义的事情。也不要过分言重,如别人帮你做了作业,你说"Thank you very much. I think I couldn't have finished it without you.(非常感谢,我想没有你我就不能完成。)"就显得太严肃了。

而老师教给我们回答感谢是"You are welcome."。其实在此之外还有许多表示"不用谢,不客气"的说法,可以根据情况选用 My plea-

sure. / All pleasure was all mines. / Don't mention it. / Any time. / Think nothing of it.等等。

"赠人玫瑰,手留余香。"刘杭(Liu Hang)和杨洋(Yang Yang)对于需要帮助的人总是能帮就帮,因为自己也会有需要他人帮助的时候。

Dialog 1

Passerby: Excuse me, where's the post office?
请问,邮局在哪儿?

Liu Hang: Go straight ahead, make a right turn at the traffic lights and the post office is just round the corner[①].
一直往前走,在交通灯那里往右拐,邮局就在拐角处。

Passerby: Thank you very much.
非常感谢。

Liu Hang: You are welcome.
不客气。

Dialog 2

Yang Yang: The boxes are too heavy for you. Do you need my help?
这箱子对你来说很重的,要我帮忙吗?

Passerby: It's very kind of you.
太谢谢您了。

Yang Yang: It's my pleasure. Where should I carry these two boxes?
别客气。我要把这两个箱子放在哪里?

Passerby: They asked me to put them in the Administration Building. It's far.
他们要我放在行政楼,很远。

Yang Yang:	It doesn't matter[2] much. I can do it. 没多大关系，我能行。
Passerby:	I appreciate what you are doing for me. 非常感谢您正为我做的。
Yang Yang:	Don't mention it. It's nothing. 别客气，没关系。

Dialog 3

Yang Yang:	Hello, may I speak to Dr. Scott? 您好，请找斯科特博士接电话，好吗？
Receptionist:	I'm sorry, sir. He's out now. May I have a message for him? 对不起，先生。他不在，可以留下口信吗？
Yang Yang:	Would you please ask him to phone me back? My name is Yang Yang. 让他回电话给我，好吗？我叫杨洋。
Receptionist:	Certainly I will. 我会的。
Yang Yang:	Thank you very much for your help. 非常感谢您的帮忙。
Receptionist:	It was my pleasure. 愿意效劳。

Typical Sentences
典型句型

1) Thanks.
   谢谢。
2) Many thanks.
   多谢。
3) Thanks a lot.
   多谢。
4) Thank you very much.
   非常感谢。

5) Thank you very much indeed.

   实在是多谢了。

6) I really don't know how to thank you enough.

   我对你真是感激不尽。

7) I am thankful to you for all this help.

   我感谢你给我的一切帮助。

8) I am grateful to you for your kindness.

   我感谢你的好意。

9) I greatly appreciate your timely help.

   我十分感谢你及时提供的帮助。

10) It's very kind (good, nice) of you to come and help us.

    非常感谢你们前来相助。

11) You are welcome.

    不客气。

12) Not at all.

    别客气。

13) Don't mention it.

    不用客气。

14) It's a / my / our pleasure.

    那算不了什么,别客气。

15) That's all right /okay.

    不谢。

背景知识

感谢的场合: 英美等国的西方人非常讲究礼貌。"请"、"对不起"、"谢谢"是经常使用的。"谢谢你"意味着某人为自己做了什么事情之后表示谢意,即使是一件无足轻重或极其普通的事情。比如,店员为你服务、餐馆里的服务员为你送上一杯咖啡、学生回答问题、丈夫为妻子倒了一杯水、丈夫协助妻子就座等等,都要说"谢谢",可

Thanks and Responses

致谢与答谢

以说是从早到晚"谢"不离口。也就是说,在英美等国家,人们对他人给予的巨大帮助要表示感谢,对举手之劳的小事,如指路、让座、找钱、回答询问、传递东西等也要表示感谢。人们不仅对上司、同事和陌生人的帮助表示感谢,而且对关系十分密切的亲戚、朋友、父母、子女等的帮助也毫无例外地表示感谢。

致谢的类别和规范: 致谢主要有口头感谢和书面感谢两种形式。口头致谢是感谢人和被感谢人之间面对面或者通过电话进行的,比如: Thanks.(谢谢。)Thank you very much indeed.(实在是多谢了。)It's very kind (good, nice) of you to come and help us.(非常感谢诸位前来相助。)对别人的感谢,被感谢者要有礼貌地做出回应。最常见的英语回答用语是 You are welcome.(不客气。)这句套话美国人用得较多,现在英国人用得也多起来。还有 Not at all.(别客气。)That's all right.(不谢。)That's okay.(不谢。)后面的两种则比较随便。对别人的感谢做出合乎礼仪的反应是社会规范的要求。

感谢信(thank-you letters)是英语国家最主要的书面感谢形式。写感谢信要诚挚,及时,语言要自然、热情,就好像你当面与被感谢者谈话一样。主要用在(1)宴请(dinner parties),(2)过夜拜访(overnight visits),(3)接受生日礼物、结婚周年纪念礼物、圣诞及其他礼物(for birthday, anniversary, Christmas and other gifts),(4)送给新娘的礼物(shower gifts),(5)送给病人的礼物(gifts to a sick person),(6)悼唁信(for notes of condolence),(7)贺卡或贺礼(for congratulatory cards or gifts),(8)婚礼礼物(wedding gifts),(9)女主人收到访客的礼物时 (when a hostess receives a gift after visitors have left),(10)商业客户受到推销员的款待时(when a client is entertained by a sales representative)等。如果赠送的礼物是一笔钱,受礼者致谢时应说明钱将如何使用。在拜访结束后的几天内写一封感谢信是绝对必要的。另一类书面致谢形式是感谢卡,它们是印制的,封面上带有"感谢您"的字样。

① round the corner 是个短语,有两个意思,一个是本义"在拐角",另一个是引申义"在附近",如:
I just live round the corner. (我就住在附近。)

② matter 这里作动词用,意思是"有关系",如:
It matters much whether you go to the meeting tomorrow or not. (你明天是否去开会,关系很大。)

Apologies and Excuses
道歉与原谅

Topic Introduction
话题导言

中国有句俗话"人非圣贤，孰能无过"，英语也有句谚语"To err is human; to forgive, divine.（犯错者是人，宽恕者是神。）"这两句话都是说，人没有不犯错误的。确实，在日常生活中，人们都难免会有某种过失或不当之处，给别人带来损失或不便，这时候一般都要表示歉意，用以修补受到损害的人际关系。从这个意义上讲，表示歉意不仅是礼貌周全、有教养、有修养的表现，而且具有维护人际和谐关系的功能。

人们表示歉意用得最多的词句是 I'm sorry. 这个说法是针对日常生活的小问题、小过失的；另一个词 apologize 则是针对比较严重错误的用语；而打搅了别人要用 excuse 这个词。具体使用哪一个说法还得细心体会。再者，道歉的时候要表现出诚挚的歉意，一边说着道歉的话，一边嬉皮笑脸会被认为是在敷衍塞责。

Situational Dialogs
情景对话

不管什么人总是容易犯点小错误，刘杭(Liu Hang)也不例外，但是最重要的是能够意识到自己的错误。

Dialog 1

Liu Hang: I'm sorry for being late.
对不起,我迟到了。

Bill: That doesn't matter. I'm often late myself. I know there are always traffic jams this hour of the day.
没关系,我自己也常迟到。我知道每天这个时候总是塞车。

Liu Hang: Actually I should go the round way, or I should leave home earlier.
其实,我应该绕道,或者早一点儿出门。

Bill: Don't blame yourself. Next time try not to be late.
别责备自己,下次尽量别迟到。

Dialog 2

Liu Hang: I'm sorry I've made the kitchen full of oily smoke.
对不起,我把厨房搞得尽是油烟。

Bill: Don't worry about that.
别担心这事儿。

Liu Hang: I had thought that smoke could go out of the machine, but it didn't. Probably there is too much smoke.
我原想烟雾能从机器里出去,可没有。可能是烟雾太多了。

Bill: No problem at all. The smoke is disappearing soon.
没有问题,烟雾很快就会没有了。

Liu Hang: I won't stir-fry dishes any more, I guarantee.
我再也不炒菜了,我保证。

Dialog 3

Stranger: Excuse me, could you spare① me several minutes?
劳驾,能耽搁您几分钟吗?

Liu Hang: Yes?
什么事?

Stranger: We're doing an investigation about college students' drinking. Could you please answer the questionnaire?
我们做一个关于大学生饮酒的调查。请您填写这个问卷,好吗?

Apologies and Excuses 6
道歉与原谅

Liu Hang:	Sure. When are you going to collect it? 好的,您什么时候收?
Stranger:	In thirty minutes. Sorry for taking up your time②. 30分钟后,对不起耽搁您的时间了。
Liu Hang:	Never mind about that. I'll finish it soon. 别在意,我会很快做完的。

Typical Sentences
典型句型

1) I'm sorry.
   对不起。
2) Sorry about that.
   这事就对不起了。
3) Sorry for not phoning you.
   对不起,没给你打电话。
4) I'm very / so / terribly / awfully / extremely sorry for that.
   我为此非常抱歉。
5) I can't tell you how sorry I am.
   我实在难以表达我的歉意。
6) Excuse me.
   请原谅。
7) Will you excuse me for a few minutes?
   对不起,我要离开一会儿。
8) I beg your pardon.
   一定请你原谅。
9) Pardon me.
   请原谅。
10) Please forgive my carelessness.
    请你原谅我的粗心大意。
11) I apologize.
    我道歉。

37

12) I've got to apologize for troubling you so much.
    给您添了这么多麻烦,我得向您道歉。

13) May I offer you my sincerest apologies for the wrongs I've done to you.
    我使您受冤枉了,谨向您表示最诚挚的歉意。

14) It doesn't matter at all.
    根本没什么关系。

15) Never mind about that.
    这没关系。

16) No problem. / That's quite all right. / It's nothing.
    没什么关系。

17) Please don't blame yourself.
    请不要责备自己了。

18) There is no reason to apologize.
    不必道歉。

19) It's really not necessary.
    这实在没有必要。

背景知识

歉意的表达:道歉,就是向对方表达出你内心深处真诚的歉意。而歉意的表达需要把握一定的技巧,否则便难以取得良好的效果。道歉的英语表达方式也很多。

I'm sorry 在因过失的行为或不当的话语而道歉时用得最多,而且比 I beg your pardon 更有诚意,这多用于事后的歉意。在无需客气的场合可直接说 Sorry,但是对上司或对长辈最好还是用 I'm sorry。若想要表示更有礼貌,可在 sorry 前加上 very, terribly, awfully, so dreadfully, really 等修饰语,如:I'm really sorry to have kept you waiting so long. 有时并非是对方的错而对方却说 Sorry。比如:你去看电影,票却卖完了,此时售票员会对你说 Sorry;在公共场所你不经意地碰到了别人,可能对方还要对你说 Sorry。

Apologies and Excuses

以下具体分析一下表示歉意的几种说法：

Sorry 多用在给别人造成了麻烦的时候，如碰撞了别人、伤害了别人、约会迟到、赴宴迟到以及不礼貌的举止，包括打嗝(belch)、打喷嚏(sneeze)、咳嗽(cough / clear your throat)等。对后面这几种不礼貌的行为也可以说 Excuse me 或 Pardon me，但还是说 Sorry 的好。

Excuse me 主要是用于向他人打听情况、请人让路、打断别人的谈话、临时离开一会儿、讲话时呛住了或打喷嚏等情况。这只是为了礼貌，避免失礼，因此不能乱用。(1)当你向不熟悉的人打听或请求某事物，如：Excuse me, could you tell me the way to the airport? 这里的 Excuse me 可以译为"请……"，"麻烦……"；(2)对有可能失礼的行为或话语时，如打喷嚏(sneeze)等；(3)打断对方的谈话等，如：Excuse me! Can you speak clearly? Excuse me..., 此处可以译为"对不起"，"请……"。(4) 对不礼貌的行为事先道歉等情况，如：Excuse me for not telling you the truth. Excuse me 还可以用来表示向对方作轻微的道歉。

I beg your pardon. 表示谢罪，"太对不起了"之意，也可以说 Pardon me. 如：Pardon me for disturbing you.（对不起，打扰你了。）若是关系密切的同事，可以用 Excuse me 来替换 I beg your pardon. 在使用过程中也可以说 I beg your pardon. / Pardon me 或 Pardon。尽量避免使用 Beg pardon，因为这被认为是粗俗的说法。当 I beg your pardon 表示请求对方"请谅解"时用降调(Falling Tone)；若是要求对方重述时用升调(Rising Tone)，这是一种礼貌的说法，在关系很密切的同事中不那么讲究时也可以说 What do (did) you say? 或 What were you saying?

Forgive me 表示请原谅，实在抱歉。用于有了过失而礼貌地表示歉意，如：Please forgive me for coming late.（请原谅我来晚了。）若要表示更有礼貌的歉意或"谢罪"时可以说：I must apologize to you for coming late. 这也是一个表示事后歉意的用语。

比较郑重地表示歉意，往往需要说明具体的问题细节和情况，有时候还要加上如何改进的想法，以显得诚心诚意。如：I do beg your pardon for the mess I've made.（我把事情搞得一团糟，一定得请您原谅。）A thousand pardons for taking up so much of your time. (占了您这么多时间，抱歉，抱歉。)

及时致歉虽然是一种美德,是有礼貌和有修养的表现,但涉及到大的事故,没有弄清责任是哪一方的,并有可能导致诉讼或赔偿时,不可随便说 I'm sorry,因为这有可能被对方视为你自己已经承认了错误,将来的官司就难办了。

在人们由于各种过错表示歉意之后,纵使接受道歉的人想发脾气也没有用,上策是做出积极友善的反应,解除犯错者的愧疚心理,使双方的关系恢复如初,如:It's nothing at all. It's one of those things.(根本不值一提,这是常有的事情。)

Notes
注释

① spare 是"抽出,省掉"的意思,如:
I cannot spare time for it.(那件事情我匀不出时间来。)

② take up one's time 的意思是"占用、耽搁某人的时间",如:
His speech took up too much time at yesterday's meeting.(他的讲话在昨天的会议上占了太多的时间。)

Weather and Time
天气和时间

Topic Introduction
话题导言

  俗话说"晴带雨伞,饱带饥粮","天有不测风云",为防患于未然,必须"未雨绸缪",这说明人们很重视天气。中国人如此,西方人对天气的重视程度也不亚于中国人。英国绅士"高礼帽、燕尾服和雨伞"的形象,想必大家并不陌生,这其中的雨伞,就表明了英国人对天气的重视。英国人关心天气不仅勤于行,而且乐于言,即爱谈论天气,这据说是因为英伦三岛天气多变。所以,人们关心天气,谈论天气,不疼不痒地谈几句,不关系到任何人的隐私(privacy),又可以用作寒暄语。正所谓人人见面谈天气,意在天气外。谈论天气可以打破僵局,作为双方结识与交际沟通的桥梁。现在,谈论天气早已成为一种国际现象,不再是英国人的专利了。很多美国人和中国人闲聊时也经常问到中国的天气情况。

  时间问题虽然不是经常的话题,但人们日常生活也会涉及到,特别是由于美国国土辽阔,被分为数个时区(time zone)以及夏令时(Daylight Savings Time,简称DST)的使用,在美国各地旅行要经常地调整钟表的指针。中国人在美国也是经常要遇到计算"中国现在是几点钟"的问题。

Situational Dialogs
情景对话

天气总是和外国朋友开始谈话的好话题,刘杭(Liu Hang)和朋友克莱尔(Clare)就在谈论天气了。

Dialog 1

Liu Hang: It's a nice day, isn't it?
天气真不错,啊?

Clare: Yes, it's terrific, especially after the long rainy season.
是,好极了! 特别是漫长雨季节之后。

Liu Hang: It is really pleasant to see the sun again. The sky is so blue and the air is extremely fresh.
又看到太阳真是开心。天空这么蓝,空气又特别清新。

Clare: I wish this kind of weather would last① a few days, so that we could go for an outing.
我希望这种天气持续一些天,我们好进行一个郊游。

Liu Hang: I agree. By the way, which season do you like best?
你说得对。另外,哪个季节是你最喜欢?

Clare: Summer is my favorite. In summer we can go swimming and go fishing in the sea on weekends.
我最喜欢夏天。夏天我们可以在周末的时候去大海里游泳和钓鱼。

Dialog 2

Clare: Hi! Beautiful day, isn't it?
嘿,多好的天气,不是吗?

Liu Hang: Yeah, it's clear and sunny. How are the winters here generally?
是啊,明媚又晴朗。这里的冬天通常是什么样的?

Weather and Time 7

天气和时间

Clare:	It snows a lot. The first snow is often in the late October or early November. In January and February it snows most, and sometimes the snow continues one week or longer. The last snow is often in late April. 下雪很多,第一场雪通常在10月末或者11月初。1月和2月下雪最多,有时候连续下一个星期或更长。最后一场雪通常在4月末。
Liu Hang:	Oh, it's very cold here. The winters are long and hard. It snows too much. 哦,这里很冷,冬天又长又难受,下雪太多了。
Clare:	How is the weather in your city? 你们城市的天气如何?
Liu Hang:	It's very hot in summer, sometimes it's near 100 degrees Fahrenheit. I can't tolerate that high temperature. 夏天非常热,有时候接近100华氏度,我受不了那么高的温度。
Clare:	How about fall[②] and spring? 秋季和春季如何?
Liu Hang:	Fall is the best season with not too much rain and it's not hot. It's humid in spring. 秋季是最好的季节,雨不多,也不热。春天太潮湿。
Clare:	And you don't have a cold winter, do you? 你们冬天不冷,是吧?
Liu Hang:	Quite right. In January it's around 70 degrees Fahrenheit, and it's not cold at all. 很对,1月有70华氏度左右,一点也不冷。

Dialog 3

Clare:	What time is it now, Liu Hang? 刘杭,现在几点?
Liu Hang:	Eight-forty. 8点40分。
Clare:	Did you set your watch one hour ahead? 你有没有将手表往前拨一个小时?

Liu Hang:	No. Why?
	没有,怎么啦?
Clare:	Daylight Savings Time began this morning. DST begins on the first Sunday in April and ends on the last Sunday in October.
	夏时制今早开始。DST 从 4 月的第一个星期天开始,10 月的最后一个星期天结束。
Liu Hang:	Thank you for your reminding me of that. I made a mistake[3] last year.
	谢谢你的提醒,我去年就犯了一个错误。
Clare:	I made the same mistake. I went to class one hour earlier last October.
	我也一样。去年 10 月我提前一个小时去上课。
Liu Hang:	I went to work one hour late last April.
	我去年 4 月上班迟到了一个小时。

Typical Sentences
典型句型

1) It's a nice (lovely, terrible) day, isn't it?
天气真好(真不错,真糟糕),不是吗?

2) Wonderful weather, isn't it?
多好的天气,不是吗?

3) What fine weather we're having today!
今天天气真好!

4) What a lovely day, isn't it?
多好的天气呀,不是吗?

5) What a terrible weather, isn't it?
多糟糕的天气呀,不是吗?

6) It looks like rain.
好像要下雨。

7) What's the temperature today?
今天气温几度?

Weather and Time

8) It seems to be clearing up.
   看来天要晴了。
9) It's rather windy today, isn't it?
   今天风真大,不是吗?
10) I hope it'll clear up tomorrow.
    我希望明天会晴。
11) Do you have the time? Sorry, I don't wear my watch.
    现在几点? 对不起,我没有戴手表。
12) What time is it? Eight forty.
    现在几点? 8点40分。
13) What's the date today? It's October 20.
    今天几号? 今天10月20号。
14) What day is it? It's Tuesday.
    今天星期几? 今天星期二。
15) Did you set your watch one hour ahead?
    你有没有将手表往前拨一个小时?

背景知识

华氏与摄氏(Fahrenheit and Celsius):中国人有个感觉,30多度就很热了,但在美国你听到30多度的气温,却很不一样,就是60多度也没有我们的30多度热。这是因为使用了不同的温度计量方法,我们中国用摄氏温度,西方国家多是使用华氏温度。

(1) 转换方法:两种温度计量方法的转换有一个很简单的公式,如下:

摄氏温度(℃)=(华氏温度−32)℉×5/9,如果知道现在是华氏68度,通过这个公式就可以换算出摄氏温度是20度。

如果知道了摄氏温度,要换算成华氏温度,公式就变成了:

华氏温度(℉)=(摄氏温度×9/5+32)℃,如果知道现在是摄氏36度,换算成华氏温度就是96.8度。所以,在美国听到这么高的温

度,不要过分害怕,这个摄氏36度在中国很多城市如武汉、重庆、南昌、南京、广州等是常见的。

(2)水的沸点、冰点和人的正常体温:我们都知道摄氏温度的这三个点分别是100℃、0℃和37℃,而华氏温度的水的沸点(the boiling point of water)是212°F、水的冰点(the freezing point of water)是32°F、人的正常体温(normal body temperature)是98.6°F。

(3)读法:华氏的读法是 degree Fahrenheit,如38°F就读作 thirty-eight degrees Fahrenheit;而38℃读作 thirty-eight degrees Celsius / centigrade。

美国的时区和夏令时:由于领土辽阔,美国被划分为六个时区(其中本土四个时区),称作标准时间(Standard Time)。全国由东往西分别是东部标准时间(Eastern Standard Time, EST)、中部标准时间(Central Standard Time, CST)、山区标准时间(Mountain Standard Time, MST)、太平洋标准时间(Pacific Standard Time, PST)、阿拉斯加标准时间(Alaska Standard Time, AKST)、夏威夷-阿留申标准时间(Hawaii-Aleutian Standard Time, HST)。

每相邻的两个时区之间的时差是一个小时,东部比西部早。例如,当处于"东部标准时间"时区的华盛顿特区(Washington D. C.)是中午12点时,处于"中部标准时间"时区的芝加哥(Chicago)是上午11点,处于"山区标准时间"时区的丹佛(Denver)是上午10点,处于"太平洋标准时间"时区的洛杉矶(Los Angeles)是上午9点,处于"阿拉斯加标准时间"时区的安克雷奇(Anchorage)是上午8点,而使用"夏威夷-阿留申标准时间"的夏威夷檀香山(Honolulu)才是早晨7点。

夏令时在美国被叫做 Daylight Savings Time,简称 DST。夏令时开始于4月的第一个星期天,每到这天人们就要把时钟往前拨一个小时,如把7点拨到8点,结束于10月的最后一个星期天。也有个别州不实行夏时制,如印第安纳州(Indiana)。

注 释

① last 在这里是动词,意思是"持续"。例如:
The war lasted eight years. (战争持续了八年。)
② 此处 fall 是一个典型的美国用法,意思是 "秋季"。美国人不用 autumn 而用 fall 来表达"秋天,秋季"。
③ make a mistake 的意思是"犯了一个错误",例如:
One can't make the same mistake twice. (人不能犯同样的错误两次。)

Parting and Farewell
道别与告辞

Topic Introduction
话题导言

当我们参加聚会或拜访朋友在告别的时候，主人总是要一再挽留，并说："时间还早哇"，"反正回家也没事儿啦"等等；真地要走时，主人要起身相送，一直送到门口，并热情地说："慢慢走哇"，"小心点儿，别碰着了"，"有空再来"。前者是表示殷情，后者是表关心。英美人士在告别时奉行主随客便，强调尊重对方。客人要走，表明客人来访的目的已经达到，现在对方提出要走，要尊重别人的意愿。即使主人有时想留一下客人，也是以征求对方意见的方式提出，不会刻意挽留。因为是真正的告别，白天说告别用 Good-bye.，而夜晚时间用 Good night.，当然也可加上客套的话，如 It's very nice talking with you. 或 Thank you for coming. 或 Nice to see you again. 等等。

人们之间的关系有时候决定了使用正式语体还是用非正式语体。美国著名语言学家 Dean Curry 编写过三本会话书，其中在《告别》这一章里，针对三种不同情况编了如下三段对话，读者可以细心揣摩。

(1) 一般相识：A: Oh, excuse me —here's my bus. Good-bye. (哦，对不起，车来了。再见！) B: Good-bye. (再见！)

(2) 普通朋友之间：A: OK. I'll see you later. So long. (好了，以后再说。再见！) B: So long. (再见！)

(3) 亲密朋友之间：A: Gotta go. (走了。) B: Okay. Check you later. (=I'll call you later.) (好吧，迟些时给你电话。)

同样是告别，由于关系的熟悉程度就有不同的表达方法。学习英语口语，懂得这一点是很有必要的。

Parting and Farewell 8

道别与告辞

欢聚的时刻总是特别短暂，刘杭(Liu Hang)和杨佳欣(Jiaxin)在迪肯逊教授(Mrs. Dickinson)家度过了一段愉快的时光后，总是要离开的。当然别忘记了谢谢主人的热情款待。

Dialog 1

Liu Hang: I'm sorry I've got to leave. I have got to finish the essay tonight.①
不好意思，我得走了。我今晚还要完成那篇文章。

Prof. Dickinson: Don't work too hard. I can review your essay when you finish it.
不要太努力了，完成以后我可以帮您看看。

Liu Hang: It's kind of you to say so. Thank you for your delicious dinner.
这样说太谢谢您了。多谢你们美味的晚餐。

Prof. Dickinson: Thank you for visiting us. Please remember me to your husband and daughter.②
谢谢你拜访我们，代我向您的丈夫和女儿问好。

Liu Hang: Yes, I will.
好的，我会的。

Prof. Dickinson: Take care of yourself.
多保重自己。

Liu Hang: Thank you. Good-bye.
谢谢，再见。

Dialog 2

Jiaxin: Oh, it's late. I've got to leave now.
哦，时候不早了，我该走了。

Prof. Dickinson: Can't you stay a little more longer?
不能多呆一会儿吗？

Jiaxin: I'm going to attend a conference at eight tomorrow morning. I must get up early.
明天上午8点钟我有一个会议，我得早点儿起床。

Prof. Dickinson: Well, I'm sorry you can't stay any longer. Thank you for visiting us.
这样呵，太遗憾你不能再多呆上一会儿。谢谢你的来访。

Jiaxin: It's very nice staying with you tonight.
今晚和你们呆在一起真的很高兴。

Prof. Dickinson: Please stop by③ again whenever you're available. You are always welcome.
有空再来看看我们，你永远受欢迎。

Jiaxin: Thank you very much. I will. Good night.
非常感谢，我会来的。晚安。

Prof. Dickinson: Tank care. Good night.
保重，晚安。

Dialog 3

Ding Tang: I'm calling to say good-bye④.
我打电话来道别的。

Mary: Oh, my God. You're leaving here?
哦，天哪。您要离开了吗？

Ding Tang: Yes, I have finished my research here. I'm taking my flight at Pullman.
是的，我的研究已经完成了。我从普尔曼乘飞机。

Mary: When is your flight?
您的航班是什么时间？

Ding Tang: Northwest Airlines, Flight 1098, tomorrow evening, eight-twenty.
明天晚上8点20分，西北航空公司的1098航班。

Mary: Is there anything we can do for you?
还有什么需要我们帮助的吗？

Ding Tang:	No, thanks. The Chinese Students' Association has made everything ready for me. 谢谢,没了。中国留学生已经把一切都给我安排好了。
Mary:	That's good. Do tell us if you need help in any way. 那太好了。如果需要帮助,请一定告诉我们。
Ding Tang:	Thank you very much. In fact, you've done a lot for me. I'm really grateful to you and the faculty⑤. 非常谢谢您,实际上,您已经为我做了很多事了。我真的好感激您和全体教师。
Mary:	It's my pleasure. Email me after you get home. 别客气,到家后给我来个电子邮件。
Ding Tang:	I will. Good-bye. 我会的,再见。
Mary:	Good-bye, and have a good flight. 再见,旅途愉快。

Typical Sentences 典型句型

1) I think I'd better be going now. I've got to get up early tomorrow.
   我想我得告辞了,明天我还要早起。

2) I hope you will excuse me, but I have to get back to my office.
   很抱歉我要告退,我必须回办公室去。

3) I think I ought to be going now. My baby sitter must leave at 11:00.
   我想我得走了,我们的保姆11点得回家。

4) I hate to say good-bye, but I've got to go now.
   我不喜欢说再见,但是我必须走了。

5) Time to hit the road.
   该走了。

6) Better get moving.
   我要走了。

7) Thank you for a lovely afternoon.

   谢谢你,我度过了一个愉快的下午。

8) Thank you, I've enjoyed this beautiful evening.

   谢谢你,这个优美的夜晚使我十分愉快。

9) Thank you for coming!

   谢谢你大驾光临。

10) See you. / So long. / See you later.

    再见。

11) Bye-bye. / Good-bye now.

    再见。

12) Have a good / nice day / weekend.

    一天愉快。/ 周末愉快。

13) Take care.

    多保重。

14) I hope you enjoy your trip.

    希望你旅途愉快。

背景知识

英语告别语:大家最为熟悉的告别语 Good-bye 能有现在这个面目,其演变是一个日渐脱离宗教而世俗化的过程。人们在中世纪(the Middle Ages)告别时常说 God be with you(愿上帝与你同在),这是一个虔诚的典型说法。其虔诚的色彩后来慢慢消失了,到莎士比亚时代就变成了 Good-bye。至于 Good bye,是 19 世纪初的变音,那时人们还可以用 So long 作告别语,显得更加亲切。当然,这两个告别语均有"直至我们彼此再见"的含义。

而 Have a nice day(祝你今天过得好!)是另一句用得最为广泛的告别语, 据说是 20 世纪 60 年代美国的加利福尼亚州青年人吸毒成风,时髦青年不信上帝,出于"今朝有酒今朝醉"的心态,根本就是"只管现在,明天都懒得去考虑",就创造出了这一告别语。这种平淡乏味的祝语后来居然大为流行，究其原因，既反映了70年代人们享乐主义(hedonism)和颓废反常(anomie)的心理，也显示了俗语强大的感染力。根据God be with you的发展轨迹，人们预测这一告别语有朝一日肯定会压缩成诸如Hayday这样的单词形式，因为它更能反映人们的上述心态。

告辞和送客：告别也是有一定之规的，长期以来形成了各民族自己独特的告辞和送客礼仪习俗。拜访结束时，一般由客人中的女士或年长者提出告辞之意。如果拜访时间比较短，客人提出告辞，再稍呆一会儿便可离去。如果拜访活动的时间较长，主人可能留客人吃饭或参加其他一些活动，而且又是在夜晚，客人在晚上10点半到11点之间告辞较为适宜。客人提出告辞和他真正离去之间应有一个短暂的时间间隔，约为15到20分钟。客人提出告辞后不应马上离去，他需反复表示告辞之意二至三次。所以，要告辞时就要把握好时间，提前说出来，否则突然说"再见"是最为糟糕的事情。

英美等国家的人们送客到大门口为止，一般不到大门以外。客人离开前自然也要说些感谢的话，而主人同样要对客人的光临表示感谢，并表示有机会再次聚首。但是我们也观察到，双方在告别时有时话长，有时话短。双方分别时还伴有握手的礼仪，就是握别。下面举例说明告辞的步骤：

第一步，客人提出要走了，正式的说法如It was nice staying with you tonight. Please give my best regards to your family.（今晚和你们呆在一起真是愉快，请代我向您家人问好。）不太正式的说法如Sorry, but I'm supposed to meet a friend.（抱歉，但是我另外有约。）比较随意的说法如Time to hit the road.（该走了。）

第二步，听到客人说要走了，主人可以略微挽留，在挽留的过程中客人并不会立即起身就走，双方会就某一个话题讨论一下。主人可以说Can't you stay a little while?（不能多呆一会儿吗？）后，就可能转到别的话题上去了。但是，如果主人觉得已经尽了留客的情谊，就不会强留客人。

第三步，从第一次说要走已经有了足够的一段时间，如话题已经谈完、茶水饮料也已经喝完等等，就可以站起来说I'd better be going.（我不走不行了。）然后开始移动脚步，边说I've very much enjoyed the dinner. Thank you very much.（这顿晚餐我吃得很好，非常感谢。）

> 第四步，主人看到客人已经真是要走了，就说 Thank you for visiting us.（谢谢您拜访我们。）并送客人到大门，到了门口时说 Have a good time.（祝您愉快。）客人回应 Thank you. We will.（谢谢，我们会的。）

① have got to 是 have to 的口语表达形式，意思也是"必须，不得不"。
② remember me to someone 的意思是"代我向某人问好"，例如：Please remember me to your parents.（请代我向你的父母亲问好）。
③ stop by 是"顺便拜访"的意思，与 drop in / drop by / stop in 等意思相同。
④ say good-bye 意思是"说再见"，后面可以加 to someone 类似的表达还有 say good morning to someone（向某人说早晨好），say hello to someone（向某人问好），say yes to someone（肯定答复某人），say no to someone（拒绝某人）等。
⑤ the faculty 指的是学校里的全体教师，而 staff 指的是职员。

Renting an Apartment
租房

Topic Introduction
话题导言

到一个英语国家,要生活下去,首先就要居有定所,租一套住房是解决这个问题的好办法。各类住房有不同的英语名称,如在美国有 house(独立一栋的房子,周围有树木草地);mobile home(工厂化生产出来的装有轮子可以用大拖车拖走的房屋,内有客厅、卧室、厨房,各种设施一应俱全);apartment(公寓,一栋房子有多套公寓,多半是多层建筑);condo(condominium 的简写,分户出售的公寓楼);studio(单间房,只有卫生间或者公用卫生间)等。

要找到自己合意的住处,要看广告、看房子、谈租约以及和朋友家人商议,特别是和房东讨论租金、设施等问题时懂得一些常用语是很有作用的。不然,被蒙了还不知道。

Situational Dialogs
情景对话

李康(Li Kang)和刘杭(Liu Hang)需要在美国呆上一段时间,租房是必需的,但是租房时问清楚一些细节问题是很有必要的。

Dialog 1

Clerk 1: Hello, C & Y Properties. May I help you?
您好，C & Y 房产公司。能帮您忙吗？

Liu Hang: Yes, I am calling for the apartment-renting ad in today's newspaper.
是的，我打电话是有关今天报纸的房屋出租广告的。

Clerk 1: We have several apartments. What kind do you prefer?
我们有几套公寓。您喜欢哪一种？

Liu Hang: I'd like the one with two bedrooms and one bathroom, on 4th Street.
我喜欢位于第四街的有两个卧室一个卫生间的那套。

Clerk 1: That's an excellent apartment. The tenants just moved out last week.
那是很不错的，房客上周才搬出去。

Liu Hang: Can I have a look?
我可以看看吗？

Clerk 1: Sure. When will you come?
当然，您什么时候来？

Liu Hang: This afternoon is good for me.
我今天下午可以来。

Clerk 1: Okay. Let's make it three thirty, shall we?
那好，我们定在 3 点 30 分，如何？

Liu Hang: Sure. Three thirty I will meet you there, at the apartment on 4th Street. The address is 327 Fourth Street[①], am I right?
当然可以，3 点 30 分我去那儿见您，就在第四街的公寓那儿，地址是第四街 327 号，对吗？

Clerk 1: Yes, right. See you later.
对的，再见。

Dialog 2

Clerk 2: Hello, nice to meet you. You are just from China?
您好，很高兴见到您，您从中国来？

Li Kang: Yes, I'm new here. I work at the university as a researcher.
是的，我刚来。我在这个大学做研究工作。

Renting an Apartment 9

租房

Clerk 2:	You are smart.② You're a university professor, aren't you? 您真聪明,您是大学教授,对吧?
Li Kang:	I am just doing research here, but I don't teach. How about the floor area of the apartment? 我在这里只做研究不教书。这套公寓面积多大?
Clerk 2:	It is quite big, around 900 square feet. Look, the living room is big enough for you to host a party and the kitchen's utensils are very new and clean. 相当大,大约900平方英尺。瞧,客厅大得您可以举办舞会,厨房设备又新又干净。
Li Kang:	It's good. 不错。
Clerk 2:	The bedrooms are wonderful, too. There is a walk-in closet in each bedroom. 卧室也非常好,每间卧室有个可以走进去的衣柜。
Li Kang:	Have you painted the walls recently? 您最近粉刷墙壁了吗?
Clerk 2:	We did a general painting the day before yesterday. The bathrooms are excellent and clean. 我们前天把整套房子粉刷了一遍,卫生间也非常好,很干净。
Li Kang:	But the carpet is so dirty. 而地毯很脏。
Clerk 2:	Don't worry about the carpet, sir. We'll get it cleaned soon. I can guarantee that everything is clean and looks new when you move in. 别担心地毯,先生。我们很快就打扫。我可以保证:您搬进来的时候一切都会干干净净,看起来像新的一般。
Li Kang:	I am satisfied with③ the apartment, but could you give a discount? 我满意这房子,但是您能否给个折扣?
Clerk 2:	We may talk about it later when we look over④ the lease. 我们可以晚些时候在看租约时讨论这个问题。

Dialog 3

Clerk 3: Please sit down. Would you like something to drink?
请坐。请问喝点儿什么?

Li Kang: A glass of water is OK for me.
给我一杯水就可以了。

Clerk 3: Just a second. This is the prepared lease. You may look it through and tell me when have any questions.
稍等,这是写好的租约。先浏览一下,有什么问题就告诉我。

Li Kang: I have to inform you of my moving out ahead of⑤ time one month, otherwise the deposit will be yours. Am I right?
我要是搬出,必须提前一个月通知您,否则押金就是您的了,对吗?

Clerk 3: Yes, quite right, sir.
很对,先生。

Li Kang: I have to pay utilities and phone bills myself, and you are responsible for the maintenance and carpet cleaning.
我付水电费和电话费,您负责维修和地毯清洁。

Clerk 3: Quite right, sir. You just pay rent, utilities and phone, and I will be responsible for everything else.
很对,先生。您付租金、水电和电话,我负责其余的一切。

Li Kang: I'm sorry I have to remind you of the discount I just referred to.
不好意思,我还是要提一下刚才说到的折扣问题。

Clerk 3: The case is that if you sign the lease for at least one year, I will give you a $100 discount.
情况是这样,如果您签至少一年的租约,我给您100美元的折扣。

Li Kang: I see.
我明白了。

Renting an Apartment

Typical Sentences 典型句型

1) I am calling for the apartment-renting ad in today's newspaper.
   我打电话是有关今天报纸的房屋出租广告的。

2) I'd like the one with two bedrooms and one bathroom, on 4th Street.
   我喜欢位于第四街的有两个卧室一个卫生间的那套。

3) How about the floor area of the apartment?
   这套公寓面积多大?

4) Is the apartment furnished or unfurnished?
   这套公寓有没有家具?

5) The bedrooms are wonderful, too. There is a walk-in closet in each bedroom.
   卧室也非常好,每间卧室有个可以走进去的衣柜。

6) Have you painted the walls recently?
   您最近粉刷墙壁了吗?

7) I can guarantee that everything is clean and looks new when you move in.
   我可以保证:您搬进来的时候一切都会干干净净,看起来像新的一般。

8) I am satisfied with the apartment, but could you give a discount?
   我满意这房子,但是您能否给个折扣?

9) I have to inform you of my moving out ahead of time one month, otherwise the deposit will be yours. Am I right?
   我要是搬出,必须提前一个月通知您,否则押金就是您的了,对吗?

Background
背景知识

租房程序：租住一套住房并不是一件容易的事情，要经过很多手续，而且在美国房费昂贵，几乎要占去一个典型美国家庭开销的 1/3 到 2/3 左右，因此要找到既廉价，又安全、舒适和方便的住房，最好先熟悉一下美国的有关租房事宜。

（1）了解房源。一是留意当地报纸的分类广告（Classifieds）中的房屋出租（Housing for Rent 或 Apartment for Rent），看到适合自己的就可以打电话询问具体情况；二是可以自己在当地网或当地大学网上发布房屋需求的信息，都是免费的，这样有房屋出租的人看到你的信息就会打电话或回 email 给你。

（2）察看房屋。在确认房屋信息后，一定要去看看房屋的实际状况，包括楼层结构、水电设施、厨房、地毯、洗衣设备、电话及网络线路、停车设施、社会治安情况等等。要注意的是，生活住房在美国一般都没有煤气管道，厨房和热水系统都是用电力的。

（3）费用分担。有的房屋看起来很便宜，但房东或房屋出租人一旦将房屋出租给你了，就什么也不管了。一般说来，租房人除了按时交纳房租以外，要负担杂费（utilities）和电话费，水费包括在房租之内。其他如房屋的简单维修、草坪的修剪、走道的打扫等所产生的费用都要考虑进去。

（4）签订租约。租房的租约英语称之为 lease，按照社会规范，就是关系特好的朋友之间租用一件什么东西也要签订租约，更别说房屋了。房东（landlord 或 landlady）或房地产经纪公司（realty 或 properties company）一般都准备了一份"格式化"的合同，要仔细阅读，不同意的地方要提出来商讨，如养宠物是一个常常涉及到的问题。签订租约时，一般要支付第一个月的租金（rent）和押金（deposit，数额等于一个月的租金）给房东，可以付支票、现金或现金汇票（money order），付支票或现金汇票不用索取收据，付现金一定要索取收据。

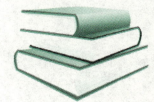

(5) 搬家入住。新到一个国家，东西不多，可以直接要求房东帮你拉一下从国内带来的行李，但说话要客气一些，一般都没有什么问题，也不会收你的钱。一切安顿之后，考虑买一些二手的家具、电器以应急需。

注　释

① 约会的时候要说清楚见面的具体地址，不然就会搞错，笔者就遇到过这种情况。英语的地址写法从小到大，与汉语相反，如 Apt 6, 722 South Washington St., Pullman, WA 36011。

② 美国人在这一点儿上与我们中国人一样，总是奉承和称赞别人。普通蓝领、白领见到大学教授，就说 You are very smart. 等。

③ be satisfied with 的意思是"对……满意"，如：
I am satisfied with your job.（我对你的工作很满意。）

④ look over 意思是"大略地看看"，单词 look 可组成很多短语，略举几例：
look at（看）
look after（照顾）
look into（调查）
look out（当心）
look out of（往外看）
look through（浏览）
look up（查阅）
look down upon（轻视，瞧不起）
look for（寻找）

⑤ 短语 ahead of 意思是"提前，在前面"，如：
You should finish the task ahead of time one week.（你应当提前一个星期完成那件工作。）

Applying for SSN
申请社会安全号

Topic Introduction
话题导言

社会安全卡的英语全称是 Social Security Card，它上面特定的号码称为 Social Security Number。该卡外表非常平常，只是名片大小的一张淡蓝色小纸片。申请社会安全卡不是什么困难的事情，只要能够说明你在美国逗留是合法的就可以了。

情景对话

社会安全卡对于要在美国逗留比较长时间的外国人非常重要。

Dialog 1

Officer: Hello, could you show me your passport, please?
您好，请出示您的护照。

Liu Hang: Hello, here it is.
您好，给您。

Officer: Why are you in the United States?
您为什么来美国？

Applying for SSN 10

申请社会安全号

Liu Hang:	I am staying here for my study. 我是来学习的。
Officer:	Do you have the offer letter with you? 您带了通知信函了吗?
Liu Hang:	Yes, here it is. 带了, 给您。
Officer:	How long will you stay here? 您将在这里逗留多久?
Liu Hang:	I will stay here for two or three years and then go back to China. 我将在这里呆两到三年, 然后回中国。
Officer:	Thank you for coming. You will receive your social security card within two weeks. 谢谢您来这里, 两个星期之内您会收到您的社会安全卡。
Liu Hang:	Thank you very much. 非常感谢。

Dialog 2

Officer:	Hello, could you show me your passport, please? 您好, 请出示您的护照?
Ding Tang:	Hello, here it is. 您好, 给您。
Officer:	This is not the first time that you came to the United States, is it? 您这次不是第一次来美国, 对吗?
Ding Tang:	No, madam. I came to the United States in 1999 for the first time and in 2001 for the second time. This is the third time. 对的, 女士。我 1999 年第一次来美国, 2001 年第二次来, 这是第三次。
Officer:	Why didn't you apply for your SSN before? 那您以前怎么没有申请社会安全号码呢?
Ding Tang:	I came here for a ten-day visit only in 1999 and for a cultural exchange program in 2001. 我 1999 年来只是访问 10 天, 2001 年也只是个文化交流项目。

Officer:	You stayed in the United States very short before. For what purpose are you here this time? 您以前来逗留的时间很短。您这次来为什么目的?
Ding Tang:	I came to do research this time and my research will last two or three years. 我这次来做研究,时间需要两三年。
Officer:	Oh, I see. Thank you for visiting us. Your SSN card will be mailed to the address you put within two weeks. 哦,我知道了。谢谢您到这里来。您的社会安全卡将会在两周之内邮寄到您填写的地址去。
Ding Tang:	I appreciate what you did.[①] 非常感谢您。

Dialog 3

Officer:	Hello, Social Security Office. May I help you? 您好,社会安全办公室。能帮您忙吗?
Ligang:	Hello, I have a question with my social security card. 您好,我的社会安全卡有一个问题。
Officer:	What's up with[②] the card? 您的卡怎么回事?
Ligang:	There is a spelling mistake in my name. What should I do with it? 我的名字拼写错了,我该怎么办呢?
Officer:	I'm sorry for that. Please mail it back and we'll correct it, and you will get a new card soon. 我为此感到抱歉。请您邮寄回给我们改正,您很快就会得到一张新卡的。
Ligang:	Okay, I will do that. Thank you very much. 好的,我会邮寄的。非常感谢。
Officer:	Thank you for calling us. 谢谢您打电话来。

Applying for SSN

申请社会安全号

Typical Sentences
典型句型

1) I am staying here because the Century Drinks Corporation provides me with a job.

   我来这里是因为世纪饮料公司给我提供了一个工作。

2) According to the contract, I will work here for one year and then go back to China.

   根据合同,我将在这里工作一年,然后回中国。

3) I came to study this time and my study will last two or three years.

   我这次来学习,时间需要两三年。

4) I have a question with my social security card.

   我的社会安全卡有一个问题。

5) There is a spelling mistake in my name. What should I do with it?

   我的名字拼写错了,我该怎么办呢?

6) Could you show me your passport, please?

   请出示您的护照?

7) For what purpose are you here this time?

   您这次来为什么目的?

8) Why are you in the United States?

   您为什么来美国?

9) Do you have the offer letter with you?

   您带了通知信函了吗?

10) Thank you for coming. You will receive your social security card within two weeks.

    谢谢您来这里,两个星期之内您会收到您的社会安全卡。

11) Your SSN card will be mailed to the address you put within two weeks.

    您的社会安全卡将会在两周之内邮寄到您填写的地址去。

Background
背景知识

社会安全卡(Social Security Card)：也称工卡，可凭护照和绿卡向社会安全办公室申请。卡上有持卡人的姓名、社会安全编号和签名，但没有相片。所以，它只是作为可以合法寻找工作的一个证明，而作为个人身份证明的作用较弱。人们常说的 SSN 就是这个卡上的号码，即 Social Security Number，是个人的终生编号，不仅每年报税时要用到它，而且你要在银行开户、申请信用卡、报考学校、申请补助等的时候都要用到它。如果你有什么信用问题，通过此号码就可以查到你的信用历史。在美国的国际学生也可以申请 SSN，但卡上注明了一个重要的限制信息，就是 VALID FOR WORK ONLY WITH INS AUTHORIZATION，意思是"只有得到移民局授权才能工作"，所以学生要想在校外工作，只有这个卡是不行的，还要寻求移民局授权。

申请的方法是亲自前往当地最近的社会安全局(Social Security Administration)，带上护照和其他文件，在等候室取号排队，叫到号码就到相应的窗口去回答询问，问话都很简单，无非是你为什么到美国来。各大学在开学不久也为国际学生申办社会安全卡而专门把社会安全局的工作人员请到学校现场办公(on-the-spot application)，就不用跑到现场去等候了。申请之后两个星期内一般会收到邮寄来的社会安全卡，如果发现名字打印错了，可以要求更改。

Applying for SSN 10

申请社会安全号

注 释

① 别人为你做了事情、提供了服务、说了有用的话等等,都要表示感谢。但说表示感谢的词语却不仅仅限于"Thank you."，为了加强谢意或更加客气,我们可以用升调,我们也可以用别的说法:

Thanks.（谢谢。）
Thanks a lot.（多谢。）
Appreciate it.（感谢。）
Thank you.（谢谢您。）
Thanks very much.（非常感谢。）
I appreciate it.（我真感谢了。）
Thank you very much.（非常谢谢您了。）
Thank you very much indeed.（实在是谢谢您了。）
I would like to thank you.（我要谢谢您。）
That's very kind of you.（太谢谢您了。）
I appreciate what you did.（我感谢您做的一切。）

后面几种是比较正式的用语。表达更加客气可以说明为什么要感谢,加上理由,如:

Thank you for your helping me finish the homework.（谢谢您帮我完成了作业。）

还有些词语书面用得更多,如 grateful、gratitude、indebted 等,如:

I am very grateful to you for inviting me to visit your college.（我对您邀请我访问你们学院非常感激。）

② What's up 意思是"怎么呢？发生什么事呢？"如:

He is very pale. What's up with him?（他脸色很苍白。怎么啦？）

Driver's License
考驾驶执照

Topic Introduction 话题导言

一到美国就会显出驾驶执照的重要性,一是因为汽车就是美国人的"腿",没有车寸步难行;二是驾驶执照是最为重要的身份证件。所以,申请驾驶执照越早越好。人生地不熟,在哪里申请以及如何申请都是问题。

先找周围的人问一问 Where's the driver's license office?(驾驶执照办公室在哪里?),然后去申请,说 I need a driver's license.(我需要驾驶执照),就会被告知如何做了。

Situational Dialogs 情景对话

新移民叶丽敏(Limin)和留学生杨洋(Yang Yang)都去申请驾驶执照,有时候难免出错。

Dialog 1

Officer: How are you today? What can I do for you?
您今天好吗?我能为您做些什么?

Limin: Fine, thank you, and you? I'd like to apply for[1] a driver's license.
很好,谢谢。您呢?我要申请驾驶执照。

Driver's License 11

Officer:	Good. Are you an American citizen, permanent resident or an alien?
	我很好。您是美国公民、永久居民还是外国人？
Limin:	I'm a new immigrant, but haven't got my green card.
	我是新移民，但还没有拿到绿卡。
Officer:	I see. We need your passport, social security card and other documents that can verify your status here.
	我清楚了。我们需要您的护照、社会安全卡以及其他能证明您身份的文件。
Limin:	Everything is here.
	都在这里。
Officer:	Did you drive before in China?
	您以前在中国开过车了吗？
Limin:	No, never.
	没有，从来没有。
Officer:	So, you need to go to any one of the three driving schools for a six hours' driving course. You will get a certificate after you successfully complete the course, and then come back here. This is the list of the driving schools. Any one is OK.
	这样，您需要去三所驾驶学校中的一所上6个小时的驾驶课程。成功完成之后您将得到一个证书，然后再回到这儿来。这是这三所学校的名单，任何一所都可以。
Limin:	Yes, I see. Thank you very much.
	是的，我明白。非常感谢。
Officer:	You are welcome.
	不用谢。

Dialog 2

Officer:	Hello, how can I help you?
	您好，我怎样帮您呢？
Yang Yang:	I'm an international student from China. This is my passport, social security card and I-20. I'd like to have a driver's license.
	我是来自中国的留学生，这是我的护照，社会安全卡和I-20表。我想要驾驶执照。

Officer: But you don't study in Louisiana.
但您并不是在路易斯安那州学习。

Yang Yang: No, madam. I've just finished my language program at the University of Idaho. I'm applying for admission of MPA program at Louisiana State University at Baton Rouge, and I'm waiting for a new I-20.
没有，夫人。我刚刚完成在爱达荷大学的语言项目。我正在申请路易斯安那州立大学巴吞鲁日校区的 MPA 项目，正在等我新的 I-20 表。

Officer: Your grace period② will end May 5th. I'm not sure if we can let you have your driver's license because there remains only 15 days of your grace period. There may be a great problem if you can't get your new I-20 within these 15 days. I have to check the Immigration Office at Baton Rouge. Please wait a second, and I'll phone them.
您呆在美国的宽限期 5 月 5 日结束，我不敢肯定我们能发给您驾驶执照，因为您的宽限期只剩下 15 天。如果您在 15 天之内得不到新的 I-20 表，可能会出现大的问题。我得联系巴吞鲁日移民办公室。请等一下，我就给他们打个电话。

Yang Yang: I'm sorry to trouble you. I can wait.
很抱歉麻烦您，我可以等。

……

Officer: It's OK now. Please fill in the form. The immigration officer asked me to remind you that you should go to Baton Rouge to extend your status as soon as possible.
现在好了，请填这张表。移民局官员让我提醒您，您应当尽快到巴吞鲁日去延长您的身份。

Yang Yang: Thank you. I will.
谢谢，我会去的。

Dialog 3

Officer: Are you ready, madam?
准备好了吗，小姐？

Driver's License 11

考驾驶执照

Limin:	Yes, sir. 好了,先生。
Officer:	Turn on the headlights, rear lights and then. ... Not bad, let's go. 打开前灯,尾灯,然后……不错,出发吧。
Limin:	Yes, sir. 好的,先生。
Officer:	Go straight ahead and then turn left at the sign. 一直往前走,然后在那个牌子处转向左边。
Limin:	Turn left? 左转?
Officer:	Right. 对的。
Limin:	So I will turn right. (Thinking to himself)③ 我要右转了。(心里想)
Officer:	Stop, please. You've made a wrong turn. 请停下,您转错了。
Limin:	I'm sorry, sir. 对不起,先生。

Typical Sentences
典型句型

1) I'd like to apply for a driver's license.
   我要申请驾驶执照。
2) I'd like to have a driver's license.
   我想要驾驶执照。
3) I'm a new immigrant, but haven't got my green card.
   我是新移民,但还没有拿到绿卡。
4) I'm sorry to trouble you. I can wait.
   很抱歉麻烦您,我可以等。
5) Are you an American citizen, permanent resident or an alien?
   您是美国公民、永久居民还是外国人?

6) We need your passport, social security card and other documents that can verify your status here.

   我们需要您的护照、社会安全卡以及其他能证明您身份的文件。

7) You need to go to any one of the three driving schools for a six hours' driving course.

   您需要去三所驾驶学校中的一所上6个小时的驾驶课程。

8) You will get a certificate after you successfully complete the course, and then come back here.

   成功完成之后您将得到一个证书,然后再回到这儿来。

9) Turn on the headlights, rear lights and then. ... Not bad, let's go.

   打开前灯,尾灯,然后……不错,出发吧。

10) Go straight ahead and then turn left at the sign.

    一直往前走,然后在那个牌子处转向左边。

背景知识

驾驶执照(Driver's License):是驾驶汽车的凭证,也是美国最重要的身份证件。驾照由各州颁发,全美没有统一的样式,办理机构名称各州也不尽相同,有的叫做 Motor Administration(机动车管理局)、有的叫做 Automobile Office (汽车办公室)、有的叫做 Vehicle Office(车辆办公室)、有的干脆就是 Driver's License Office(驾驶执照办公室),不管名称如何,这些机构都是州交通厅(Department of Transportation)的下设机构。

申请时带上护照、绿卡、I-20 表等原始证件前往当地的相应机构去当面申请,有的州会安排你到经过核准的驾驶学校(Driving School)学习交通规则和安全常识,然后参加所学内容的考试;有的州不要求你去驾驶学校学习,自己看书就可以直接参加交通规则和安全常识的考试了。大城市可以选择用汉语进行考试,小城市和个别州规定只能用英语。知识考试合格后才能在有驾照的他人指导下学习驾车,待掌握驾车技术后再申请路试(Road Test),通过路

Driver's License 11

考驾驶执照

试后即可获得驾照。不管是知识考试还是路考，一次不及格可以多次考。

　　知识考试合格而路考不合格者可以要求发一个学习证件，通常称作 Learner's Permit，实际上跟正式驾照在外观上没有什么区别，而且名称也叫做 Driver's License，只是限制项增加了一条：W/lic driver only，意思是 You can drive with licensed driver only.（您只能在有驾照者的陪同下才能驾车。）

　　驾驶执照主要内容为本人的照片、本人的姓名以及签名、本人的出生日期、本人的性别、本人的住址、本人的个人特征资料（体重、身高、肤色等）、证件编号、发证机构、发证日期以及限制条件（如必须配戴眼镜）。由于驾驶执照包含了以上各项内容，因此驾照在美国生活中成为一项重要的个人身份证件。

注　释

① apply for 意思是"申请，请求"，如：apply for job / post / passport / visa （申请工作 / 职位 / 护照 / 签证）。

② 按照美国移民局的规定，外国学生在学业完成之后只能在美国再逗留 60 天，这 60 天就被称作 grace period（宽限期）。对于获得学位的留学生可以申请逗留 12 个月以找工作或实习。

③ 因为 right 是多义词，即"右边"和"正确"，这位女士想确认一下是左转还是右转，结果考官回答说 right，实际上这里的意思是"正确"，即应该向左转，然而这位女士理解成右转了。

Buying a Used Car
购买二手车

Topic Introduction
话题导言

美国人上班、上学、购物、游览都离不开汽车。新到一个地方只呆上几天还可以租车来对付，而一旦定居在一个城市，有时公共交通又不方便，买辆车是必须考虑的事情。

经济上很有实力，当然可以买新车。而初到美国的人士一般并不富裕，买二手车或者说旧车(used car)的还是绝大多数。与买卖其他物品不同，旧车交易可以讨价还价的空间比较大，如果不是对汽车很在行，很可能会吃亏，特别是美国的汽车没有报废期更会令人摸不着门。因此带上一个懂行的朋友帮你谈价钱、试车、买保险、上牌照、纳税等是很有必要的。

Situational Dialogs
情景对话

拿到了驾照，下一步，叶丽敏(Limin)想买一部二手车，但是二手车市场似乎没有合适的，幸好朋友的姐姐有合适的车要出售。

Buying a Used Car 12

购买二手车

Dialog 1

Clerk: Hi, how are you? What kind of car do you like best?
嗨,您好吗? 哪一种车您最喜欢?

Limin: I'm pretty good. How are you? I'm just looking around.
我很好,您也好吗? 我只是看看。

Clerk: I'm fine. Do you need any recommendations?
我很好。需要推荐吗?

Limin: Sure, I need one about three years old Japanese car, like Honda or Toyota or something like that①.
当然,我需要一部三年的日本车,像本田或丰田或诸如此类。

Clerk: How about the price limit?
您的价格上限是多少?

Limin: My budget is 3000 dollars.
我的预算是 3000 美元。

Clerk: OK. This Mazda is three years old, automatic transmission with a power steering, power brakes and air-conditioning, and the price is 3800.
好的,这辆马自达有三年了,自动变速,动力方向盘,动力刹车和空调,价格是 3800 美元。

Limin: But the price is too high. Would you give me a discount?
但这价格太高,您能给我折扣吗?

Clerk: You can have a trial drive first and if you are really interested in it we can discuss it later.
您可以先试开,如果真的感兴趣,我们再讨论。

Limin: But my driver's license is only a learner's permit. Could you accompany me?
可我的驾驶执照只是个学习证,您能陪我吗?

Clerk: Sure, madam. Let's go.
当然,小姐。我们上路吧。

75

Dialog 2

Limin: I have been thinking about getting a newer car, but I can't afford a brand-new one.
我一直想搞到一辆较新的车,可崭新的车我又买不起。

Peter: My sister is going to take a job in Los Angeles and she wants to sell her car. It's a 2006 Nissan Altima with only 70,000 miles.
我姐姐正要到洛杉矶去工作,她想卖掉她的车,是一辆2006年的尼桑奥体马,只有70,000英里。

Limin: That sounds not bad. Is it automatic or manual?
听起来不错,自动还是手动?

Peter: Automatic. I have driven it several times. It runs very well.
自动。我开过几次,很不错。

Limin: By the way②, how much does your sister ask for?
顺便说一下,您姐姐要多少钱?

Peter: I don't know for sure③. You may talk with her.
我也搞不确切,您可以和她谈谈。

Limin: Can you arrange me to have a look?
您能否安排我看看?

Peter: Okay. I'll phone her this evening.
好的,我今晚给她打电话。

典型句型

1) I'd like to see if there is a used car I'm interested in.
   我想看看是否有我感兴趣的二手车。

2) I'm planning to buy a used car.
   我正计划买一部旧车。

3) I'm looking for a used Japanese car, like Honda or Toyota or something like that.
   我在找一辆日本二手车,像本田、丰田或者类似的。

Buying a Used Car 12

4) I'm looking for a model less than three years old.

   我在找一辆车龄低于三年的车。

5) Is the car on the ad a four-door or a two-door?

   广告上的车是四门的还是两门的？

6) Is it automatic or manual?

   是自动的还是手动的？

7) I'm feeling the car too expensive because you have used it for four years.

   因为您已经用了四年了，我觉得太贵了。

8) This price is far beyond my budget.

   这个价格远远超过我的预算。

9) Would you like to buy the car by check or pay cash?

   您买这车是付支票还是付现金？

10) The engine of thi`s car is very excellent.

    这车的发动机非常好。

背景知识

　　二手车信息：要买二手车车，可以通过各种渠道了解二手车的信息。(1)互联网(internet)，很多汽车交易商都在网上公布了他们的交易范围、车型、报价。一般买当地交易商的比较好，因为你查到信息后可以直接到车行去。不要贪图网上的便宜车，但网上外地车的价格可以作为讨价还价的一个参考。(2)报纸广告(newspaper advertisements)，特别注意当地报纸的分类广告(classifieds)和专版汽车广告，然后再去实地了解。(3)汽车广告(wheel sales)，很多地方都有专业的二手车广告，一个星期或半月出版一期，在各大超市、机构等都可以免费取阅。(4)车身广告(poster)，很多人想把汽车卖掉时就直接在自己的车上贴一个招贴"For Sale"，上面注明电话、价格或更加详细的内容。(5)旧车市场(used car market)，一般在城市的边缘都有很大的旧车交易市场，大公司的展场甚至有数个足球场那么大，车上都有出厂年月、型号、价格、什么零件大修过等信息。

生活流畅美语

汽车种类：买车就要知道车的名堂，如型号、类型等，略列几个词语：full-size（大型）、mid-size（中型）、subcompact（小型）、new model（新车）、used car（二手车）、hardtop（硬顶小客车）、sedan（轿车）、coupe（双座小轿车）、jeep（吉普车）、van（面包车、旅行车）、sports car（跑车）、runabout（敞篷车）、truck（卡车）、pickup（小卡车）等。

还有值得一提的就是美国汽车协会（American Automobile Association，简称AAA），购买汽车后到机动车管理局（Department of Motor Vehicles）登记注册，就可以加入到AAA了。成为其会员就会享受很多低廉或免费的服务，如修理、拖车等，只需按照要求缴纳会费就可以了。

注　释

① something like that 是"诸如此类，类似"的意思，有时候略为 something，例如：
Are you crazy or something (like that)? （您是疯了还是怎么了？）
She is called Yukovsky or something like that. （人们叫她尤科夫斯基之类的。）
否定句中 something 要改为 anything，如：
She is not a professor at all or anything like that. （她根本不是教授或类似的人物。）
口语中还可以听到：and things like that（等等）。

② by the way 是插入语，意思是"顺便问一下"。

③ for sure 是口头用语，意思是"确定，肯定"，等于 certainly so 或 exactly 等。

At the Supermarket
超市购物

Topic Introduction
话题导言

美国的超市和近几年中国发展起来的超市本质上没有什么区别,只是规模大得多,多数位于城市郊区,步行是难于到达的,因而新到美国者要结伴去购物,邀一个有车的同伴一块儿去。

美国的大型超级市场雇用的工作人员是很少的,即使如此,也免不了要和店员交谈,特别是当你不知道找你所需要的东西时,要学会问:Where can I find... (我在哪里可以找到……)?进门和结账时也要用到英语,还要了解他们是否接受个人支票或者信用卡以及退货的规定,而且同伴之间还要交谈。

Situational Dialogs
情景对话

逛超级市场总是一件惬意的事情,在这里什么都可以买到。刘杭(Liu Hang)和杨洋(Yang Yang)和朋友去逛超级市场,但是若找不到需要的东西的时候,那就要求助工作人员了。另外去之前了解该超市的结账方式也是很重要的哦。

Dialog 1

Liu Hang: Oh, what a nice large supermarket.
噢,多么好的一个大超市!

Mark: So it is. Things are cheaper in a supermarket than in an ordinary store.
是很大。超市的东西要比一般商店的东西便宜。

Liu Hang: Let's get a shopping cart, shall we?
让我们拿一辆购物手推车,好吗?

Mark: All right. You can get almost everything you need in a supermarket.
好的,你在超市可以买到你需要的几乎一切东西。

Liu Hang: Which section do we go to first?
我们先去哪个部呢?

Mark: Let's first look at the fruit.
先看看水果吧!

Liu Hang: OK. And then I am going to buy some pork.
好的,然后,我想买些猪肉。

Mark: If I were you, I would rather① buy a larger package. Larger packages are usually cheaper. That also saves you the trouble of shopping every day or two.
如果我是你,我宁愿买大包的。大包的东西通常会便宜些。这也避免了你一两天就买一次东西的麻烦。

Liu Hang: Perhaps you are right. I'm worrying that this large bag is beyond my need these days.
也许您是对的。我正担心这一大包超过了我这些天的需要。

Mark: It can't be so. You eat every day.
怎么会呢。你每天都要吃的。

Liu Hang: Is there the bean curd② here? It's a typical Chinese food.
这里有豆腐吗? 这是一种典型的中国食品。

Mark: That will be at the section of vegetables.
那东西在蔬菜部。

Liu Hang: I'm short of cookers. I need a pan, a pan turner and some scoops.
我缺少炊具,我需要一个锅、一个锅铲和几个勺子。

At the Supermarket 13

超市购物

Mark:	It is a better choice to buy a non-stick frying pan.
	买一个不粘炒锅是个更好的选择。
Liu Hang:	You said it.③
	你说对了。

Dialog 2

Cashier:	That comes to④ forty-eight dollars and ninety-five cents, sir.
	总共是48美元95美分,先生。
Yang Yang:	Will you take a check?
	你们收支票吗?
Cashier:	Sorry, sir. You'll have to pay in cash or by credit card.
	对不起,先生。您必须支付现金或使用信用卡。
Yang Yang:	All right. I'd like to pay by credit card.
	好的,我用信用卡支付。
Cashier:	Certainly, sir.
	当然可以,先生。
Yang Yang:	Here it is. Do I have to enter my PIN⑤?
	好的。我要输入密码吗?
Cashier:	No, sir. But would you please sign your name here, at the bottom of the slip?
	不用,先生。请您在这儿签名,在单子的下端,好吗?
Yang Yang:	Yes. It's finished.
	好的,完成了。
Cashier:	Thank you very much. Welcome again.
	非常感谢,欢迎再来。

Typical Sentences 典型句型

1) Excuse me, where can I find leather shoes?
   请问,皮鞋在哪里卖?
2) Things are cheaper in a supermarket than in an ordinary store.
   超级市场的东西要比一般商店的东西便宜。

3) Let's get a shopping cart.
   让我们拿一辆购物手推车。
4) You can get almost everything you need in a supermarket.
   你在超级市场可以买到你需要的几乎一切东西。
5) Which section do we go to first?
   我们先去哪个部呢?
6) Let's first look at the fruit.
   先看看水果吧!
7) I am thinking of buying some pork.
   我想买些猪肉。
8) If I were you, I would rather buy a larger package.
   如果我是你,我宁愿买大包的。
9) Larger packages are usually cheaper.
   大包的东西通常会便宜些。
10) That also saves you the trouble of shopping every day or two.
    这也避免了你一两天就买一次东西的麻烦。
11) Is there the bean curd here?
    这里有豆腐吗?
12) That will be at the section of vegetables.
    那东西在蔬菜部。
13) It's a typical Chinese dish.
    这是一种典型的中国食品。
14) It is a better choice to buy a non-stick frying pan.
    买一个不粘炒锅是个更好的选择。
15) I am afraid it's beyond my means.
    我怕这会超过我的财力。
16) Can I use my credit card or personal check?
    我可以用信用卡或者个人支票吗?

At the Supermarket 13

超市购物

Background 背景知识

　　超级市场,即大型自选市场,是美国最为大众化的购物场所。超级市场起源于上世纪初的加利福尼亚州。经过一个世纪的发展,美国的超级市场在数量和规模上有了惊人的变化,全美目前有40,000多家超级市场,每个超级市场占地30,000多平方英尺,出售商品18,000多种。美国最为有名的超级市场是沃尔玛(Wal-Mart)和凯玛特(K-Mart)。一般位于城市的郊区,有宽大的停车场,价格低廉,吸引了大量的顾客。其他大型连锁超市还有克罗杰(Kroger)、艾伯森(Albertsons)、萨夫威(Safeway)等。

Notes 注释

① would rather... (than)意思是"宁愿,宁可",如:
She would rather die than lose the children. (她宁愿死也不愿失去孩子。)

② 词语 bean curd 很多美国人听不懂,不知道你说的是"豆腐",他们更多地使用"tofu"一词。

③ You said it.的意思是"你说对了,你说的对极了"等。类似的说法还有:
You can say that again. (你说得没错。)
Right on! (说得没错。)
You're telling me. (就跟你说的一样。)
That makes two of us. (我的想法也一样。)

④ come to something 指"共计为某数,等于某数"。

⑤ PIN 是 personal information number 的缩写,有时候也用 password 或 code 代替这个词。

Buying at Farmer's Market
逛农民市场

Topic Introduction 话题导言

星期六上午,去逛农民市场(Farmer's Market)可以买到新鲜的蔬菜和水果,明码标价,不用讨价还价,比起超市里的商品要便宜很多。但在冬季比较漫长的寒冷地区,农民市场并不是一年四季都有,只是在春季比较暖和之后才开市交易,到秋季天气转凉就要停市。如果你是冬天到的美国,等到第二年春天发现还有农民市场这一古老商业的遗留,你一定会很惊讶。虽然类似的市场在芝加哥等大城市也有,但摆摊设点的主体不是农民,买卖的商品也主要是日常生活用品,且讨价还价之声不绝于耳。

Situational Dialogs 情景对话

农民市场上蔬菜水果既便宜又新鲜,刘杭(Liu Hang)就经常去逛星期六上午的农民市场。

Dialog 1

Liu Hang: Excuse me, which kind of chilies is hotter?
请问,哪种辣椒辣一些?

Buying at Farmer's Market   14

逛农民市场

Farmer:	Those at that end. 那一头的那些。
Liu Hang:	I like to buy some medium hot chilies. Do you have some recommendations? 我要买些不太辣的。您介绍一些好吗？
Farmer:	This one in the middle. 中间的这种。
Liu Hang:	Oh, I see. You've lined your baskets of chilies from extremely hot to slightly hot, am I right? 哦，我明白了。您把您的辣椒篮子按照辣的程度从非常辣到有一点点辣排成队了，对吗？
Farmer:	Quite right. Which kind do you like now? 很对，您喜欢要哪一种？
Liu Hang:	I like this kind. They are big and juicy. 我要这一种，又大又多汁。
Farmer:	Okay, just choose what you think is the best. 好的，选些您认为最好的。

Dialog 2

Kevin:	Hello, Liu Hang. It's a coincidence to meet you here. 您好，刘杭。真巧在这里见到您。
Liu Hang:	I'm coming to buy some vegetables for next week. How are you and your family? 我来买些蔬菜下周吃。您和您家人都好吗？
Kevin:	All are pretty good. I like eating vegetables, such as cucumbers, eggplants, lettuces, and green beans. 全家都好。我喜欢吃蔬菜，如黄瓜、茄子、生菜和青豆。
Liu Hang:	The same vegetables can be cooked into different styles. 同样的蔬菜可以做成不同的风味。
Kevin:	Yes, you're an expert and Chinese people are all experts in① cooking. I'd like you to cook some delicious food when we have parties some day. 是的，您是烹调专家，中国人都是烹调专家。哪天我们聚会，我喜欢您做些美味的食品。

Liu Hang: I'm flattered②, but I will cook when I'm needed some day.
您过奖了，不过哪天需要我，我愿意做。

Typical Sentences
典型句型

1) Will you go to the Farmer's Market this Saturday?
这个星期六你去农民市场吗？

2) Not only cheap, but also fresh and something is very special.
不只是便宜，而且新鲜，有些东西还很有特色。

3) I saw you and your husband last Saturday on the Market.
我上个星期六在市场上看到你和你丈夫。

4) Excuse me, which kind of chilies is hotter?
请问，哪种辣椒辣一些？

5) You've lined your baskets of chilies from extremely hot to slightly hot.
您把您的辣椒篮子按照辣的程度从非常辣到有一点点辣排成队了。

6) Okay, just choose what you think is the best.
好的，选些您认为最好的。

7) I'm coming to buy some vegetables for next week.
我来买些蔬菜下周吃。

8) The band is also very excellent.
乐队也非常有些优秀。

9) The performances are very popular there.
那里的表演很受欢迎。

Background
背景知识

农民市场(Farmer's Market)：可以说是美国部分地区古老集市贸易商业文化留下的一个剪影。实际从表象上看，类似于我们中

Buying at Farmer's Market 14

逛农民市场

国的集市贸易。

笔者在美国大部分时间生活在一个只有两万多人口的小城市。每当春暖花开时节到来时，在星期六的清早，离城市不远处农场的农民就开上小卡车，装满自家产的各种水果、蔬菜、鲜花以及各种家庭制作(homemade)的工艺品到距离城中心(downtown)不远处的广场上摆摊设点。部分城市居民和附近大学的一些师生也趁这天是周六而赶来凑热闹，有的卖衣服，有的卖小吃，也有外国留学生来兜售具有本民族特色的物品，更有甚者把锅碗瓢盆搬到市场上去亮出自己煎、烧、炸、蒸、煮等各样厨艺。各种商品都是明码标价，没有人讨价还价，因为比起超市里的商品要便宜很多。整个集市热闹非凡。

还有一点很有美国特色，在广场的一端有一支乐队从早晨一直演奏到中午时分，乐队服装艳丽，乐曲时而威武雄壮，时而欢快流畅，但他们不是为了赚钱卖艺，而是为周末生活增姿添彩。

注 释

① expert in ... 的意思是"……(方面)的专家"，如：
Dr. Smith is an expert in mathematics. (史密斯博士是数学方面的专家。)

② flatter 在这里用作被动语态，指"使某人感到高兴或荣幸"，如：
I was very flattered by your invitation. (承蒙您的邀请，不胜荣幸。)

Going Yard-Sale
逛庭院售卖

Topic Introduction
话题导言

　　从春天转暖直到深秋季节，天气冷暖适宜，人们乐于进行室外活动，很多家庭抓住这个时机，把自家多余的物品或旧货摆在房前屋后的空地、草坪、车库等处对外进行低价销售。这一活动一般在周末两天的每天早上 7:00 至中午 12:00 进行。此前，家庭主人把广告牌贴在附近一些主要十字路口的电线杆上，说明时间、地点和特色，如果销售规模较大，还会在星期三或星期四推出报纸广告。所以，一到周六、周日的早晨大家三五成群开着车就逛开了。

　　"逛 Yard-Sale"成为新移民和留学生中比较流行的词语，因为人们经常在这种活动中买到异常便宜而实用的物件，如台灯、电话机、平底锅、成套餐具、沙发、床垫、皮衣、书包、名牌服装等都是商店售价的几十分之一。有时物主甚至不叫价而由顾客随意给些钱算了。在这方面有一个转变观念的问题，因为大部分东西都是用过的，所以中国人开始都不乐于接受旧物品。入乡随俗，慢慢习惯就好了。

Situational Dialogs
情景对话

逛 Yard-Sale 总是能买到不少好东西，杨洋 (Yang Yang) 和刘杭 (Liu Hang) 总是有所收获。

Going Yard-Sale 15

逛庭院售卖

Dialog 1

Marry:	Hi, Yang Yang. Will you go Yard-Sale tomorrow morning?
	你好,杨洋。明天早晨逛 Yard-Sale 吗?
Yang Yang:	I don't have a car. If you go Yard-Sale, can I go with you?
	我没有车。你要是去,我可以和你一起去吗?
Marry:	Yes. I need a table lamp and a phone answering machine.①
	可以。我想买一个台灯和一个电话答录机。
Yang Yang:	When are we starting out then?
	那我们什么时候出发?
Marry:	I think it better to go earlier. How about 7:30?
	我想早一点比较好,7:30 怎么样?
Yang Yang:	That's OK. Have you got some ads?
	好的,你拿到广告了吗?
Marry:	Yes, I've got today's and yesterday's *Daily News*.
	拿到了,我有今天和昨天的《每日新闻》。
Yang Yang:	That's great. So please pick me up 7:20 at my place.
	很好,那么就请你 7:20 来我这里接我。
Marry:	All right. See you tomorrow morning.
	好的,明早见。

Dialog 2

Yang Yang:	Hello, Good morning.
	早晨好。
Seller:	Good morning. Can I help you?
	早晨好,买东西吗?
Yang Yang:	Yes. How much is the shirt?
	是的,这件衬衣多少钱?
Seller:	Two dollars, sir.
	两美元,先生。
Yang Yang:	How about this table lamp?
	这个台灯多少钱?
Seller:	One dollar.
	一美元。

Yang Yang:	What does this pan cost? 这个平底锅多少钱?
Seller:	One and a half, sir. 一美元五十美分,先生。
Yang Yang:	Could you charge me four dollars for all these three things, I mean,② this shirt, the table lamp and the pan? 我买所有这三样东西,我是指衬衫、台灯和平底锅,您收我四美元怎么样?
Seller:	All right. Please pay to the young lady. 好的,请把钱付给那位年轻女士。

Dialog 3

Liu Hang:	Excuse me, sir? 打搅一下,先生。
Seller:	Yes, may I help you? 好的,您要点儿什么?
Liu Hang:	These books are useful for me. How much are they? 这些书对我来说很有用,多少钱?
Seller:	Pay as you like, madam. 小姐,给多少钱随意。
Liu Hang:	If I add this pair of blue jeans, how much all together? 如果我加上这条蓝色牛仔裤,总共多少钱?
Seller:	We have no price, madam. Pay as you think. 我们没有价格,小姐。想给多少就给多少。
Liu Hang:	I take five books and a pair of jeans. I'm wondering if it's suitable for me to pay six dollars in all③. 我要这五本书和一条牛仔裤,我不知道总共六美元是否合适。
Seller:	Six dollars is enough. 六美元足够了。
Liu Hang:	Thank you for your generous offer. 谢谢您的慷慨。

Going Yard-Sale 15
逛庭院售卖

Typical Sentences
典型句型

1) Will you go Yard-Sale tomorrow morning?
   明天早晨逛 Yard-Sale 吗？

2) If you go Yard-Sale, can I go with you?
   你要是去逛 Yard-Sale，我可以和你一起去吗？

3) I need a table lamp and a phone answering machine.
   我想买一个台灯和一个电话答录机。

4) Have you got some ads?
   你拿到广告了吗？

5) Could you charge me four dollars for all these three things, I mean, this shirt, the table lamp and the pan?
   我买所有这三样东西，我是指衬衫、台灯和平底锅，您收我四美元怎么样？

6) If I add this pair of blue jeans, how much all together?
   如果我加上这条蓝色牛仔裤，总共多少钱？

7) We have no price, sir. Pay as you think.
   我们没有价格，先生。想给多少就给多少。

8) I take five books and a pair of jeans. I'm wondering if it's suitable for me to pay six dollars in all.
   我要这五本书和一条牛仔裤，我不知道总共六美元是否合适。

9) Thank you for your generous offer.
   谢谢您的慷慨。

Background
背景知识

家售服务：巨型购物中心、超级市场和连锁店是美国商业文化的主体背景，显现出市场发达、购销两旺的火暴场面。另一种销售方式却与之形成强烈反差，即居家销售：

（1）Yard-Sale，庭院销售，在自家门前的草坪上举行，是居家销售最多的一种形式，人们就用"Yard-Sale"一词统称诸如此类的销售形式。

（2）Moving Sale，搬家销售，美国人因调换工作或寻找喜欢的气候条件，一生中多次迁徙，如果搬到较远的地方去，要处理掉大部分家用物品。家庭主人发出搬家销售的广告后，把物品分类摆放在室内室外、楼上楼下，欢迎惠顾。

（3）Garage Sale，家庭主人平时把准备销售的物品存放在车库里，当天卖不完的物品也不用收拾移动，第二天继续开张。

（4）Porch Sale，家庭主人平时把准备出售的物品存放在走廊，这样销售活动就在走廊举行了。

（5）Multi-Family Sale，多家销售，是互为邻居的几个家庭把各种物品集中到其中一家的草坪上，联合出售。

（6）Block Sale，街区销售，是一个街区的多个家庭预约同日进行。多个家庭在相同的销售日把物品摆在各自户外的草坪上，供人们选购。

（7）Basement Sale，地下室销售，冬天室外气温偏低，主人就在地下室售卖多余物品，并在房前的草坪上安放指示牌，引导人们直接入室选购。

（8）Boutique Sale，美国一些家庭妇女不外出工作，利用操持家务的空余时间制作妇女和儿童针织品，比如披肩、围巾、枕巾和头饰等，图案精美，工艺考究，具有浓厚的民族特色，然后会选准一个时机把这些物品出售。

Going Yard-Sale 15 逛庭院售卖

注释

① phone answering machine(电话答录机),是具有录音功能的电话机,在美国广泛使用,当主人不在或不愿意接听电话时,就打开它以便让打进电话的人留言。提示音内容大同小异,如:
Hello, John here. I'm sorry I can't answer your call now, but if you leave your name and phone number at the tone, I'll get back to you as soon as I can. Thank you. (您好,我是约翰。很抱歉现在不能接听您的电话,如果能在一声响后留下姓名和电话,我会尽快和您联络。谢谢。) 有的非常简单,如:
Sorry Bill is not available now, please leave a message. (对不起,比尔不在,请留言。)

② I mean 是插入语,用于解释或改正所说出的话。

③ in all 和 all together 的意思相同,都是"一起,总共"的意思。

At an Electric Appliance Shop
在电器商店

Topic Introduction
话题导言

　　电器商品是人们的日常生活必需品之一，购买电器是必不可少的活动。在美国，购买电器可以去专门的商店，也可以到超市去选购。专门商店品种齐全，可供选择的余地很大，超市的电器品种较少，往往是一些大众的品牌，价格可能会低一些。Circuit City 是比较有名气的连锁店，全国有很多分店，也可以通过网上购买。电器商品是耐用消费品，售后服务是必须考虑的因素，你在一家店购买了商品到同一公司的另一家连锁店也可以退换和维修。

　　一段时间没有某种电器使用不会给生活带来很大的不便，因此购买时机也是应该选择的，因为某个时段的价格会大大低于平时的售价。根据经验，感恩节后的两三天是购买家用电器的黄金时期，一般商品的降价幅度在 40% 或更多，更有一些小家电免费赠送。平时 9 点钟才开门营业的商店，这几天清晨时段大门外已经排起等待购物的长队，商店 7 点钟也开门营业了。这种场景在美国只有这个时候才有，与平时商店生意稀稀拉拉形成了强烈对比。据报道，很多商店这三天的营业额占到全年的 20% 或更多。

At an Electric Appliance Shop 16

在电器商店

Situational Dialogs 情景对话

电器是人们生活必不可少的必须品,杨洋(Yang Yang)和刘杭(Liu Hang)要去买一些电器。

Dialog 1

Yang Yang: Hello, where are you going shopping tomorrow morning?
你好,明天早晨到哪里去买东西?

Mary: I have no idea.① CostCo. has a lot of good buys②. Something is free, like laptop case, CD case and something like that.
我也不知道,CostCo.有很多便宜货,有些甚至不要钱,像手提电脑包、CD 包以及类似的东西。

Yang Yang: But I hear Circuit City will have a lot of cheap things, and something is just half price.
但我听说 Circuit City 有很多便宜货,有些东西只是半价。

Mary: That's true. This is really a steal.③ What do you need to get?
是的,真是很便宜的。你需要买什么?

Yang Yang: I need a laptop, a digital camera, and a CD player for my daughter.
我需要一台笔记本电脑,一个数码照相机,给我女儿买个 CD 播放机。

Mary: Better go to Circuit City in Spokane. These stuffs are a dime a dozen④.
最好还是斯波坎的 Circuit City,这些东西便宜得很。

Yang Yang: You mean they are dirt cheap⑤?
你说它们很便宜?

Mary: You got it.
对了。

95

Dialog 2

Shop assistant: Good morning. Can I help you?
早晨好,您要买点儿什么?

Liu Hang: I'd like to buy a Walkman.
我想买一台随身听。

Shop assistant: Is there any particular brand you are interested in?
有什么你感兴趣的品牌吗?

Liu Hang: I would certainly prefer a Japanese brand.
我当然喜欢日本牌子的了。

Shop assistant: How do you think of this Sony? It is digital, has an auto-reverse, and a super bass.
你觉得索尼怎么样呢? 这是数码的,自动回转和超低音。

Liu Hang: What about the price of these brands?
这些牌子的价格都怎么样?

Shop assistant: This Sony is 99 dollars, and... .
这台索尼是 99 美元,还有……

Liu Hang: Why is the price so different?
价格为什么有所不同呢?

Shop assistant: Sony offers the best quality.
因为索尼的质量最好。

Liu Hang: I see. I'd like to take a Sony.
我明白了,就买台索尼的吧。

Dialog 3

Shop assistant: Would you tell me what I could do for you, sir?⑥
先生,我能帮您什么忙吗?

Yang Yang: Do you have any camcorders here? I'd like one that can be used both in the United States and China. What would you suggest?
你们这里卖摄像机吗? 我要买一台在美国和中国都能用的。你有什么建议吗?

Shop assistant: This Panasonic meets your needs, which is made in Malaysia.
这台松下符合您的要求,是马来西亚生产的。

Yang Yang: It looks nice. How much is it?
看上去不错,多少钱?

16 At an Electric Appliance Shop
在电器商店

Shop assistant: 520 dollars plus tax.
520 美元,外加税金。

Yang Yang: What kind of warranty does it carry?
保修期间提供什么样的服务?

Shop assistant: Parts and labor for 90 days, and parts only for nine more months.
三个月内零件和人工全部免费,以后九个月只有零件免费。

Yang Yang: It's too short.
太短了。

Shop assistant: Yes, you can extend the warranty to three years by paying an extra $130 dollars.
是啊,您多付 130 美元就可以将保修期延长到三年。

Yang Yang: Free parts and labor for three years?
三年零件和人工都免费?

Shop assistant: That's right. This is my recommendation.
对的,这是我的建议。

Yang Yang: You talked me into it. OK, I'll take this camcorder with an extended warranty.
您说服我了,好的,我就要了这台摄像机并延长保修期。

Typical Sentences
典型句型

1) CostCo. has a lot of good buys.
   CostCo.有很多便宜货。

2) But I hear Circuit City will have a lot of cheap things, and something is just half price.
   但我听说 Circuit City 有很多便宜货,有些东西只是半价。

3) I need a laptop, a digital camera, and a CD player for my daughter.
   我需要一台笔记本电脑,一个数码照相机,给我女儿买个 CD 播放机。

4) These stuffs are a dime a dozen.
   这些东西便宜得很。

5) You mean they are dirt cheap?
   您说它们很便宜?
6) I'd like to buy a Walkman.
   我想买一台随身听。
7) I would certainly prefer a Japanese brand.
   我当然喜欢日本牌子的了。
8) What about the price of these brands?
   这些牌子的价格都怎么样?
9) What kind of warranty does it carry?
   保修期间提供什么样的服务?
10) I'll take this camcorder with an extended warranty.
    我就要了这台摄像机并延长保修期。
11) There're so many different kinds here that I really can't make up my mind.
    这么多种类,我还无法决定。
12) What price range do you have in mind?
    你要的价格范围是什么?
13) If you prefer one with digital tuning, you may take this Panasonic.
    如果你喜欢数码调台,你可以买这台松下的。

购买家电:在美国购买家电需注意如下几个问题:

(1) 时机,感恩节的本意是要感谢上帝的恩赐,现在商家利用这一节日来感谢顾客一年来的关照,节后降价成为美国商业界的一大风景。一般人选择在感恩节后第一天或第二天购买电器,早晨7点之前赶到商店门口排队,因为去晚了很多减价商品或免费赠送商品会被一抢而空。事先就要通过互联网或报纸查阅广告,了解减价动态。

At an Electric Appliance Shop 16 在电器商店

（2）税率，商店货品的标价都不包括消费税在内，税率各州不同，住在几个州交界地带的人们经常利用这一点"越境"购物。电器属于价格较高的商品，税率低就可以少付钱。如爱达荷州为5%，而华盛顿州为10%，但华盛顿州食品免税，爱达荷州北部和华盛顿州东部交界地区的人们经常利用这一点。

（3）回扣，除了降价以外，商家或厂家在感恩节期间也派发现金返还券，称作rebate。方法是顾客把收据复印件和rebate，连同商品包装上的条码一起邮寄到指定的地址，几个星期之后就会收到返还的现金支票或转账支票。

（4）保修，家用电器保修是人所共知的，购买时一定要弄清楚保修期限多长以及保修内容，如果觉得保修期太短，可以"购买"更长的保修期。

（5）电压，经常有中国人在美国买了电器带回中国后发现被烧坏了，原因就是电压不一样。美国家用电的电压是110伏，而中国是220伏。一定要问清楚是否可以两用，输入电压介于110至240伏之间的既可以在美国用也可以在中国用。从中国带电器到美国也存在这个问题。

注 释

① I have no idea. 的意思是"我不知道"，和 I don't know. 意思一样。
② a good buy 指的是"便宜货"。
③ This is really a steal. 不是说"偷的东西"，而是表示"便宜得跟偷来的东西一样"，与 cheap 或 inexpensive 意思相同。
④ a dime a dozen 直接翻译过来就是"一角一打"，这里是"非常便宜"的意思。
⑤ dirt cheap 形容价钱很便宜，"便宜得跟尘土一样"，比说 very cheap 让人觉得更便宜。

⑥ Would you tell me what I could do for you, sir?（先生，我能帮您什么忙吗？）是一种非常客气礼貌的称呼，用在这里显示服务人员的用语有些过分。

⑦ You talked me into it. 的意思是"你把我说服了，我就听你的了。"这里 talk 成了及物动词。

At the Barber's
在男美发厅

Topic Introduction
话题导言

讲究容颜是人们日常必需的生活内容之一,对于男士来说理发是必不可少的事情。英语中为男子理发的店叫做男美发厅(Barber's Shop),理发师称作 barber。不同的理发店,价格迥异,有的光是一个剪发(haircut)就是十几、二十美元,也有便宜到七八美元的。因此,临时出国在国外理发绝不是好主意。

不管是贵的店,还是便宜的店,都要事先预约(make an appointment)才行,说清楚是去干什么:理发(haircut)、洗头(shampoo)还是烫发(permanent),还要问清楚你应该几点钟到那儿。对于发型,好像用英语很难说明白,其实只要记住几句话和一些常用术语,就足够应付自如了。

Situational Dialogs
情景对话

理发对于男士来说总是一件不可缺少的事情,李康(Li Kang)和杨洋(Yang Yang)当然也不例外了。去理发不要忘记要事先预约比较好。

Dialog 1

Receptionist: Hello, this is Red Rose. May I help you?
您好,红玫瑰美发厅。能为您服务吗?

Li Kang: I'd like to make an appointment for 4 o'clock this afternoon.
我想预约到今天下午 4 点来理发。

Receptionist: Certainly, sir. But could you come half an hour later?
当然可以,先生。不过,您能否晚来半个小时?

Li Kang: OK. I will be there at 4:30.
好的,我 4:30 到你们那里。

Receptionist: We're expecting you then. By the way, may I know your name, please?
到时我们等着您。顺便问一下,您贵姓?

Li Kang: Li Kang. L-I K-A-N-G.
我叫李康,写作 L-I K-A-N-G。

Receptionist: Thank you. And see you later.
谢谢,再见。

Li Kang: Good bye.
再见。

Dialog 2

Barber: Good afternoon, sir.
先生,下午好。

Li Kang: Good afternoon. I have an appointment at 4:30.
下午好。我跟你们预约的四点半。

Barber: So you are Mr. Li, am I right?
那么,您就是李先生了,对吗?

Li Kang: Yes, I am. My name is Li Kang.
是的,我叫李康。

Barber: Please sit here and take off your glasses. Now, how would you like your hair cut?[①]
请坐在这里,取下眼镜。那么,您想怎样理呢?

Li Kang: Er...
哦……

At the Barber's 17

在男美发厅

Barber: Would you keep the same fashion?
您要保持原来的样式吗?

Li Kang: No. Please cut the sides and back fairly short, but leave the front as it is.
不,请把两边和后边剪短些,前面就留成现在这个样子。

Barber: What about the top then?
头顶上怎么理?

Li Kang: Just a trim, please.
请只修整一下。
……

Barber: Please have a look. Is it all right?
请看一看。行吗?

Li Kang: Could you cut a bit more off the temples?
请把鬓角剪掉多些,好吗?

Barber: Yes, sir. Now, do you want me to shampoo your hair?
好的,先生。您要洗头吗?

Li Kang: Yes, I like it shampooed.
要,我要把头洗一下。

Barber: And now for the shave. Do you want me to trim your moustache?
现在到刮脸了,您要把胡子修整一下吗?

Li Kang: Oh, please don't.
哦,不用了。

Barber: And do you want some spray?
要喷发胶吗?

Li Kang: No, nothing at all.
不要,什么都不要了。

Barber: Then, it is finished. I hope you are satisfied.
那么,完成了。我希望您满意。

Li Kang: Yes, you've done your work quite well. Thank you very much.
满意,您做得不错。非常感谢您。

Barber: I'm glad you like it.
您喜欢,我很高兴。

Dialog 3

Yang Yang: Do you receive walk-ins, miss?
小姐,临时来的客人,你们接待吗?

Barber: Certainly, sir. But you have to wait about ten minutes.
当然,先生,但您得等大约10分钟。

……

Barber: Would you like me to shampoo your hair?
要洗头吗?

Yang Yang: Yes, please.
要洗头。

Barber: How do you want your hair cut?
你要理什么发式?

Yang Yang: I have no idea. Please do what you think is nice.
我也不知道,您认为怎么好看就怎么理吧。

Barber: Here are some patterns of hairstyles② for your choice.
这里有一些发型的式样,请你选择。

Yang Yang: That's wonderful. Just this fashion, please.
真是好极了。请就按这种发式。

……

Barber: It's finished. Do you like a body massage, sir?
现在理好了。你要全身按摩吗,先生?

Yang Yang: No, thanks. I'm afraid there's no enough time.
不了,谢谢。我恐怕时间不够。

Barber: Thank you for coming. Welcome again.
谢谢光临。欢迎再次光临。

Typical Sentences
典型句型

1) Hello, is that Red Rose? I'd like to make an appointment for 4 o'clock this afternoon.
您好,是红玫瑰美发厅吗?我想预约到今天下午4点来理发。

At the Barber's 17
在男美发厅

2) Do you receive walk-ins, miss?
   小姐,临时来的客人,你们接待吗?

3) Certainly, sir. But you have to wait about ten minutes.
   当然,先生,但您得等大约10分钟。

4) Would you like me to shampoo your hair?
   要洗头吗?

5) How do you want your hair cut?
   你要理什么发式?

6) Here are some patterns of hairstyles② for your choice.
   这里有一些发型的式样,请你选择。

7) Would you keep the same fashion?
   你要保持原有发型吗?

8) How about the sideburns?
   鬓角怎么办呢?

9) Do you want me to shave your beard?
   要我把你的胡子刮掉吗?

10) Do you want your hair parted?
    你要把头发分开吗?

11) Do you want it short or just trimmed?
    你要剪短些还是修修整齐?

12) Would you like your moustache trimmed?
    要修小胡子吗?

13) Do you like a body massage, sir?
    先生,你要全身按摩吗?

14) Do you need a pedicure, sir?
    先生,你要修脚吗?

15) Thank you for coming. Welcome again.
    谢谢光临。欢迎再次光临。

生活流畅美语

Background 背景知识

打理头发：走在美国的大街小巷，你会发现人们的发型多种多样，个别青年还把头发弄得五彩斑斓。很多在美国生活的中国人都觉得其实美国理发店的手艺也不怎么样，而且还奇贵。所以，一般的平民百姓大多习惯于自备理发工具，他们在家人、朋友的帮助下也能整出一头美观的发型。

小费：洗头、剪发、烫发、按摩以及吹风等都是分开计费的，在你按照服务人员开的账目付费之后，还要给理发师加上10%到15%的钱作为小费，不然就显得不够礼貌。

理发常用词汇：

bang 前刘海　　　　　　　part hair 分发
permanent wave 烫出的波浪发型　　crop 平顶头
setting lotion 头发定型液　　cutting & styling 做发型
shock 乱发　　　　　　　electric hair curler 电烫发机
snood 束发结　　　　　　hair fixer 压发
thinning 打薄　　　　　　hairdo 女子做发
trim 修剪　　　　　　　　hairnet 发网

Notes 注释

① "你想剪成什么样的发型？"还可以说成："How would you like your hair done today?"或者"What will it be today?"对于此问题的回答也要注意：Just a trim, please.（只要修一修。）也可以加上 I like long sideburns.（我的鬓角要留长一点。）如果要剪得很短，就回答说：Short cut, please. 若要剪成平头就说：Crew cut, please.

② hairstyle 也可以说成 hairdo，也有人用法语词 coiffure。

At the Beauty Salon
在女美发美容厅

Topic Introduction
话题导言

柔软的青丝、美丽的发型可以打造靓丽的女性,秀出自我风采。这不但是为了整洁美观,而且也是人际交往的需要。英语中为女士理发的店叫做美容院(beauty shop, beauty salon, beauty parlor 或者 hair salon),为女士理发的理发师则叫做 hairdresser,也叫做 hairstylist 或 beautician,美容院主要为客人剪发(cut)、洗头(shampoo)、做发型(set),也给客人化妆(make-up)和修指甲(manicure)。

Situational Dialogs
情景对话

刘杭(Liu Hang)晚上要去参加一个晚会,因此预约去美容厅做头发。

Dialog 1

Hairdresser: Hello, this is Fancy Beauty Salon. Can I help you?
您好,我们是梦幻美容厅。可以帮您吗?

Liu Hang:	Hello. I'd like to dress my hair Wednesday morning. 您好。我想星期三早上来做头发。
Hairdresser:	What time is it convenient for you? 您什么时间方便?
Liu Hang:	I think I will come at eight. Could you make it? 我想8点钟来,能行吗?
Hairdresser:	Certainly, madam. May I know your name? 当然可以,女士。可以告诉我您的姓名吗?
Liu Hang:	Liu Hang. 刘杭。
Hairdresser:	All right. We're looking forward to your arrival then. 那好,我们期待您的光临。
Liu Hang:	See you then. 到时候见。
Hairdresser:	See you at 8 Wednesday evening, Miss. Liu. 周三早上8点见,刘女士。

Dialog 2

Hairdresser:	Good afternoon, madam. How would you like your hair done? 下午好,女士,您喜欢做什么式样的发型?
Liu Hang:	Can you show me some patterns of hair styles first? 能不能先让我看看你这里的发型式样?
Hairdresser:	Certainly, madam. Here are the photos for various kinds of patterns. Which one would you prefer? 好的,女士。这是各种式样的发型照片。您喜欢哪一种?
Liu Hang:	I'm going to attend a party. I think the chaplet hairstyle would be suitable. 我要参加一个晚会。我觉得盘花冠式发型比较合适。
Hairdresser:	Yes, madam. Do you wish to dye your hair? 是的,女士。您想要染发吗?
Liu Hang:	Yes, please. But I've brought my own dyestuff. Please use it after washing my hair. 是的,不过我已经带了染发剂。请你在替我洗发后使用。

At the Beauty Salon 18 在女美发美容厅

Hairdresser: Yes, Madam. Now would you please cover your eyes with this towel? I'm going to give you a rinse.
好的,女士。请您用这条毛巾蒙上眼睛好吗?我要给您冲洗了。

Liu Hang: O.K. I'm ready.
好吧,我准备好了。

Hairdresser: All right. Please sit under the dryer.
好了。请坐到干发器下面来。

Liu Hang: Thank you for your help.
谢谢您的服务。

Hairdresser: I'm always at your service.
我随时乐意为您服务。

Dialog 3

Hairdresser: Good evening, Madam. Would you like your hair done?
晚上好,女士。要做头发吗?

Liu Hang: Yes, I'd like to have my hair shampooed and set①.
是的,我要洗头,并做头发。

Hairdresser: Certainly, madam. Take this chair, please. Shall I make your curls inward or outward?
当然可以,女士。请坐在这把椅子上。您的头发要向内卷还是向外卷?

Liu Hang: Outward, please.
请向外卷吧。

Hairdresser: Styling mousse?
要定型摩丝吗?

Liu Hang: Yes, how much do I owe you?②
要,我该付多少钱?

Hairdresser: That'll be 40 dollars altogether.
总共 40 美元。

Typical Sentences
典型句型

1) Hello, this is Kate. I'd like to dress my hair this evening.
   您好,我是凯特。我想今晚来做头发。

2) I think I will come at eight. Could you make it?
   我想8点钟来,能行吗?

3) So, you're Mrs. Zhou. We're looking forward to your arrival.
   那么,您就是周太太了。我们正期待您的光临。

4) Madam, how would you like your hair done? Washed or dressed?
   夫人,您的头发要怎样处理?洗一洗,还是做一做?

5) Shall I make your curls inward or outward?
   给您的头发做成向里卷还是向外卷?

6) How about some hair tonic? Some hair tonic would be good to your hair.
   来些护发素怎么样?搭点护发素对您的头发有好处。

7) Some hair tonic is good for the scalp and it prevents dandruff.
   来点护发素对头皮有益,可以防止生头皮屑。

8) Would you just hold this towel over your eyes while I give you a rinse?
   请你用这毛巾遮住眼睛,我要给你冲洗一下。

9) Now please come over here to sit under the dryer, madam.
   现在请您坐到干发器下面来,女士。

10) Your hair is graying. Do you want to have it dyed?
    您的头发在变白了。你是否要染一下?

11) This hair tonic is especially good for dry hair.
    这种护发素对干燥的头发特别有用。

12) Do you want a face massage?
    您要做一下脸部按摩吗?

13) Would you like to have a manicure or are you planning to get a manicure later?
    您要修指甲,还是打算以后修指甲?

14) Would you like a facial, madam?
    您要脸部按摩吗,太太?

15) What color would you prefer for your nail-polish?
您喜欢什么颜色的指甲油？

背景知识

　　美发美容院：预约虽然非常重要，但是如果你到了的时候，不到接待台去报到(check in)，服务人员会误认为你是临时进来的客人(walk-in)而让你排队等候。所以，到达的时候一定要说：I have an appointment here.(我有个预约。)一旦确定你按时到了，马上就可以得到服务。

　　费用：遇到在做头发的过程中，理发师问你是否需要别的项目时，可以大胆地问清楚是否另外收费以及收费多少，不要一味地说Yes 或 No，不懂的时候可以请他解释一下具体内容。

注　释

① 这种句型（have something done）在英语中使用得非常广泛。其中 something 与 done 是被动的主谓关系，如"我要理发"就可说成：I'd like to have my hair cut.(字面意思是"我想我的头发被剪")，这里没有说明希望谁做这件事。

② 也可以说：How much shall I pay you?（我该付多少钱？）
How much do you charge for a haircut?（剪发多少钱？）
此种表达可以用于咨询价格。

Eating at a Restaurant
餐馆就餐

Topic Introduction 话题导言

生活习惯的不同体现在方方面面,在英美上餐馆也是这样。进门时没有"迎宾小姐"迎接,而且需要自己动手推开门。一进门就看到迎面有个牌子"Please wait to be seated"(请等候安排座位),要先在柜台附近等一等,切忌自己入座,这时会有人上来打招呼:How are you today? How many are there in your group?(您今天可好? 你们一起有几位?)然后根据人数和空座情况带你入座,不要自己选择桌位,如遇到自己不喜欢的地方,可以礼貌地提出换个桌位。等大家坐定了,侍者先问你需要什么饮料,再给你菜单,由就餐人点菜。

点菜时点到有些菜时,侍者可能会问:How do you want it?(想要菜做得如何?),意思是 Rare, medium, well done?(嫩些、中等、还是老一些?)。根据自己的口味回答,可以是 medium-rare(略嫩些),或 medium-well done(略老些),或 rare(嫩些),或 medium(中等),或 well done(熟透)。如果你买单,记住按照消费金额的 10%到 15%给小费,直接放在餐桌上就可以了。

Eating at a Restaurant

俗话说,民以食为天。但各国饮食文化则千差万别,在美国去餐馆吃饭就有很多与我们不同的方面值得注意。

Dialog 1

Waitress: How are you today, sir?
先生,您今天好吗?

Li Kang: Pretty good, thanks. And how are you?
很好,谢谢。您好吗?

Waitress: I'm fine, sir. How many in your group today?
我很好,先生。你们今天多少人?

Li Kang: We're five altogether.
我们总共五个。

Waitress: Do you smoke or not?①
吸烟吗?

Li Kang: No, we don't.
不吸烟。

Waitress: How about the table near the window?
靠近窗户的那张桌子如何?

Li Kang: That table is nice.
那张桌子不错。
……

Waitress: Okay, sir. What would you like to drink?
好的,先生。要什么饮料?

Li Kang: Er, one hot tea, a coke, two sweetened ice tea and one sprite.
呃,一个热茶,一个可乐,两个冰冻甜茶和一个雪碧。

Waitress: Just a second, and this the menu for you.
稍等,这是菜单。

Dialog 2

Waitress: May I take the order now?
现在可以点菜了吗？

Li Kang: I think so. I need a share of steak.
我想是的，我要一份牛排。

Waitress: How do you want it, rare, medium, or well-done?
您要做成什么样，嫩一些，中等还是熟透？

Li Kang: Medium is OK.
中等就可以了。

Waitress: What do you like to have, sir?
先生，您要吃点什么？

Li Kang: I need something special. Do you have any recommendations?
我要特别的东西，您有什么推荐吗？

Waitress: We have roast oyster, and borsch to go with it.
我们有烤牡蛎，配菜是罗宋汤。

Li Kang: That's good. I'd like to have a try.
那不错，我尝一尝吧。

Waitress: OK, sir.
好的，先生。

Dialog 3

Li Kang: May I have the check[2], please?
我可以结账了吗？

Waitress: Separate or together?
分开算还是一起算？

Li Kang: Today it's my treat. Can I pay by credit card here?
今天我请客。我可以用信用卡吗？

Waitress: Yes, we accept MasterCard, Visa, Discover and American Express.
可以，我们接受万事达卡、维萨卡、发现卡和美国运通卡。

Li Kang: Here it is.
给您。

Waitress:	Okay, 48 dollars in all, and please sign here. If you like to tip the waiter, please put the amount below. Then add them together, and put the total here.③
	好的,总共48美元,请您在这里签字。如果您要给服务员小费,把数字写在下面,然后加在一起,把总数写在这里。
Li Kang:	It's finished. May I keep the carbon?
	签好了,我可以保留副本吗?
Waitress:	Yes. Thank you and have a nice weekend.
	可以,谢谢,祝您周末愉快。
Li Kang:	You, too.
	您也一样。

典型句型

1) Let's go for lunch together. It's my treat.
   我们一起吃午饭,我请客。
2) How many in your group today?
   你们今天多少人?
3) How about the table near the window?
   靠近窗户的那张桌子如何?
4) Er, one hot tea, a coke, two sweetened ice tea and one sprite.
   呃,一个热茶,一个可乐,两个冰冻甜茶和一个雪碧。
5) I think so. I need a share of steak.
   我想是的,我要一份牛排。
6) How do you want it, rare, medium, or well-done?
   您要做成什么样,嫩一些,中等还是熟透?
7) I need something special. Do you have any recommendations?
   我要特别的东西,您有什么推荐吗?
8) May I have the check, please?
   我可以结账了吗?
9) Today it's my treat. Can I pay by credit card here?
   今天我请客,我可以用信用卡吗?

10) May I keep the carbon?
我可以保留副本吗?

Background
背景知识

英美餐馆常规:(1)主要菜肴品种:roast beef(烤牛肉),beef stew(红烧牛肉),pork chop(猪排),fried/roast chicken(炸/烤鸡),egg(鸡蛋),牛排(beefsteak)等。(2)生熟程度:well-done(全熟),有时太老;medium(半熟),比较合适一般口味;medium-rare(半熟),略生一点;rare(半生不熟),多半外熟内生。(3)色拉(salad)类的不同调味酱称为"dressing",一般有:French(法式,较酸);Blue Cheese(乳酪,带酸奶味);Thousand Island(千岛式,酸中略甜,比较适合一般人的口味);Italian(意大利式,带蒜味);House Dressing(该饭店特制的酱)。(4)上菜:最先是饮料,然后上色拉或汤,等吃完了侍者把盘子或碗收走后再上主菜。吃完后侍者把碗盘收走,然后问你要吃什么甜点。

餐馆付账:餐馆服务员估计客人吃得差不多的时候,就会送上账单结账。与美国人一起到餐馆就餐时,谁来付账是一个很重要的问题。通常男女一起进餐,习惯上由男士做东请客。但现在美国的女学生和职业女子已逐渐习惯于上餐馆时自己付账。当你遇到有人说 Let's go for lunch together.(我们一起去吃午饭吧。)时,就表示"只是一起去吃饭,没表明要买单",没有说要请对方,那就是在餐后大家均摊 (go Dutch)。如果其中一方说 Let's go for lunch together. It's my treat.(我们一起吃午饭,我请客。)时,就意味着他打算要一起付账。

值得注意的是,有时英语国家的人们,主要是美国人,说的一些话听起来像是请吃饭,但实际上并不具备请吃饭的内容。如果听者是外国人,不清楚这一点,误认为对方向自己发出了邀请,就容易造成误解。例如: I haven't seen you for a long time. You must come round for dinner sometime.(好久不见了。什么时候你一定过来吃饭啊！）或者 It's good seeing you. I'll invite you to tea later.（见到你很高兴，过些天我请你喝茶。）这些例子对非英语国家的人们来说，听起来的确像请吃请喝，但一琢磨便发现了问题，没有讲时间和地点，也没有征求对方的意见。这种话完全是社交应酬的需要，表示亲近以保持双方良好的人际关系，说话人完全没有请吃的意思，只是客套话而已，不具备任何实质内容。恰当的回答方式应当是：Thank you. I'd love to very much.（谢谢，我很乐意），切记不要问"When?"（什么时候？）或者"Where?"（什么地点？）一旦问了，那会令说话人十分窘迫，因为他毫无请客的思想准备。

女士优先:在美国，女士比较受到尊重。通常总是把女士放在优先考虑的地位。如果男女一起走进一道门，男士要替女士开门。进房间或进餐馆时，女士多走在前面，除非男士必须在前面选择餐桌、开车门或作其他效劳。进出电梯时，男士按住按钮侧身请女士出入，除非电梯拥挤时男士不得不先行出入。在街上行走或穿过马路时，男士要走在女士身旁靠来车方向的一边。宴会上，主人把客人领进客厅时，如果客人是位女士，她进客厅时，厅中的大多数男子都要站起来以示尊敬，特别年长或地位高得多的除外。如果女主人带一位男客人进入客厅，女主人的女儿若在，她要把客人向女儿介绍。通常是把男士介绍给女士，除非他年长得多或地位高得多。一般的惯例是把年轻的介绍给年长的。不管进入客厅的是男士还是女士，在客厅里就座的女士都不必起身示礼。女士需要入座时，男士要帮助女士就座。

注　释

① 餐馆内通常分为吸烟区和非吸烟区，所以服务员要问客人是否吸烟，这是安排座位的需要。

② check 这里指的是消费后结账的清单，上面列明了各项费用以及总额。

③ 如果没有现金付小费，可以在用信用卡付账时加在消费的金额后面，当天营业结束后收银员再把这部分从餐馆的账上扣回，餐馆再以现金的形式支付给服务员。tip 这里用作动词，是"给……小费"的意思。

Spending Holidays
过节日

Topic Introduction
话题导言

中国人在国内过节日,最隆重的莫过于春节了。在英国、美国这样的西方国家,人们要过圣诞节、复活节、感恩节等,这些节日很多都与宗教有关,这与宗教在人们的生活中占有重要位置是分不开的。

到了异域他乡,就要入乡随俗,不说完全融入他们的节日生活,但要与"老外"们打交道,总得有所了解。中国过春节,人们总要问候一声"新年好"或者道一声祝福"恭喜发财"。西方人过圣诞节、新年等节日时,也要说一声"Merry Christmas!"和"Happy New Year!"虽然各民族的节日风俗各不相同,但大家都把节日当作休闲和聚会的好时机。

Situational Dialogs
情景对话

丁唐(Ding Tang)和李康(Li Kang)很喜欢节日,在节日里可以抛开平时单调的工作,与朋友、家人欢聚在一起,也可以利用这段时间去旅游景点游览一番。

Dialog 1

Li Kang: Happy Easter!
复活节快乐!

Kate: Thanks a lot. And you too!
谢谢。您也一样!

Li Kang: What's your plan during the Easter vacation?
复活节假期您有什么计划?

Kate: My friends and I are going to give a party[①]. Why not join us?
我和我的朋友们要举行一个晚会。要不要和我们一起呢?

Li Kang: No, thanks. I'm going to Denver and Atlanta tomorrow.
不了,谢谢。我明天要去丹佛和亚特兰大。

Kate: That's a big trip. You'll travel around the country, right?
那是很远的旅行,您要周游全国,对吗?

Li Kang: I think so.
我想是的。

Dialog 2

Ding Tang: Have a merry Thanksgiving Day!
祝您感恩节愉快!

Mandy: The same to you! Where are you going to spend your holiday?
您也一样! 到哪里去度假呀?

Ding Tang: My parents and my sister will be here tomorrow morning, and I'll show them around here.
我父母和姐姐明天上午要来这里,我带他们到周围看看。

Mandy: Great. You're missing them, I guess.
很好,我想您很想念他们的。

Ding Tang: Sure. After that we'll go to Canada for a visit. I've never been there. You know, we have nine days in all.
当然了, 此后我们要去加拿大旅行, 我从没有去过。您知道,我们有九天假期。

Mandy: Yes, we have a long vacation, too. So I'll fly to California to stay with my parents for most of the vacation.
是啊,我们假期也很长。所以,我要飞往加利福利亚,大部分时间和父母呆在一起。

Spending Holidays 20

过节日

Dialog 3

Ding Tang: Could you tell me something about your Christmas Day?
给我谈谈你们过圣诞节的一些事情,好吗?

Mandy: Well, it's celebrated every year by Christians for the birth of Jesus Christ on December 25.
好的,是基督徒每年庆祝耶稣基督12月25日降生。

Ding Tang: How do you celebrate it?
你们怎么庆祝呢?

Mandy: We can have fun, and forget everything else. Also,② we have a very big dinner, and all the family members return home.
我们可以玩乐,忘掉一切别的事情。而且,我们还有大的聚餐,所有的家庭成员都回到家里。

Ding Tang: Do you have a long vacation?
你们有很长的假期吗?

Mandy: Yes, we don't need to be busy working③ all day long until after New Year's Day.
是的,我们不必整天忙于工作,一直玩到过了新年。

Ding Tang: That's full of fun.④ I've never spent a Christmas Day.
太有意思了。我从来没过一个圣诞节。

Mandy: Wish you a merry Christmas!
愿您有个愉快的圣诞节!

Ding Tang: You, too!⑤
您也一样。

Typical Sentences 典型句型

1) Happy Easter!
   复活节快乐!

2) Wish you a merry Christmas!
   祝您圣诞节快乐!

3) Have a merry Thanksgiving Day!
   祝您感恩节愉快!

4) Are you planning anything for Thanksgiving Day?
   感恩节有什么打算？
5) What's your plan during the Easter vacation?
   复活节假期您有什么计划？
6) My friends and I are going to give a party. Why not join us?
   我和我的朋友们要举行一个晚会。要不要和我们一起呢？
7) Could you tell me something about your Christmas Day?
   给我谈谈你们过圣诞节的一些事情，好吗？
8) Christmas Day is in honor of Jesus Christ.
   圣诞节是为了纪念救世主耶稣基督降生。
9) Christmas Day is a reunion day.
   圣诞节是个团聚的日子。
10) It's celebrated every year by Christians for the birth of Jesus Christ on December 25.
    它是基督徒每年庆祝耶稣基督12月25日降生。
11) We can have fun, and forget everything else. Also, we have a very big dinner, and all the family members return home.
    我们可以玩乐，忘掉一切别的事情。而且，我们还有大的聚餐，所有的家庭成员都回到家里。

Background 背景知识

元旦(New Year's Day)：元旦是辞旧迎新的时候，每年的最后一天，人们怀着激动的心情等待着钟声敲击12点的最后一响。此刻，大家拥抱亲吻，举杯祝愿新的一年的到来。

圣诞节(Christmas)：顾名思义，就是圣人诞辰之节。12月25日是基督徒所认定的耶稣基督(Jesus Christ)降生纪念日，因而这天成了具有浓重宗教色彩的节日。据《圣经(Bible)》记载，耶稣为拯救人类降生在伯利恒客栈的马厩里。人类以耶稣基督降生的那一年为新的纪年。基督徒纪念他是因为人类从此有了得救的希望。举家

Spending Holidays 过节日

团聚和去教堂做礼拜都是这个节日最美好、也是最有意义的活动，还有圣诞晚餐、圣诞树、圣诞礼品、圣诞贺卡、圣诞颂歌、圣诞弥撒、圣诞老人送玩具等富有想象力的有趣习俗。许多家庭在圣诞前夜前往教堂吟颂几段《圣经》或在圣诞节一早去教堂聆听布道。人们在圣诞节的早上一家围坐在圣诞树(Christmas Tree)旁，打开圣诞礼物，互致"圣诞快乐(Merry Christmas)"。晚上，人们便享受传统的圣诞晚餐——火鸡、白薯、火腿、坚果、酸果蔓果酱、色拉、布丁、苹果饼和冰淇淋等。

节日往往最青睐儿童，圣诞节给孩子们以丰富的想象力。传说圣诞前夜会有"圣诞老人"(Santa Claus)在人们熟睡时从烟囱中爬下来给孩子们送礼物，孩子们睡前把一只长筒袜挂在床头或烟囱附近等待"圣诞礼物"。

复活节(Easter day)：每年3月21日或该日后月圆以后第一个星期日，也叫做复活节礼拜天(Easter Sunday)，指的是耶稣复活的日子。据《四福音书》记载，耶稣是道成肉身，为人类赎罪而降生于世的，耶稣的名字就是"神将他的百姓从罪恶里拯救出来"之意。他在世时带了12个门徒。耶稣的言行引起犹太教当局的不满和愤恨，最后被钉死在十字架上。耶稣死后第三天从死人中复活。现在美国等西方国家的复活节，是为了纪念耶稣的复活(Resurrection)。

现代复活节有两个重要标志，一个是染成红色的鸡蛋，表示他们确信耶稣复活的喜悦心情；二是小兔子，象征新生命。基督徒们借用极具生命力的象征物，喻示耶稣基督的生命再现。

万圣节前夕(Halloween)：11月1日，Halloween的意思是所有圣徒之除夕(Eve of All Saints' Day)。在法国、意大利、西班牙等许多欧洲国家，万圣节是严峻、肃穆的，人们在教堂、广场举行大型的弥撒活动，在墓地为已故亲戚朋友祈祷祝福。然而，在美国和英伦三岛，万圣被看作是寻欢作乐、装神弄鬼、占卜算命、搞恶作剧的日子。据说，在10月31日的那天晚上，所有的鬼都会出现，面目丑陋的女巫也会出现，身后还跟着一群黑猫和一些稻草人(scarecrows)。于是，过节的人们也把自己打扮成妖魔鬼怪相互逗乐。最高兴的还是孩子们，到了晚上，拿上一只南瓜灯笼(jack-o'-lantern)，戴着假面具，装扮成骷髅、幽灵、恶魔、巫婆、海盗等模样，成群结队地挨家挨户地去讨糖果，口中叫着"Treat or trick（不好好招待，我们就捣蛋）"，大人们赶紧拿出糖果点心给他们，否则，他们可能会搞些恶作剧。

感恩节(Thanksgiving Day)： 每年11月的第四个星期四是美国最重要的、最具有民族特色的，也是最具有美国传统的节日之一。感恩节起源于1621年。这一年，美国的第一代移民(当时的英国清教徒)在今天的马萨诸塞州普利茅斯(Plymouth, Massachusetts)，在当地印第安人的帮助下度过了一个寒冬，战胜了饥饿和疾病，取得了第一个大丰收。这些虔诚的清教徒认为这是上帝的恩赐，请来印第安人分享他们猎取的火鸡、自己种的南瓜、玉米等食物。此后，这一庆祝活动便年复一年地沿袭下来。家庭聚餐是感恩节的重要纪念活动，主食是烤火鸡(roast turkey)和南瓜饼(pumpkin pie)，说着 We have a lot to be thankful for.(我们有许多值得感谢的东西)。

情人节(Valentine's Day)： 也叫圣瓦伦丁节。2月14日是个充满激情、温馨浪漫的节日。据说情人节的习俗来自于古罗马节日，也有人说这个节日来源于公元三世纪殉教的瓦伦丁修士的逝世纪念日。人们庆祝情人节是借以表达对爱情的祝福。情侣们交换的贺卡上一般都会有象征爱情的红心(heart)或带箭的丘比特(Cupid)，卡上有充满激情的甜言蜜语和一些柔情的诗句。此外，还互送礼物，最好的礼物是鲜花和心形糖果、巧克力等。

愚人节(April Fools' Day)： 愚人节的历史可以追溯到中世纪，从那时起人们就开始在每年的4月1日相互开玩笑，让轻易上当的人吃一点儿苦头。

母亲节(Mother's Day)： 每年5月的第二个星期日，政府部门和各家门口悬挂国旗，表示对母亲的尊敬。在家里，儿女们和父亲给母亲买些礼物或做些家务。

父亲节(Father's Day)： 每年6月份的第三个星期天，表示对父亲的尊敬。在家里，儿女们和母亲给父亲买些礼物。

哥伦布日(Columbus Day)： 每年10月12日，纪念哥伦布在北美登陆，为美国的联邦假日。

华盛顿诞辰纪念日(George Washington's Birthday)： 每年2

Spending Holidays 20

月 22 日,庆祝华盛顿诞辰,为美国的联邦假日。

劳动节(Labor Day):每年 9 月的第一个星期一,表示对劳工的敬意,为美国的联邦假日。

林肯诞辰纪念日(Abraham Lincoln's Birthday):每年 2 月 12 日,庆祝林肯诞辰,为大多数州的节日。

退伍军人节(Veterans Day):每年 10 月份的第四个星期一,表示对退伍军人的敬意。

阵亡将士纪念日(Memorial Day):每年 5 月的最后一个星期一,纪念为美国献身的阵亡将士,为美国的联邦假日。

注 释

① give a party 的意思是"举行晚会",类似的表达如下:give a lecture(举行一个讲座);give a report(举行一个报告会);give a lesson(讲一节课);give a talk(举行一次演讲)等。

② also 在这里的意思是"而且",意思接近的词还有 besides, moreover, furthermore 等。

③ be busy doing/at/with something 都可以表示"忙于某事",如: She is busy writing letters. (她正忙于写信。)

④ full of fun 意思是"充满了乐趣",full of 是"充满"的意思,如: The room is full of people. (房间里装满了人。)

⑤ 对于别人的祝贺、问候,有时可以简单地回答:You, too! 或 The same to you!,意思都是"您也一样!"如:
—Merry Christmas! (圣诞快乐!)
—The same to you! (您也快乐!)

Chinese Festivals
中国节日

Topic Introduction 话题导言

中国人到了国外,同样丢不下自己的文化传统,特别喜欢聚集在一起,就连一些临时而去的留学生、访问学者也喜欢"扎堆",想到大家毕竟是"老乡",彼此之间有个照应。于是,照样烹调着中国菜,穿着中国式的服装,说着夹有英文的中国话,保留着中国式待人接物的习惯,也过着中国的节日。

但另一方面,中国人周围的西方人又越来越多地对中国文化传统产生兴趣。所以,中国人过"自己的"节日的时候,就会邀请他们的当地朋友从某个侧面来领略中国的文化,这在唐人街、大学城等中国人"扎堆"的地方成为了一道亮丽的风景线。虽然,对于推进世界了解中国来说,这样做还差得很远很远,但毕竟是一种不错的形式。

Situational Dialogs 情景对话

春节是中国的传统节日,热情好客的丁唐(Ding Tang)和刘杭(Liu Hang)邀请对中国文化十分感兴趣的外国朋友共度佳节。

Chinese Festivals 21

中国节日

Dialog 1

Mandy: Do many people in China celebrate Christmas Day?
中国有很多人庆祝圣诞节吗？

Ding Tang: No, not very many. Only a few① people know about Christmas Day.
不是很多，在中国了解圣诞节的人不太多。

Mandy: I hear the Chinese New Year is the most important.
我听说中国新年是最重要的。

Ding Tang: That's right. We Chinese celebrate our Spring Festival, also called the Lunar New Year's Day, and it is the most important festival in China.
是的。我们中国人过春节，也叫做阴历新年，春节是中国最重要的节日。

Mandy: When do you celebrate it?
春节是在什么时间？

Ding Tang: It depends on the lunar calendar. Generally, it falls on a certain day of the second half of January or the first half of February.
这取决于阴历，一般在阳历一月下半月或二月上半月。

Mandy: Oh, I see. What does it mean? Does it mean the beginning of spring?
哦，我知道了。春节意味着什么？是否意味着春天的开始？

Ding Tang: Yes. It also means the family reunion. On New Year's Eve we have the Family Reunion Dinner. Nearly everyone is given several days off②.
对。也意味着全家团圆。除夕，我们都吃团圆饭。几乎人人都放好几天假。

Mandy: Why do you use red color?
为什么用红色？

Ding Tang: Because in Chinese culture, red color is the lucky color. It's the symbol of happiness and good luck.
因为在中国文化中，红色代表吉祥，是幸福和好运的象征。

Mandy: Oh, that's very interesting.
噢，那倒很有意思！

Dialog 2

Nicholas: I'm very happy to spend Chinese New Year's Eve with you.
和你们度过除夕,我很高兴。

Liu Hang: It's our pleasure you could come. The dinner is ready. Let's go in.
您能来是我们的荣幸。晚餐好了,我们进去吧。

Nicholas: Oh, my goodness[3]! So many dishes and they all smell wonderful.
噢,我的天哪! 这么多菜,闻起来都这么美妙。

Liu Hang: Please help yourself[4]. Let's drink for the coming New Year!
请随便吃。让我们为新的一年干杯!

All: Cheers!
干杯!

Liu Hang: This is a traditional food called jiaozi. Northern Chinese people usually eat some jiaozi at this dinner. Please help yourself.
这是一种传统食物叫饺子,中国北方人在这顿晚餐通常吃一些饺子。请随便吃。

Nicholas: Thank you. Very delicious.
多谢,味道很好。

Liu Hang: Everything is typically Chinese. Just eat what you like.
每样东西都是典型的中国口味,随意吃您所喜欢的。

1) I hear the Chinese New Year is the most important.
我听说中国新年是最重要的。

2) The Dragon Boat Festival is in the honor of an ancient poet.
端午节是为了纪念一位古代诗人。

3) We Chinese celebrate our Spring Festival, also called the Lunar New Year's Day, and it is the most important festival in China.
我们中国人过春节,也叫做阴历新年,春节是中国最重要的节日。

Chinese Festivals 21

中国节日

4) Generally, it falls on a certain day of the second half of January or the first half of February.
一般在阳历一月下半月或二月上半月。

5) Spring Festival also means the family reunion.
春节也意味着全家团圆。

6) On New Year's Eve we have the Family Reunion Dinner.
除夕,我们都吃团圆饭。

7) Nearly everyone is given several days off.
几乎人人都放假好几天。

8) Because in Chinese culture, red color is the lucky color. It's the symbol of happiness and good luck.
因为在中国文化中,红色代表吉祥,是幸福和好运的象征。

9) I'm very happy to spend Chinese New Year's Eve with you.
和你们度过除夕,我很高兴。

10) Please help yourself. Let's drink for the coming New Year!
请随便吃。让我们为新的一年干杯!

11) This is a traditional food called jiaozi. Northern Chinese people usually eat some jiaozi at this dinner.
这是一种传统食物叫饺子,中国北方人在这顿晚餐通常吃一些饺子。

背景知识

中国节日的英语说法:虽然中国人过西方节日,如圣诞节和情人节的越来越多,但毕竟不是大多数。这里列出我国全国性节日的英译。

春节(农历正月初一) the Spring Festival

端午节(农历五月初五) the Dragon Boat Festival

国际妇女节(公历三月八日) International Working Women's Day

国际劳动节(公历五月一日) International Labor Day / May Day

国庆节(公历十月一日) National Day

教师节(公历九月十日) Teachers' Day

六一儿童节(公历六月一日) International Children's Day

清明节(公历的每年四月四日至六日之间) the Qing Ming Festival

五四青年节(公历五月四日) Chinese Youth Day

元旦(公历一月一日) New Year's Day

元宵节(农历正月十五) the Lantern Festival

中秋节(农历八月十五) the Mid-Autumn Festival / the Moon Festival

重阳节(农历九月初九) the Chong Yang Festival / the Double Ninth Day

注 释

① a few 和 few 修饰可数名词的复数形式，注意 a little 和 little 则是修饰不可数名词。

② give several days off 意思是"放几天假"。还有类似表达法:ask three days off(请三天假)。

③ my goodness 常用于口语中表示惊异,译为"天哪！"同样用法还有 Goodness me!/Goodness gracious (me)!

④ help oneself (to something) 常用在口语中表示"请随便(什么东西)"。如：
Help yourself to a cigarette.（请随便抽根烟吧。）

Going to a Dinner Party
参加宴会

Topic Introduction
话题导言

以宴请的方式款待客人绝不是一般意义上的吃吃喝喝,通常都具有某种目的或含义。邀请别人参加可以是电话或口头邀请,也可以书面邀请。

口头邀请的语言一般很不正式,表达方式因人因事而异,但真正的邀请都包含有四个特征,即内容(for what)、地点(where)、时间(when)和请求回答(Can you come?)。如:I would like to invite you for a dinner party in University Hotel at six Friday evening. Can you come?(我邀请您在星期五晚上六点到大学酒店参加宴会。您能来吗?)就包含了上述四个必要项。对于口头邀请的回答要明确表明是接受还是拒绝,比如:Yes, thank you. It's my pleasure to be invited to such a dinner.(我去,谢谢,被邀请参加这样的宴会我感到荣幸。)如果拒绝,除了说明不能去以外,要表示谢意,还要说明不能去的原因,否则就显得太无礼貌了,比如:I'm sorry I can't. Thank you all the same. I have to take care of my daughter at home.(很抱歉我不能去,还是要谢谢您,我得在家照顾我的女儿。)

书面的邀请,如请柬(Invitation Card)或邀请信(Letter of Invitation),是正式的,一般应当做出回答(response),明确告知对方你是否能接受邀请,否则是很失礼的。

Situational Dialogs
情景对话

李康(Li Kang)受到帕克博士邀请去参加她的晋职庆祝晚宴。

Dialog 1

Secretary: Hello, Dr. Li. Dr. Parker would like to invite you to a dinner party this Saturday evening. Would you come?
李博士,您好。帕克博士邀请您参加这个星期六的晚宴,您能来吗?

Li Kang: Yes, it's kind of her to invite me[①]. I'd be delighted to go.
能,她邀请我真是太客气了。我很高兴去参加。

Secretary: So I'll go to your home to pick you up at 5:30 Saturday evening. Is it suitable for you?
那么,我就星期六晚上5:30到您家来接您,适合吗?

Li Kang: Yes, I'll be waiting for you then. By the way, for what is the dinner party?
好的,我那时就等您了。顺便问一下,这个晚宴是为什么目的?

Secretary: It's for Dr. Parker's promotion. She was promoted as an associate professor last week. The dinner is at her home.
是为帕克博士的晋升,她上个星期被晋升为副教授,宴会就在她家里了。

Li Kang: She deserves the position.
她应该得到这个职位。

Dialog 2

Dr. Parker: Welcome to my home, Dr. Li.
李博士,欢迎到我家来。

Going to a Dinner Party 22

参加宴会

Li Kang: Thank you for inviting me to the dinner party. Congratulations② on your promotion, Dr. Parker.
谢谢您邀请我来参加晚宴,帕克博士,祝贺您得到晋升。

Dr. Parker: Thank you very much. Please take a seat. What would you like to drink?
非常感谢,请坐。想喝点儿什么？

Li Kang: A cup of coffee is all right for me, I guess.
我想,一杯咖啡就可以。

Dr. Parker: OK, just a second. … Oh, Dr. Li, would you like to meet my husband, Bill?
好的,稍等。…… 哦,李博士,见见我的丈夫比尔,好吗？

Li Kang: I'm glad to meet you, Mr. Parker.
帕克先生,很高兴见到您。

Dr. Parker: Bill, this is Dr. Li from China.
比尔,这是从中国来的李博士。

Mr. Parker: Very nice to meet you, Dr. Li. My wife has told me about you before.
李博士,很高兴见到您。我妻子跟我谈起过您。

Dr. Parker: Now please be seated at the table, and help yourself to the food.
那请坐在桌子这边来吧,随便吃些东西。

Dialog 3

Department head: The honored guests③ are welcome to our dinner. I suggest a drink for Dr. Julia Parker's promotion and all the guests present today. I wish everyone good luck and good health.
我们欢迎各位贵宾来参加今天的宴会。我提议为朱利亚·帕克博士的晋升以及今天所有的来宾干杯,并祝大家万事顺利、身体健康。

Dr. Parker: Thanks for our department head's suggestion and wishes, and now cheers!
谢谢系主任的提议和祝愿,现在请干杯！

All: Cheers!
干杯！

……

Li Kang:	All the dishes are so delicious, and I like them very much! 所有的菜都这么美味，我很喜欢它们。
Dr. Parker:	It's kind of you to say so. Please help yourself to some fruit. 您这么说真是太客气了。请随便吃些水果吧。
Li Kang:	Thank you. 多谢。

……

Li Kang:	This is a wonderful dinner party. I think I must be going now. 这真是一个不错的宴会，我想我该走了。
Dr. Parker:	Would you stay a little while for a second cup of coffee? 多呆一会儿，再喝一杯咖啡，好吧？
Li Kang:	I've had enough. Thank you for your dinner. 我已经喝得够多了，谢谢您的晚餐。
Dr. Parker:	Thank you for coming. 多谢您的光临。
Li Kang:	Good night. 晚安。
Dr. Parker:	Good night. 晚安。

Typical Sentences 典型句型

1) I would like to invite you for a dinner party in University Hotel at six Friday evening. Can you come?
我邀请您在星期五晚上6点到大学酒店参加宴会。您能来吗？

2) Dr. Parker would like to invite you to a dinner party this Saturday evening. Would you come?
帕克博士邀请您参加这个星期六的晚宴，您能来吗？

3) It's my pleasure to be invited to such a dinner.
被邀请参加这样的宴会我感到荣幸。

Going to a Dinner Party 22

参加宴会

4) It's kind of her to invite me. I'd be delighted to go.
   她邀请我真是太客气了。我很高兴去参加。

5) I'm sorry I can't. Thank you all the same. I have to take care of my daughter at home.
   很抱歉我不能去,还是要谢谢您,我得在家照顾我的女儿。

6) Thank you for inviting me to the dinner party. Congratulations on your promotion, Dr. Parker.
   谢谢您邀请我来参加晚宴,帕克博士,祝贺您得到晋升。

7) A cup of coffee is all right for me, I guess.
   我想,一杯咖啡就可以了。

8) All the dishes are so delicious, and I like them very much!
   所有的菜都这么美味,我很喜欢它们。

9) This is a wonderful dinner party. I think I must be going now.
   这真是一个不错的宴会,我想我该走了。

10) Would you stay a little while for a second cup of coffee?
    多呆一会儿,再喝一杯咖啡,好吧?

背景知识

宴会:比较隆重、正式地宴请招待客人称为宴会,有国宴、正式宴会和便宴之分。国宴(state banquet)是国家元首或政府为招待国宾、其他贵宾或在重要节日为招待各界人士而举行的正式宴会。宴会厅内悬挂国旗,乐团演奏国歌和席间音乐,还有席间致辞或祝酒。正式宴会(banquet 或 dinner 或 feast)有时也称为"盛宴"(grand banquet 或 magnificent banquet),是为某些重要人物或重大事件而举行的。正式宴会十分讲究,请柬上标明对客人服饰的要求,比如男士须穿礼服,女士须着晚礼服。便宴(informal dinner)比较随便,多见于朋友间日常友好交往。便宴有午宴和晚宴(lunch 或 dinner)。

招待会(reception):规模较大,也比较正式,但比不上宴会(banquet),经常是为了某项庆祝活动如开幕式、闭幕式、庆祝代表访问和文艺、体育表演等。主要有冷餐会(buffet 或 buffet-dinner)和酒会(cocktail)两种形式。冷餐会不设席位且以冷餐为主,食物和餐具放在桌上供客人自行取用。客人们可以自由走动、相互交谈。冷餐会可在室内,也可在室外、花园举行。酒会形式活泼,更便于客人广泛接触交谈。酒会主要以酒水和水果为主招待客人,还有三明治、面包、香肠和糕点,酒会延续时间也比较长,客人们有的已经吃完走了,有的却还没有来。

工作餐(working dinner)和茶会(tea party):工作餐是现代交往中的一种非正式宴请形式,客人们可利用一起共同进餐的时间,边吃边聊,气氛显得轻松随便,招待普通的生意伙伴和客人都可以这样做。茶会是一种很简单的招待方式,大学的学生组织负责人或者系主任邀请校友参加的庆祝会、联欢会都属于此类,通常备有咖啡、点心和小吃等。客人可随便找个地方或站或坐,地板椅子随意选择,人们无拘无束,自由交谈感兴趣的话题。

不吸烟(No smoking)和二次致谢(Thank twice):在英语国家的饭店一般都标有"No smoking"的字样,如果有吸烟室可以到吸烟室去吸烟。即使没有标示,也不能随意吸烟而要征求周围人的意见,可以说:Would you mind if I smoke?(我吸烟您介意吗?),在得到许可的答复后才能吸烟,否则被认为是不礼貌的。宴会完毕表示谢意是必要的,但美国人有二次感谢(thank twice)的习惯,即除了当面表示感谢之外,回家之后还要写信或打电话再次表示谢意,也可以同时回请主人。

英语请柬的样式:英语请柬的格式很有讲究,也比较固定。通常第一行是主人的姓名全称;第二行是 request the pleasure of;第三行是客人的姓名全称;第四行是 company at...;第五行是日期;第六行是宴会举行的钟点;第七行是地点。请柬下方的 R. S. V. P. 或 rsvp 是要求答复的意思,右下方是主人的电话号码。全文用第三人称的口气。主人和客人的姓名都出现在请柬里面的正文里,称呼和结束语就省略了。特示例如下:

Going to a Dinner Party 22

参加宴会

DR. WILLIAM STEINHORST AND MRS. JULIA STEINHORST
REQUEST THE PLEASURE OF
MR. TOMMY NELSON AND MRS. HEATHER NELSON'S
COMPANY AT DINNER
ON FRIDAY, SEPTEMBER THE TENTH
AT SIX O'CLOCK PM
NEW CENTURY HOTEL

R. S. V. P.

TELEPHONE: 888-888-8888

翻译成中文就是：

兹定于九月十日(星期五)下午六点在新世纪酒店
敬治菲酌，恭请
汤米·纳尔逊先生和希瑟·纳尔逊夫人光临
威廉·施泰因霍斯特博士和朱利亚·施泰因霍斯特夫人谨订

敬请回复

电话：888-888-8888

注 释

① It's kind of you to do something. 是一种表示谢意的说法，属于比较客气也比较正式的用语。
② 表示祝贺要用这个词的复数形式，如：
   Congratulations on your success. (恭喜您获得成功。)
③ honored guests 意思是"贵宾"，也可用"guests of honor"。

At a Birthday Party
生日晚会

Topic Introduction 话题导言

不仅中国人将庆祝生日(birthday)看作是一件大喜事,西方人也是如此。在英美等西方国家,人们过生日一般都有庆祝活动,亲朋好友都会被邀请前来参加生日聚会,这也是人们增进友谊、密切关系的一个好时机。应邀而来的客人都要准备一份礼物送给过生日的人,并热诚地向他或她表示祝贺,离开时要再次表示祝贺。但对于已经成年的人过生日尤其是女士,不要问他们多少岁,这是不礼貌的。

收到生日礼物要当众打开,并表示感谢。生日晚会的高潮是人们围坐在一起,同唱《祝你生日快乐》(Happy Birthday to You)这首歌,以向过生日的人表示祝贺。然后是主人公吹熄生日蜡烛,共同分享生日蛋糕。也有人到餐馆去庆祝生日,其中有来宾会悄悄地告诉服务人员,这时服务员就会齐集而来共唱"Happy Birthday to You",使得主人公感到惊喜不已。

Situational Dialogs 情景对话

生日总是一件值得庆祝的大事情,今天是刘杭(Liu Hang)的朋友埃里克(Eric)的生日,看一下大家是怎么为他庆祝生日的。

At a Birthday Party 23

生日晚会

Dialog 1

Mrs. Nelson: Welcome, Liu Hang. Give me your coat and hat, and make yourself at home.①
欢迎您,刘杭。把您的大衣和帽子给我,就当成在自己家里吧。

Liu Hang: Thank you. Mrs. Nelson.
谢谢您,纳尔逊太太。

Mrs. Nelson: All boys and girls are in the living room. Let's meet Eric there.
所有的孩子们都在客厅里,我们去见埃里克吧。

Liu Hang: Hello, Eric. Happy birthday to you. Many happy returns of the day. Here's the present for you.
您好,埃里克。祝您生日快乐,年年有今日,岁岁有今朝。这是给您的生日礼物。

Eric: It's so beautiful. Thank you very much, Liu Hang.
好漂亮,谢谢您,刘杭。

Liu Hang: I'm glad you like it. It's 100% silk.
我很高兴您喜欢,这是100%的丝织品。

Dialog 2

Eric: Come into the dining room, Liu Hang.
刘杭,到餐厅里来吧。

Liu Hang: What wish would you like to make?
您会许下什么愿望?

Eric: I'd like it a secret.
我想保持秘密。

Liu Hang: Your secret wish will come true, I believe.
我相信您的秘密愿望会成真的。

Eric: I remember you're just several weeks younger than I am. So your birthday is also nearing②. When is it then?
我记得您只比我小几个星期,您的生日也快到了。是什么时候?

Liu Hang: A few weeks to go. I'll ask you to go to my birthday party that day.
还有几个星期,那天我会请您参加我的生日晚会的。

Dialog 3

Liu Hang: Oh my goodness, who's that girl?
天啦！那个女孩是谁？

Eric: Which one?
哪一个？

Liu Hang: The one in red. I think I've never seen her before. She is cute③.
穿红衣服的那个，我觉得以前没有见过她。她真漂亮。

Eric: You did. She's Mike's sister. You saw her at David's birthday party the month before last.
您见过的。她是迈克的妹妹，上上个月在大卫的生日晚会上您见过她。

Liu Hang: Oh, it's her. But I feel she's getting prettier.
哦，是她！但我觉得她越长越漂亮了。

Eric: Yes, she is. She's eighteen next semester, still at high school now.
是漂亮些了。下个学期她就18岁了，现在还在读高中。

Liu Hang: She is my kind of girl.④ It's a good chance to make friends with her.
她是我喜欢的类型。这是和她交朋友的一个好机会。

Eric: Yes. Let me blow out the birthday candles and cut the cake. Ah shhhhhh……
是啊。我来吹熄生日蜡烛，切蛋糕。啊嘘—嘘……

All: (Sing) Happy birthday to you! Happy birthday to you! Happy birthday, my dear friend! Happy birthday to you! ...
(唱)祝你生日快乐！祝你生日快乐！祝你生日快乐，我的朋友！祝你生日快乐！……

Eric: Thank you all.
多谢大家。

典型句型

1) Are you going to have a birthday party?
您要举行生日晚会吗？

At a Birthday Party 23

生日晚会

2) What wish would you like to make?
   您会许下什么愿望？
3) Your secret wish will come true, I believe.
   我相信您的秘密愿望会成真的。
4) Wish your dream come true.
   愿您的梦想成真。
5) My birthday is December 12.
   我的生日是12月12日。
6) Make a wish first.
   先许个愿吧。
7) Make yourself at home.
   当成在自己家里吧。
8) It's nice of you to come to my birthday party.
   您来参加我的生日晚会真是太谢谢您了。
9) Many happy returns of the day!
   年年有今日，岁岁有今朝！
10) Happy birthday to you!
    祝您生日快乐。
11) I'm glad to meet you.
    很高兴见到您。
12) It's a good chance to make friends with her.
    这是和她交朋友的一个好机会。

背景知识

"生日快乐"歌：关于"祝你生日快乐(Happy Birthday to You)"一歌是如何产生的故事，一开始是件令人愉快的事，到后来就变了味，令人很扫兴。事情是这样的：有姐妹俩，一个叫米尔德丽德·希尔 (Mildred Hill)，路易丝威尔市肯塔基实验幼儿园 (Louiseville, Kentucky Experimental Kindergarten) 教师，一个叫帕蒂·希尔 (Dr. Patty Hill)，该校的校长。姐妹俩一道为儿童们谱写了一首歌，歌名为"大家早上好(Good Morning to All)"。米尔德丽德是当地赞美诗的专家,再加上她的音乐天分,又是当地教堂的风琴师,而且她姐姐在幼儿教育方面也很有经验,"大家早上好"一歌无疑是个巨大的成功。

1893年,两姐妹发表了一部歌曲集,题名为"幼儿园的故事(Song Stories of the Kindergarten)"。31年以后,在帕蒂·希尔出任哥伦比亚大学幼儿教育系(the Department of Kindergarten Education at Columbia University)系主任之后,一个名叫罗伯特·H·科尔曼(Robert H. Coleman)的男士未经姐妹俩的允许,私自出版了这首歌,在这首歌后又加上了一段,即大家熟悉的"祝你生日快乐",这就构成了对姐妹俩的侵权。科尔曼增加的第二段歌词使这首歌很快就更加流行起来。

最终,姐妹俩的第一段歌词消失了。"祝你生日快乐",这首唯一的生日歌完全取代了姐妹俩原来的歌曲"大家早上好!"。

米尔德丽德于1916年逝世后,帕蒂与其另一个妹妹杰西卡出面将科尔曼告上了法庭。在法庭上,她们证明,实际上她们拥有这首歌曲调的版权。最后她们终于收回了这首歌的著作权。

注 释

① **make yourself at home** 的意思是"就当成在自己家里吧",用于招待客人时让客人不要客气的用语。
② 这里的 **near** 是动词,"接近"的意思。
③ **cute** 是形容词,"漂亮"的意思。
④ **She is my kind of girl.** 意思是"她是我喜欢的那类女孩"。也可以说成:She is my type of girl.

Going to a Wedding
参加婚礼

Topic Introduction
话题导言

  不论是在中国还是在西方，结婚都被看作是人生的一件大喜事，婚礼是一个大喜大庆的庆典。新婚男女往往是最高兴的，因为他们从此要踏上新的生活征程。举行婚礼应该穿最好的衣服，但与中国的习俗不同的是，新娘穿白色结婚礼服，披白纱，手拿一束白色的鲜花，而新郎通常穿黑色结婚礼服。

  应邀参加婚礼应该向新婚夫妻表示祝贺，尽管都是表达"恭贺新婚"，对男方和对女方说的话是不同的，对男方要说：Congratulations(祝贺)；对女方要说：Wish you happy(祝你幸福)。送结婚礼物不是在婚礼之上，而是在婚礼之前的单身告别会上送礼，女方的告别会叫做 Bridal Shower；男方的告别会叫做 Bachelor/Stag Party。

Situational Dialogs
情景对话

> 丁唐(Ding Tang)的朋友爱丽丝(Alice)要结婚了，国外的婚礼和中国的总是有很大的不同。

Dialog 1

Ding Tang: I hear Alice is getting married.
我听说爱丽丝要结婚了。

Mandy: Really? That's great. My best wishes to her. Who's the lucky guy?
真的吗？那好极了。真是要最好地祝愿她。谁是那个幸运的人？

Ding Tang: Steve will be the bridegroom.
史蒂夫将是新郎。

Mandy: Oh my, how romantic!
哦，天啦，好浪漫啊！

Ding Tang: Could you tell me what a church wedding is like?
您能告诉我教堂婚礼是个什么样子吗？

Mandy: The bride has her maid of honor and bridesmaids, and the bridegroom has his best man, and all the relatives and friends will go to the church, and the minister① will chair the whole ceremony, and ... I can't describe it exactly. Let's go to Alice's wedding that day, and you will know everything yourself.
新娘有伴娘和花童，而新郎有伴郎，所有的亲戚和朋友都去教堂，牧师将主持整个仪式，还有…… 我说不上来了。我们那一天去参加爱丽丝的婚礼，您就会自己了解一切了。

Ding Tang: That'll be good. I must buy something for her.
那是不错，我一定得买些东西给她。

Dialog 2

Ding Tang: I'm told of something about② throwing the bridal bouquet. I haven't got everything.
有人告诉过我扔结婚花环的事情，我还没有完全搞清楚。

Mandy: Well, when the ceremony is ending, the bride throws her bridal bouquet to the single girls, and they each try to catch it.
哦，当整个仪式即将结束时，新娘就把她的结婚花环扔向单身的姑娘们，他们每个人争相抢得这个花环。

Ding Tang: Why?
为什么？

Going to a Wedding 24

参加婚礼

Mandy: It's said the one who gets it will be the next one married.
据说得到花环的人将是下一个结婚的人。

Ding Tang: That's really amazing. Where's the reception?
那很有意思,在哪里举行结婚酒宴?

Mandy: The reception is often held at a public place, such as a hotel, a restaurant, a club, a big room in the church, or sometimes at the home of the bride.
酒宴经常在公共的地方举行,如酒店、餐馆、俱乐部或者就在教堂的大房间,有时候还在新娘家里。

Ding Tang: You mean the bride's home?
您是说在新娘的家里?

Mandy: Correct. The bride's family is responsible for the entire wedding, including arrangements, costs, and so on.
没错。新娘的家里负责整个婚礼,包括一切安排、开支等等。

Ding Tang: That's quite different from③ what we do in China.
那跟我们中国的情况有很大的不同。

Typical Sentences 典型句型

1) Will it be a church wedding or a civil wedding?
   他们将举行教堂婚礼还是普通婚礼?

2) Are you going to hold a bridal shower for Alice?
   你们要为爱丽丝举行一个新娘送礼会吗?

3) May every happiness be yours on your marriage.
   愿你们新婚美满如意!

4) The bride and groom will go to Europe for their honeymoon.
   新娘和新郎将要到欧洲去度蜜月。

5) I hear Alice is getting married.
   我听说爱丽丝要结婚了。

6) Steve will be the bridegroom.
   史蒂夫将是新郎。

7) Could you tell me what a church wedding is like?
   您能告诉我教堂婚礼是个什么样子吗?

8) I'm told of something about throwing the bridal bouquet. I haven't got everything.

   有人告诉过我扔结婚花环的事情,我还没有完全搞清楚。

9) It's said the one who gets it will be the next one married.

   据说得到花环的人将是下一个结婚的人。

10) That's quite different from what we do in China.

    那跟我们中国的情况有很大的不同。

背景知识

结婚礼物: 在美国遵守传统规矩的人是越来越少了,但旧的习俗仍然存在。年轻人在结婚之前有一个新娘送礼会(bridal shower),是一个只有女性参加的party,关系密切的亲朋好友要送礼品给女方,即马上就要结婚的新娘。可以送蜜月旅行的行李用品、女用内衣、床上用品、浴室毛巾、厨用毛巾、桌布或餐巾、瓷制塑像、绢花等。赠送的礼物要求实用、得体、新颖。传统上这些礼品都是手制的,今天仍被视为是最理想的馈赠物品。礼品必须当面赠与,不能让商店转交;礼物上应附有一张贺卡以让受礼人知道是谁人所送;礼物当面打开并当场向馈赠者表示感谢。新郎和他的同性朋友也有称为bachelor或stag party的晚会,也会收到朋友们的礼物。

美国人的婚礼: 对任何人而言,结婚都是人生的一件大事,各国婚礼却因文化的差异而不尽相同。美国社会的传统是:年轻人从相爱到准备结婚之前,有一个比较正规的订婚仪式。订婚之后,女方父母要向双方亲友发出婚礼邀请,接到邀请的人要回信表示祝贺,如果不能出席婚礼,要提前回信表示歉意;收到邀请的人还要筹备贺礼。为了避免收到重复的礼物,新娘一般会事先拟好所需物品的清单发给亲友。

美国人的婚礼可以概括为四个字:新、旧、借、蓝。新(new),是新娘的白礼服必须是新做的,寓意新娘要开始新的生活;旧(old),是新娘头上的白纱必须是母亲的旧纱,以示不忘父母的养育之恩,

Going to a Wedding 24 参加婚礼

特别是不忘母亲养育子女的恩情；借(borrow)，是新娘手里的白手帕必须是从女朋友那里借来的，以示不忘朋友的情谊；蓝(blue)，则是新娘身上吊袜束腰带(garter belt)必须是蓝色的，象征对爱情的忠贞。尽管20世纪60年代后，开始有人在户外举行简单婚礼(open air espousal)，就像平时就餐一样，双方家庭成员快快乐乐地一起聚餐就算是举行了婚礼，双方的父母和亲属也就理所当然地成了法律上的证婚人。也有些人主张婚礼从简，不请客不受礼，只在当地法院举行，由一名法官当证婚人，但近年来多数婚礼仍按传统方式进行。

注 释

① minister 在这里指"(英国)非国教派牧师"。英国国教派牧师叫 vicar, rector, curate。
② be told of something about... 是一个被动表达法，但翻译成中文时往往用主动式，意为"有人告诉……"。
③ be quite different from... 是"与……有很大不同"的意思。

At a Potluck Party
家常聚餐会

Topic Introduction
话题导言

　　日常生活中聚会实在是很多，同学、朋友、师生、同事、商业伙伴等等都可以为了什么或不为什么而在一起聚会。聚会的时间一般在周末，特别是星期五的晚上以及节日休假时间。这类聚会的邀请在以前通常是发出书面邀请，现在由于科技的发展，发个电子邮件给所有受邀人就可以了。一般没有明确要求回复的可以不回复，但出于礼貌最好还是回复为好，只要表明是去还是不去就行了。

　　家常的聚会有时候很难确定人数，因此常常采取自带食物的方法，叫做 potluck party（"百乐餐聚会"，也有的译为"聚餐会"），这样主人就不必为准备多少人的食物而发愁了。节日、课程结束、周末、晋升等都是聚会的理由，通知上一般都写明了是 potluck party，你若参加就要准备一些吃的东西，有时候会明确要求只要是小吃就可以了。

　　到了主人家里，主人一般会把其他家庭成员介绍给你认识，并会和你交谈一些感兴趣的话题。特别是当知道你是来自于中国的时候，与中国有关的话题就会被提出来，尤其是如果主人家有人以前到过中国就更会谈一谈关于中国的见闻。这时候也是让他们了解中国的时机，你可以将中国近几年发生的巨大变化告诉他们。

At a Potluck Party 25

Situational Dialogs 情景对话

刘杭(Liu Hang)和丁唐(Ding Tang)受邀去汤米(Tommy)家参加聚餐会，跟大家见面无疑是快乐的，不论是谈公事还是社交聚会，都可以让新朋老友聚在一起进行交流。

Dialog 1

Ding Tang: I've received a notice of a potluck party.
我收到了一个聚餐会的通知。

Mandy: Which one, at Tommy's or Cory's?
哪一个，是汤米家的还是考利家的？

Ding Tang: You've got two? I've received only one, and it's a potluck party at Tommy's house Friday evening. Will you go there?
您收到两个？我只收到一个，是汤米家的聚餐会，在星期五晚上，您去吗？

Mandy: Sure. How about your plan?
当然了。您怎么计划的？

Ding Tang: I'm thinking if I could go with you because I don't have a car.
因为我没有车，我在想我能否和您一块儿去。

Mandy: Sure, you could go in my car.
当然，您可以坐我的车去。

Ding Tang: Thank you for your offer. And what should we take for the potluck?
谢谢您主动让我坐您的车。我们应该带点儿什么去呢？

Mandy: Anything, I think. But if you have something special, that's better.
我觉得什么都行。但如果您有什么特别的东西，那就更好。

Ding Tang: I will stir-fry something typically Chinese, I think.
我想，我炒一些典型的中国菜。

Mandy: Great. But don't worry about it too much. There'll be too many potlucks, and almost every weekend, you'll get several notices.
好极了,但别太担心这件事情。会有很多的聚餐会的,几乎每个星期您都会收到好几个通知的。

Ding Tang: Oh, really?
哦,真的吗?

Dialog 2

Tommy: Hello, Liu Hang. Welcome to my home.
刘杭,您好。欢迎到我家来。

Liu Hang: Hello, Good evening. I feel honored to be invited for tonight's party.
您好,晚上好。被邀请来参加今晚的聚会,我感到荣幸。

Tommy: Please make yourself at home. Liu Hang, this is my wife Catherine.
请您就当成在自己家里吧。刘杭,这是我的妻子凯瑟琳。

Liu Hang: Very nice to meet you.
很高兴见到您。

Tommy: Catherine, this is Liu Hang from China.
凯瑟琳,这是从中国来的刘杭。

Catherine: Nice to meet you. Please take a seat and have something to drink.
很高兴见到您。请坐,喝点什么东西吧。

Liu Hang: All right. Thank you very much.
好的,非常感谢。

Catherine: How do you pronounce your Chinese name?
您的中文名字怎么发音?

Liu Hang: Liu Hang.
刘杭。

Catherine: Hang, ni cong zhongguo nage chengshi lai?
杭,你从那个城市来?

Liu Hang: Oh, your Chinese is good. I'm from Wuhan, the capital of Hubei Province.
哦,您的中文不错。我从武汉来,就是湖北省的省会。

At a Potluck Party 25

Catherine: Oh, my Goodness!① I've been there for one year.
哦,我的天啦！我到那里呆了一年。

Liu Hang: No wonder② you can speak Chinese so well.
难怪您会讲这么好的中文。

Catherine: Thank you. I taught English at Wuhan University ten years ago.
谢谢,十年前我在武汉大学教英语。

Liu Hang: What a coincidence! I used to③ study at the very university.
多么巧啊！我过去也就是在这个大学学习。

Dialog 3

Tommy: Okay, it's time for us to eat. Please help yourself to some food, Liu Hang.
好了,该吃饭的时间了。刘杭,请随便吃点东西吧。

Liu Hang: Thanks a lot.
多谢了。

Tommy: Do you have something in China similar to④ a potluck?
在中国有类似这种聚餐会的活动吗？

Liu Hang: No, we don't. It's strange for us Chinese to bring food to other people's home and then share the food together.
没有。对于我们中国人来说,把食物拿到别人家里去再和别人一起吃拿去的食物,令人感到奇怪。

Tommy: But it's not strange here. Just eat what you like.
但在这里不奇怪,吃您喜欢的吧。

Liu Hang: Certainly I will. There goes the saying, "When in Rome do as the Romans do."
我当然会的。有谚语说,"入乡随俗"嘛。

Tommy: Correct. My wife often tells me about Chinese people's hospitality, and the real Chinese food can only be found in China.
对了。我妻子经常说中国人很好客,并说真正的中国菜只有在中国才能找得到。

Liu Hang: That's true.
没错。

Typical Sentences
典型句型

1) I've received a notice of a potluck party.
   我收到了一个聚餐会的通知。
2) I've just received only one, and it's a potluck party at Tommy's house Friday evening. Will you go there?
   我只收到一个,是汤米家的聚餐会,在星期五晚上,您去吗?
3) I'm thinking if I could go with you because I don't have a car.
   因为我没有车,我在想我能否和您一块儿去。
4) What should we take for the potluck?
   我们应该带点儿什么去呢?
5) I will stir-fry something typically Chinese, I think.
   我想,我炒一些典型的中国菜。
6) I feel honored to be invited for tonight's party.
   被邀请来参加今晚的聚会,我感到荣幸。
7) Please help yourself to some food, Larry.
   拉瑞,请随便吃点东西吧。
8) Do you have something in China similar to a potluck?
   在中国有类似这种聚餐会的活动吗?
9) It's strange for us Chinese to bring food to other people's home and then share the food together.
   对于我们中国人来说,把食物拿到别人家里去再和别人一起吃拿去的食物,令人感到奇怪。
10) There goes the saying, "When in Rome do as the Romans do."
    有谚语说,"入乡随俗"嘛。

At a Potluck Party 25

家常聚餐会

Background 背景知识

聚会(Get-together)：美国人平时工作很忙碌，社交活动也很频繁，也因此产生了各式各样的聚会，但实际上很多聚会都是混合式的：

（1）家常聚餐会(Potluck Party)：身在美国，你常常会收到举办"potluck"的邀请，这就表明你得带上自己所做的精美食品到别人家里，这些食品通常摆在搭起的长桌上，让客人们共同享用。主人家会提供一些葡萄酒和饮料，主要是大家有一个交流的机会。

（2）暖屋会(House-Warming Party)：正如中国人庆祝乔迁之喜有"烧锅底"之类的活动，美国人乔迁新居之后也举行的一种庆贺宴会，应邀参加某人的乔迁喜宴，客人总要带点小礼品，如烟灰缸、毛巾、带框的墙画、壁炉毛刷等，以耐用物品为好，或者是记事薄、集邮薄、当地的地图、交通时刻表、旅游说明书等，以助主人开始新的生活。

（3）圣诞树装饰会(Christmas Tree Decorating Party)：每当圣诞节来临，家家都要精心装饰一棵圣诞树，为此还要举行不同形式的圣诞树装饰会，参加者只要带一两件装饰品凑凑热闹就可以了。

（4）摘苹果郊游会(Apple-Picking Party)：每当秋天正值水果收获之季，不少大学的国际学生办公室(International Students Office)会邀请外国学生和他们的家属前往农村果园，边摘苹果边品尝，这时你可以随便吃个够，但要带走的话就要出钱购买，不过价格倒是很便宜。有时邻居三五成群也会自发组织这样的活动，只要知道的人都可以参加。这是秋天过周末的一种形式。

（5）其他聚会：雪利酒会(Sherry Party)一般安排在周五下午，席间有各种饮料(雪利酒是产于西班牙南部的烈性葡萄酒)；男人交际会(Stag Party)，参加聚会者一般不带妻子、女友；家庭招待会(House Party)，常在乡间别墅里举行，要持续一夜；以及游园会(Garden Party)、野餐会(Picnic Party)、茶会(Tea Party)、生日喜庆会(Birthday Party)等等。

① My goodness! 是表示吃惊的用词,意思同 Oh dear,多为女性所使用。而男性则用 Damn! 或 I'll be damned!(该死!)表示吃惊。还有一些常听到的词汇,如:

比较粗俗的说法 (多为男性使用)	比较委婉的说法 (女性多用)	中文意思
Damn!	Darn!	该死!
God!/By God!	Gosh!/Golly!/By gosh!	天啦!
Jesus!	Gee!/Geez!/Jeepers!	喔!
Shit!	Shoot!	可恶!
Hell!	Heck!	下地狱吧!

② no wonder 是"难怪"的意思,如:
It's no wonder that you know everything about him.(难怪您对他了如指掌。)

③ used to 是"过去常常,现在不再"的意思,如:
She used to stay with her uncle in Seattle.(她以前在西雅图和她叔叔住在一起。)

④ similar to 是"与……相似"的意思,如:
Our house is similar to yours here.(我们的房子和你这里的相似。)

At a Public Library
在公共图书馆

Topic Introduction 话题导言

这是一个信息时代(information age),人的流动性也空前无比,流动的人们要获取信息的渠道很多,而图书馆是一个理想的去处。在美国,大大小小的社区都有自己的图书馆,许多专业和社会团体也建立了自己的图书馆,以至于一些学者把美国说成是"世界的图书馆"。此说法绝不夸张,因为不管走到哪里你都能找到图书馆,都能找到你需要的信息和资料。

到了一个新的地方,图书馆是值得一去的地方。可以去借书、看报,也可以去上网,还可以有很多的视听资料供你使用。只要有合法的证件,就可以申请一张免费的图书证(library card),然后便可自由使用图书馆的一切设施,哪怕是临时到一个地方,也可以要求图书管理员允许你使用图书、网络、阅览室等。

Situational Dialogs 情景对话

杨洋(Yang Yang)平时最大的兴趣就是去图书馆看书,到了一个新的地方,他当然不会忘记先找当地的图书馆了。

Dialog 1

Yang Yang: Hello, I'd like to apply for a library card.
您好，我想申请图书证。

Librarian: Do you have any ID card[①] with you, like driver's license?
您带了身份证件吗，像驾驶执照？

Yang Yang: I don't have a driver's license. I am a foreigner here. Can I use my passport instead?
我没有驾驶执照。我是外国人，我可以用护照代替吗？

Librarian: Sure you can. Please fill the application form and sign it.
当然可以，请填这个表并签字。

Yang Yang: Yes, thank you.
好的，谢谢。

Librarian: That's all right.
不用谢。

Dialog 2

Yang Yang: Excuse me, may I use one of the computers?
请问，我可以用这里的电脑吗？

Librarian: Yes, you can. But all the computers are occupied now. Could you wait a second?
可以用。但是现在所有的电脑都有人在用。您能等一会儿吗？

Yang Yang: Yes. How long can a person use a computer?
好的。一个人可以用多长时间的电脑？

Librarian: You are allowed to use a computer for thirty minutes every time. If no one is waiting there, you may use as long as[②] you like.
您可以一次用电脑 30 分钟。如果没有人等候，您想用多长时间就用多长？

Yang Yang: Oh, I see. Can I go to the Internet?
哦，我知道了。我能上互联网吗？

Librarian: Yes. There comes a computer available for you. No. 18, please.
能。有一台电脑您可以用了。请用第 18 号。

At a Public Library 26

在公共图书馆

Yang Yang: Thank you very much.
非常感谢。

Librarian: It's OK.
不用谢。

Dialog 3

Yang Yang: I'd like to check out③ these videotapes.
我想把这些录像带借出去。

Librarian: Sure. How many would you like to have this time?
好的,这次您要借多少盘?

Yang Yang: Can I get ten, please?
请问我可以借十盘吗?

Librarian: I'm sorry, sir. Every reader can get five at most④ at a time.
对不起,先生。每位读者一次最多只能借五盘。

Yang Yang: Never mind. I take these five first and I'll get the rest next time.
没关系。我先借这五盘,下次再借剩余的。

Librarian: Sure. Do you need a plastic bag?
好的,您需要塑料袋吗?

Yang Yang: Yes, thank you. How long can I keep them?
要,谢谢。我可以用多长时间?

Librarian: Two weeks. You will be fined if you could not return on time.
两个星期。不按时归还将会被罚款。

Yang Yang: Okay. I see. Thank you. Good-bye.
好,我明白了,谢谢,再见。

Typical Sentences 典型句型

1) What are the opening hours of the library?
图书馆什么时间开放。

2) Is the library open on Sunday?
图书馆星期天开放吗?

3) How can I find a particular book?
   我怎么找我要的书呢?
4) I'd like to apply for a library card.
   我想申请图书证。
5) I am a foreigner here. Can I use my passport instead?
   我是外国人,我可以用护照代替吗?
6) Excuse me, may I use one of the computers?
   请问,我可以用这里的电脑吗?
7) I'd like to check out these videotapes.
   我想把这些录像带借出去。
8) Every reader can get five at most at a time.
   每位读者一次只能借五盘。
9) How long can I keep them?
   我可以用多长时间?
10) You will be fined if you could not return on time.
    不按时归还将会被罚款。
11) You have a book that's three days overdue.
    你有一本书迟还了3天。
12) Where is the copy machine?
    复印机在哪里?
13) May I check these books out?
    这些书可以借出馆外吗?
14) How many books can I check out each time?
    一次可以借几本书?
15) We are closed on Sundays, but open on Saturdays.
    我们星期天关门,但星期六开门。

Background 背景知识

公共图书馆(public library):出示有效证件,如驾驶执照、学生证、绿卡、护照、身份证等中的任何一种都可以,填写一张简单的表

At a Public Library

格,包括姓名、性别、年龄、住址、电话等个人基本信息以及社会安全号码,并签名,图书管理员就会发一张编号的图书证(library card)给你。每次借书、上网、借录像带等都要出示此证并登记,而归还所借的图书时则只要投入到图书馆或者路边图书馆专用的归还箱就可以了。美国的每个县(county,路易斯安那州叫做 parish)都有数家图书馆,小的城市有一家,稍大的城市就会有多家。一般你在一个图书馆办理了图书证,全县其他图书馆也可以使用。

公共图书馆一般规模不大,但功能齐全,而且设备先进。据观察,一个公共图书馆一般由四个部分组成:书报阅览区、电脑网络区、视听区、儿童图书区。工作人员多为已婚女性,并配有一名警察负责安全。开放时间一般为上午 8:30 到晚上 9:00,星期天关门。读者最多的时候在下午 3:30 之后,因为中小学都放学了,学生纷纷到图书馆去查资料做作业,即使在这个时候馆内也非常安静。星期六则是成年读者最集中的时间。

注　释

① **ID card** 即身份证,是 Identification card 的缩写。
② **as long as** 相当于从属连词,意思是"只要",如:
We'll elect you our group leader as long as you like. (只要您愿意,我们就选您当组长。)
③ **check out** 也可以指"办理旅馆结账或者退房手续"。
④ **at (the) most** 意思是"最多,至多",如:
There were 50 people there, at the very most. (那里满打满算有 50 人。)

Arranging Children to School
安排子女上学

Topic Introduction
话题导言

孩子到了入学读书的年龄，家长有义务送孩子到学校接受教育。各个国家对学龄儿童入学都有明确的规定。到了美国，任何人的孩子不分种族、来源、性别、国籍，都必须入学接受免费的中小学 12 年义务教育。在中国已经上了几年学的孩子，可以直接插到相应的班级上课。家长可以找到当地中小学的校长谈谈孩子各方面的情况，面谈之前先打电话预约个时间，同时也可以把孩子带到学校去。

谈话的内容包括孩子的学习程度、当地的教育制度、师资水平、教材难度等，特别要提到孩子英语的学习问题。可以说：My child is 11 years old and she was in Grade 4 in China.（我孩子 11 岁，在中国时上四年级。）I'd like to listen to your suggestions about my child going to school.（关于孩子上学的事情，我想听听您的意见。）She is very good at math and science.（她数学和科学很好。）Do you have any specialized teacher to teach her English?（你们有没有专门老师教她英语？），等等都可以提出来。

Arranging Children to School 27

Situational Dialogs 情景对话

刘杭(Liu Hang)的女儿也来到了美国,不管怎样,孩子的教育始终是个大问题。

Dialog 1

Principal: Hello, McDonald Elementary School.
您好,麦当劳小学。

Liu Hang: Hello, may I speak to Mr. O'Neill, the principal[①]?
您好,可以跟奥尼尔先生,就是校长,通话吗?

Principal: Speaking. How can I help you?
我就是。我能怎么帮您呢?

Liu Hang: My family just moved here and I have a daughter of 9 years. I'd like her to go to school. Could you arrange a meeting with us?
我家刚搬到这里来,我有一个9岁的女儿。我想让她上学,您能安排见我们吗?

Principal: Let me see. Oh ... would you come to meet me at our school about 9:30 tomorrow morning?
我看看,哦……您明天上午9:30到我们学校来见我,好吗?

Liu Hang: 9:30 is good for me. How can I find your office?
对我来说9:30没问题。我怎么能找到您的办公室呢?

Principal: My office is Room 012. Someone at the main entrance will show you the way.
我的办公室在012房间,大门口会有人给您指路的。

Liu Hang: So, I will meet you at 9:30 tomorrow morning. Thank you very much.
这样,我明天上午9:30去见您。非常感谢。

Principal: Sure.
不用谢。

Dialog 2

Liu Hang: Good morning, Mr. O'Neill. I am the person who phoned you yesterday afternoon. My name is Liu Hang.
早晨好，奥尼尔先生。我是昨天下午给您打电话的人。我叫刘杭。

Principal: Nice to meet you, Liu Hang. Tell me about your daughter.
很高兴见到您，刘杭。谈谈您的女儿。

Liu Hang: She is 9 years old now and has finished two years' elementary school education in China.
她今年9岁，已经在中国读了两年小学。

Principal: How about her English?
她的英语怎么样？

Liu Hang: She's just learned English for one year. I'm worrying about that.
她刚刚只学了一年英语，我正为此担心。

Principal: That's not a problem. Children learn a new language very fast, besides we have a specialized teacher who teaches ESL② for children here.
那不是问题，孩子学新语言是很快的，而且我们有专门的老师教母语不是英语的孩子。

Liu Hang: I'm glad to hear that. Mr. O'Neill, I have a question.
很高兴听到这点。奥尼尔先生，我提个问题。

Principal: Go ahead③, please.
请提吧。

Liu Hang: I'm wondering if she can enroll in Grade Three at your school and we are worrying if there may be someone who will bully her.
我想她能否入读您学校的三年级，我们也担心是否有人欺负她。

Principal: She will enter a suitable grade according to her schooling background. As for④ what you are worrying about, I can guarantee that we'll take good care of her during school and no one will bully her.
根据她以前上学的情况，她会进入到适当的年级的。至于您所担心的，我能保证她上学期间我们将很好地照顾她，也没有人会欺负她。

Arranging Children to School 27

安排子女上学

Liu Hang:　　It's kind of you.⑤ Could I bring her here tomorrow?
　　　　　　太谢谢您了,明天我能带她来吗?
Principal:　　Certainly.
　　　　　　当然。

1) May I speak to Mr. O'Neill, the principal?
   可以跟奥尼尔先生,就是校长,通话吗?
2) My family just moved here and I have a daughter of 11 years. I'd like her to go to school.
   我家刚搬到这里来,我有一个11岁的女儿。我想让她上学。
3) She has finished four years' elementary school education in China.
   她已经在中国读了四年小学。
4) She's just learned English for one year. I'm worrying about that.
   她刚只学了一年英语,我正为此担心。
5) I'd like to listen to your suggestions about my child going to school.
   关于孩子上学的事情,我想听听您的意见。
6) She is very good at math and science.
   她数学和科学很好。
7) Do you have any specialized teacher to teach her English?
   你们有没有专门老师教她英语?
8) We have a specialized teacher who teaches ESL for children here.
   我们有专门的老师教母语不是英语的孩子。
9) Could I bring my daughter to school tomorrow?
   明天我能带我女儿来学校吗?

Background 背景知识

美国初等教育(grammar school education)：是指对1到12岁儿童的教育，包括：(1) 幼儿园教育(kindergarten education)，这是初等教育的第一步。4到6岁为学前教育 (preschool education)阶段，开设的主要课程是：讲故事(story-telling)、做游戏、音乐、图画、手工等。(2) 初等学校教育(elementary school education)，是指对6到12岁儿童的教育。教师多是已婚的妇女，课堂气氛轻松愉快，开设的课程主要有：数学、语言、书法、自然、美术、音乐、体育和社会知识等，在有些学校高年级还开设了外语课。学生管理形式各地不相同，有的是董事会(Board of Directors)，有的是"家长教师联合会"(Parent-Teacher Association，简称为 P. T. A.)。美国小学教师大都拥有大学文凭，但地位、收入比较差。

美国中等教育(high school)：中等教育仍然属于义务教育范畴，分为两个阶段，即(1) 初中教育阶段(junior high school education)，是对12到15岁的孩子进行的教育；(2) 高中教育阶段(senior high school education)，指对15到18岁的学生进行的教育。18岁以下的青少年可以免费读完中等教育。大多数中等教育学校开设数学、英语、物理、化学、社会学科(包括历史、地理、公民学和经济学)和体育，以及计算机、商业、工业贸易等课程，包括必修课(required courses)和选修课(elective courses)。实行学分制，一个学分大约等于120个小时，一般学生需要达到近20个学分才能毕业。美国中学85%是公立学校，只有少数有钱人家子女进入私立中学。美国初、高中除了传授基础文化知识以外，普遍重视学生的课外活动，注重培养学生的兴趣、性格和社会活动能力。学生办报、组织戏剧社团、参加航模兴趣小组等课外活动组织在各中学里都十分普遍。同时，美国的中学教育面临着许多问题，如辍学、暴力、吸毒、酗酒、抢劫、自杀等事情经常出现。中等教育的弊端也不断暴露出来，如学生普遍缺少地理知识，不知伊拉克(Iraq)在亚洲还是在欧洲，不关心时事，单词拼写错误较严重等。所有这些问题都使美国许多教育家、教师和父母忧心忡忡。

Arranging Children to School 27

安排子女上学

美国中小学学制(school system)：从小学入学至高中毕业的12年教育中，由于中小学教育由各州自行管理和制定教育政策，各州教育法都规定6岁至16岁的少年和青少年必须上学读书，但各州的学制很不统一，主要有四种学制形式：(1) 4年小学＋4年中学＋4年高中；(2) 6年小学＋3年初中＋3年高中；(3) 8年小学＋4年高中；(4) 6年小学＋6年初、高中。在美国各州，大多数小学实行6年制，但也有一些小学实行4年制或8年制。实行4年制或8年制的小学，一般把小学与中学或高中直接连通，增加或减少中学或高中的学年。总之不管如何划分，从小学到高中的总年数为12年。

注 释

① Mr. O'Neill 与 the principal 指的是同一个人，the principal 是 Mr. O'Neill 的同位语。
② ESL 是 English as a Second Language(英语作为第二语言)的缩写。
③ Go ahead 意思是"继续，走吧，说吧"，用于让对方开始或接着说话的时候。
④ as for 意思是"至于某人(某事物)"，如：
As for you, you ought to be ashamed of yourself. (至于你，你应该感到羞愧。)
⑤ It's kind of you. 意思是"您太好了"，表示感谢的时候使用比 Thank you. 的语气要强。

At the Post Office
在邮局

Topic Introduction
话题导言

人们的交往采用书信的方式越来越少了,使用邮局的机会也少了很多。但是,在像美国这样的西方发达国家,邮局的重要性仍然不减当年,原因主要是商业信函的数量在不断增加,特别是广告大量地通过邮局发送到千家万户。

作为外来"人口",使用邮局的时候还是不少,如邮寄信函、明信片给亲朋好友,给国内有关人士寄回资料等重要物品,还有人爱好集邮。而更多的时候则是我们常常收到通过邮寄送达的商业机构、政府部门、学校等单位的广告、通知、说明、回复等邮件。

Situational Dialogs
情景对话

对于特别热爱集邮的杨洋(Yang Yang)来说,会经常给国内的朋友和家人邮寄一些贺卡和信函,所以经常和邮局打交道。

Dialogue 1

Clerk: Can I help you, sir?
先生,要我帮什么忙吗?

At the Post Office 28

Yang Yang:	Yes. I'd like to mail some letters to China.
	是，我要邮寄几封信到中国去。
Clerk:	How do you want them sent? By airmail or EMS[1]?
	您想用什么方式邮寄？航空还是特快？
Yang Yang:	How long will it take by airmail, miss?
	小姐，航空信要多长时间？
Clerk:	About ten days or two weeks. But a mail by EMS can reach China within five days.
	大约十天到两个星期。但特快信五天就可以到达中国。
Yang Yang:	These letters are very urgent and important, so I'd like to mail them by EMS. What's the postage for them?
	这些信很紧急，很重要，我想寄特快。多少邮费？
Clerk:	Let me weigh them. Er ... 28 dollars in all. And here are the special envelopes for your letters. Please fill them hard.
	让我来称一称。哦……总共28美元。这是您寄信的特殊信封。请用力填写。
Yang Yang:	Excuse me, miss. I've finished it.
	打搅了，小姐。我填写好了。
Clerk:	This is the postal receipt. Please keep it, and you can check the status of your mail by this tracking number[2].
	这是邮政收据，请保管好，您可以用这个追踪号码查询您的邮件状态。
Yang Yang:	Thank you. Good bye.
	谢谢，再见。

Dialogue 2

Yang Yang:	Excuse me, miss. Is this the counter for sending parcels?
	打搅了，小姐。这是邮寄包裹的柜台吗？
Clerk:	Yes, sir. What can I do for you?
	是的，先生，要我帮什么忙吗？
Yang Yang:	Yes, I want to post this parcel to Sydney, Australia.
	是的，我要把这个包裹邮寄到澳大利亚的悉尼去。
Clerk:	What's in it?
	里面是什么？

Yang Yang:	Some books and magazines. 一些书和杂志。
Clerk:	Could you open it so that I could inspect its contents? 您能打开让我检查一下里面的东西,好吗?
Yang Yang:	Must I? 必须这样做吗?
Clerk:	I'm afraid you must. All parcels have to be inspected before they are accepted. 我恐怕必须这样做。所有包裹在接收之前必须接受检查。 ……
Clerk:	Well, please fill in the two forms. 好的,请填写这两张表格。
Yang Yang:	How much is the postage, please? 请问,多少邮费?
Clerk:	Would you like it insured? 要保险吗?
Yang Yang:	What's the insurance premium rate? 保险费率是多少?
Clerk:	One percent of the declared value。 声明价值的百分之一。
Yang Yang:	Yes, I'd like it insured. 好的,保险吧。
Clerk:	We have a special rate for the printed matter. Let me see. It comes to 21 dollars in all. 我们对印刷品有一个特殊费率。我看看,总共 21 美元。
Yang Yang:	Can I use my credit card here? 我可以使用信用卡吗?
Clerk:	Sure. Thank you. 当然,谢谢您。

Dialogue 3

Clerk:	Good morning, sir. 早晨好,先生。

At the Post Office 28

在邮局

Yang Yang: I'd like to buy some stamps.
我想买几张邮票。

Clerk: What kind of stamps do you like? Would you like to have a complete set or just the newest issue?
您喜欢什么样的邮票？您要买整套的还是最新出的？

Yang Yang: I'm a stamp collector. I want to buy a few complete sets first.
我是个集邮者，想买几个整套。

Clerk: Here are the samples. You may choose any sets you like.
这是样票，您可以选择您喜欢的。

Yang Yang: Thank you. These look very nice. I take four sets.
谢谢您。这些看上去不错，我买四套。

Clerk: I suggest you buy some new sets, and I'll cancel them for you.
我建议您买几套新出的邮票，我来给您盖销。

Yang Yang: A good idea. I prefer these two sets.
好主意。我喜欢这两套。

Clerk: Anything else?
您还想买什么？

Yang Yang: Nothing else, thank you very much.
不要别的了，非常谢谢您。

Clerk: $32 altogether, please.
总共请付 32 美元。

1) I'd like to send this letter to China by airmail, please.
请把这封信件航空邮寄到中国。

2) Er, it is quite a bit overweight.
呃，有点超重。

3) This will cost 80 cents.
邮费 80 美分。

4) I'd like to buy five 37 cents stamps.
我想买五张 37 美分的邮票。

5) Shall I give this letter to you or drop it in the mailbox outside.

我是把这封信交给你,还是投到外边的信箱里呢?

6) The parcel can be sent as printed matter.

这个包裹可当作印刷品邮寄。

7) Is there any way to mail this letter faster?

是否还有别的更快的寄信方式呢?

8) You can send it by Global Express Mail Service.

你可以发全球快递。

9) It should reach anywhere in the Mainland of China within three days.

在三天内,信件可以到达中国大陆任何地方。

10) Please use this envelope.

请使用这种信封。

11) What is the least expensive way to mail some books to China?

把这些书寄到中国,最便宜的办法是什么?

12) You can do it by surface mail.

你可以采取平邮的方式。

13) We have a one-destination mailbag delivery service.

我们提供单一目的地邮袋配送服务。

背景知识

普通邮寄业务: 在美国邮寄平信(ordinary letter, surface mail)、明信片(postcard)或小包裹(package),只需要投入到街区的邮筒(mailbox)即可。但国际航空信函(airmail)、特快(special express)、挂号信函(registered mail)等则必须到邮局去办理。邮局还出售邮票,非营业期间可以在自动售邮票机上购得邮票。邮局的营业时间通常为上午8:00到下午4:00,中午不休息。

住址变更: 在美国,人们经常搬家,住址常变动。这时,你只需要到邮局去要一张地址变更表(Address Change Form),认真填写好并签字,邮局就把你的信件转送到新的住址了,不用担心信件丢

At the Post Office

失的问题。

其他业务：这里有两项业务与邮局似乎沾不上边儿。(1)外国居留者可以在邮局领取"外国人登记卡(Alien Registration Card)"，填好后寄到移民局(Immigration & Naturalization Department)，目的是告知你的新地址。以前是每年的1月才填，"9·11"之后要求变动地址的10天以内必须向移民局报告。否则，就可能有违反法律的嫌疑。这种表格也可以在大学的"国际学生办公室(International Students/Scholars Office)"领得。(2)邮局也出售面额为整数的现金汇票(Money Order)，这种汇票相当于现金，但注明了是由谁付的钱，收款人是谁，与现金支票(Cashier's Check)的用途差别不大，遗失了可以查出来谁是最终持有人。银行以及一些大的公司(如Wal-Mart, Winn Dixie)也出售此类汇票。

注 释

① EMS 是"express mail service"的缩写。
② 办理特快邮寄的时候，邮局会给你一个号码，凭借这个号码就可以在网上或者打免费电话查到你的邮件目前到哪儿了，这个号码就是 tracking number。

Phone Service I
电话服务 1

Topic Introduction
话题导言

美国的电话服务运营商(phone service provider)很多,如 AT&T 和 SBC 等。不同的公司资费标准差异很大,所提供的服务内容也不同,人们要根据自己使用电话的具体需要进行选择。

安装电话和搬家移机一定要和电话公司讲清楚地址、姓名、性别和社会安全号码,特别是姓名和地址的拼写要说正确,这涉及到以后电话公司进一步为你提供服务和账单邮寄的问题。比方说,很多时候由于口音的问题,分辨不清 Z 和 G、S 和 X、B 和 D 等,但凡是问题都有解决的办法,像说出字母所在的单词就是一种方法,人们常说 Z as in zebra,B as in bicycle 等等。数字的读法也是多种多样,很多人有不同的习惯,有人喜欢把 99 读成 double nine,也有人爱读成 nine nine,不一而足。

查号服务是世界各地电话服务的基本要素之一,查本地用 411,查外地用 1-区号-555-1212,查免费电话用 1-800-555-1212。也可以自己在黄页(Yellow Pages)上查到,排列是先姓后名并按照姓氏字母顺序,姓和名之间有一个逗号,如 John-David Tovey 排列为 Tovey, John-David,就要先查 T,找到 Tovey 后再找 John-David,如果遇到同名同姓,就要区分住址。

Phone Service I
电话服务 1

Situational Dialogs
情景对话

叶丽敏(Limin)来到一个陌生的环境居住,安装一个电话是首要的事情。这方便她同熟人联系,也可以通过电话查询熟人的号码。

Dialog 1

Clerk 1: Hello, AT&T. May I help you?
您好,AT&T 公司,需要帮什么忙吗?

Limin: Hello, I've just moved here and need a phone at my home.
您好,我刚搬到这儿来,家里需要电话。

Clerk 1: May I know your name, madam? And, what's your address?
女士,可以问您的名字吗?还有,您的地址是什么?

Limin: My name is Limin Ye[①]. My address is seven twelve, South Carlton Street, Number Two, Sulphur, Louisiana and the zip code is seven zero six six three.
我叫叶丽敏,我的地址是路易斯安那,萨尔弗,南卡尔顿街 712 号之二,邮政编码是 70663。

Clerk 1: What's your social security number, Ms. Ye?
叶女士,您的社会安全号码是什么?

Limin: 318-27-2099. Three one eight, two seven, two zero double nine. How much should I pay each month?
318-27-2099,就是三一八,二七,二零两个九。我每个月要付多少钱?

Clerk 1: We have several plans for you. You may choose one of them. You may pay $19.95, $24.95, $29.95, $49.95 or $99.95 per month. It depends on your needs. If you phone very often to other states, you may choose the highest rate, for you could phone freely, no time limit.
我们有数个方案供您选择,您可以从中选一个。您每月可以付 19.95 美元、24.95 美元、29.95 美元、49.95 美元或 99.95

|||||||美元。这取决于您的需要。如果您打到外州的电话很多，您可以选择最高的费率，这样您就可以随意打电话，没有时间限制。

Limin: I phone very little other than② within the area code 314. I think the lowest rate is all right for me.
我除了在区号 314 内打电话外，很少打电话。我觉得最低的费率适合于我。

Clerk 1: All right. So, your phone can be used within 48 hours, your number will be 518-8177. You may have a try Sunday afternoon. If you can't use the phone till next Monday morning, please give us a call and the number is 1-800-323-5858.
好的。这样您的电话在 48 小时内就可以使用了，您的号码是 518-8177。星期日下午您可以试一下。如果到星期一早晨还不能用，请给我们打电话，号码是 1-800-323-5858。

Limin: All right. Thank you.
好的，谢谢。

Clerk 1: You are welcome, and thank you for choosing At&T.
不客气。也谢谢您选择了 At&T 公司。

Dialog 2

Limin: Hello, is that 1-800-555-1212?
您好，是 1-800-555-1212 吗？

Clerk 2: Yes, how can I help you?
是的，能帮您什么？

Limin: I need to know the toll-free number of Federal Express. Could you tell me that, please?
我需要知道联邦快递的免费电话号码，能告诉我吗？

Clerk 2: Just a second. ... (Voice from system) The toll-free number of FedEx is 1-800-212-6788. Thank you very much.③
请稍等，……（来自系统的声音）联邦快递的免费电话号码是 1-800-212-6788。非常感谢。

Phone Service I

Dialog 3

Limin: Hello, is that 411?
您好,是 411 吗?

Clerk 3: Yes?④
查询谁的电话?

Limin: Please give me the phone number of Miss Beibei Wang.
请告诉我王蓓蓓小姐的电话号码。

Clerk 3: How do you spell her name?
怎么拼写她的名字?

Limin: Her given name is B-E-I-B-E-I, and her family name is W-A-N-G.
她的名是 B-E-I-B-E-I,她的姓是 W-A-N-G。

Clerk 3: Hold on⑤ a second. ...... Sorry I can't find it. What city do you know she lives in? Or, tell me the area code, please.
稍等,……对不起,没有这个人。请问她住在哪个城市?或者请您告诉我那里的区号。

Limin: Lake Charles, Louisiana. I don't know the area code.
路易斯安那的查尔斯湖市。我不知道区号。

Clerk 3: Hold on please. The area code is 314, and I'll transfer you to Lakes Charles 1-314-555-1212.
请稍等。那里的区号是 314,我就把您转接到查尔斯湖市的 1-315-555-1212。

Limin: Thank you.
谢谢。

Functionary: Hello, Lake Charles Inquiring Station. May I help you?
您好,查尔斯湖咨询台,能帮您忙吗?

Limin: Could you tell me the number of Miss Beibei Wang? Her given name is B-E-I-B-E-I, and her family name is W-A-N-G.
告诉我王蓓蓓小姐的电话号码,好吗?她的名是 B-E-I-B-E-I,她的姓是 W-A-N-G。

Functionary: Hold on please. ... (Voice from system) Her number is 1-314-123-5678. Thank you very much.
请稍等,……(来自系统的声音)她的号码是 1-314-123-5678。

Typical Sentences
典型句型

1) I need to open phone service at 722 South Carlton Street.
   我需要开通南卡尔顿街722号的电话服务。

2) I've just moved here and need a phone at my home.
   我刚搬到这儿来,家里需要电话。

3) I am intending to transact phone moving procedure, for I've moved.
   我搬家了,因此想办理移机手续。

4) Can I still use the present number after phone moving?
   请问移机后我现在的电话号码还能继续用吗?

5) Will you please tell me how to make a long-distance call?
   你能告诉我如何打长途电话吗?

6) Why are you still making the long-distance call in this way?
   你怎么还在用这样的办法打长途。

7) How much should I pay each month?
   我每个月要付多少钱?

8) I think the lowest rate is all right for me.
   我觉得最低的费率适合于我。

9) By the way, what's the opening fee?
   顺便问一下,开通费是多少?

10) It's 21 dollars and will be charged together with your first month phone bill.
    21美元,并和第一个月话费单一同缴纳。

11) I need to know the toll-free number of Federal Express. Could you tell that, please?
    我需要知道联邦快递的免费电话号码,能告诉我吗?

12) Please give me the phone number of Miss Beibei Wang.
    请告诉我王蓓蓓小姐的电话号码。

13) Could you tell me the number of Miss Beibei Wang?
    告诉我王蓓蓓小姐的电话号码,好吗?

Phone Service I

Background 背景知识

电话服务种类(一)：美国的电话服务公司竞争激烈，各运营商和电话卡公司都争相笼络客户，以扩大业务量。作为一个在美国的中国人，常常要用到的电话服务有：

(1) 装机移机：装一部电话的手续与国内差别很大，只要首先找一部公用电话或在朋友家里给电话公司打个电话，告诉他们你需要装一部电话以及你的住址，并在他们提供的几个方案中选一个，把电话机插上早已有的接线口就可以用了。移机也是这样，告诉他们你的地址变了，他们就会把你的这个号码改到新地址，但超过一定区域就要重新装机换号了。装机和移机都要缴纳数十美元的服务费，相当于国内的初装费。

(2) 通话方案：各电话公司都提供多个话费方案，一般地，用户每月缴纳固定的月费，在一定的范围内可以无限地打电话，超过这个范围就要按照长途在月费的基础上另外计费；不同的方案月费不同，月费不同可以不限时间通话的区域不同，月费越高，不限时间通话的区域越大。如果很少打美国国内长途电话，就选择最低月费的那种；如果打往其他州的电话很多，就选择包美国国内长途的那种。

(3) 查号服务：国内都知道114，但美国电话号码查询有两种，一个是在本区号内(area code)查号拨411就可以了；另一个是超过本区号要拨1和区号，再拨555-1212。若不知道对方区号，告诉查号台城市名称就可以了。美国查号不仅可以查到单位办公电话，也可以查到私人住宅电话，除非主人要求不公开其电话。但如果你要求不公开你的电话，则反而要付费，奇怪得很吧。

注 释

① 东方人到了西方国家,因为姓名的顺序不同经常惹出不必要的麻烦。所以,要入乡随俗,在办理正式业务时将姓名的顺序说成或写成"名+姓"。

② other than 多用于否定词之后,可以表示"除了",如:
She has no clothes other than this one. (除了这件衣服外,她没有别的了。)
或者可以指"不同于,而不",如:
He seldom appears other than happy. (他很少有不高兴的时候。)

③ 这是电话公司的自动语音系统发出的信息,不用回答。

④ Yes?相当于问句:What number do you need to know? (你需要知道谁的电话号码?)

⑤ 短语 hold on 相当于 wait 的意思。

Phone Service II
电话服务 2

Topic Introduction
话题导言

没有电话不行,有了电话,出了问题也不行。所以,问题咨询、故障报修、错收话费反映等都是需要和电话公司打交道的。打这类电话也有学问,遇到故障而导致电话不能正常使用的时候,就一定要正确地叙述故障的具体表现,如没有拨号音叫做 no dial tone,杂音多叫做 lots of static, 听不见响铃叫做 no ringing/sound,没有电流叫做 no current 等等。如果不懂这些词汇,也可以具体地描述故障的表现,电话公司服务人员跟母语不是英语的人打交道的情况很多,很有经验。

紧急电话(emergency calls)属于比较特殊的一类,不仅免费,而且线路总是畅通。遇到紧急事件需要打紧急电话,最为重要的就是要把事件的地点和究竟发生了什么事情简明扼要地说清楚,以争取得到最为及时的帮助。

Situational Dialogs
情景对话

丁唐(Ding Tang)和杨洋(Yang Yang)遇到些不顺心的事,不仅电话出故障,杨洋竟然还碰到抢劫的,幸好可以通过电话报警。

Dialog 1

Clerk: AT&T Repair Service. What can I do for you?
AT&T 维修服务部,能为您帮什么忙吗?

Ding Tang: My phone doesn't work right.
我家电话工作不正常。

Clerk: What's wrong with it?①
是怎么回事儿?

Ding Tang: From last Friday, I often receive strangers' phone calls, but there're no such people they want to speak to. When I call my home number, I am connected to other people's home. My number has been transferred to their home and their number to my home. I don't know why.
从上周五起,我经常接到陌生人的电话,而我家没有他们要找的人。我打我自己家的号码时,却接到了别人的家里。我家的号码换到了别人的家里,而别人的号码换到了我家。我不知道为什么。

Clerk: All right. I see.
好的,我明白了。

Ding Tang: I should have very important calls these days. When can it be OK?
这几天我应该有几个重要电话,什么时候能够修好?

Clerk: I'm sorry for that. I'll let them check as soon as possible and have it repaired.
对此我感到抱歉,我会让他们尽快检查并修好。

Ding Tang: Thank you.
谢谢。

Dialog 2

Clerk: At&T Repair Service, may I help you?
At&T 公司维修部,能给您帮什么忙?

Yang Yang: My phone is out of order②.
我家电话出故障了。

Clerk: What seems to be the problem?
可能是什么样的故障呢?

Phone Service II

Yang Yang:	There is no current at all. I think the phone wire is probably broken.
	完全没有电流,我想电话线路可能断了。
Clerk:	Is the indicator red when you pick up the receiver?
	拿起听筒时,指示灯变红了吗?
Yang Yang:	No. We cannot phone out and nobody can phone in. There's no reaction when picking up the receiver.
	没有,我们不能打出去,别人也打不进来。拿起听筒就没有反应。
Clerk:	All right. What's your phone number?
	好的,您的电话号码是多少?
Yang Yang:	528-7263.
	528-7263。
Clerk:	Okay, we'll take care of that. Have a try after six this evening.
	好的,我们会帮您处理的,今晚6点之后再试一下。
Yang Yang:	I will. Thank you.
	好,谢谢。

Dialog 3

Officer:	911 Emergency. May I help you?
	911 报警台,需要协助吗?
Yang Yang:	Yes. I met a young man, white with blond hair, about 25 years old and he is very strong. He stopped me and forced me to give him 100 hundred dollars at the back of the University Students Union Building.
	是的,我遇到了一个年轻人,白人,金色头发,大约25岁,长得很结实。他在大学学生联合会大楼后面拦住我并强行要我给他100美元。
Officer:	Did you give him the money?
	你给他钱了吗?
Yang Yang:	No, sir. We began quarrelling and another Asian guy heard us and ran to help me. They began to fight. So I ran away to phone you.
	没有,先生。我们开始争吵,另一个亚洲人听到我们就跑过来帮我。他们开始打起来,我就跑来打电话。

Officer: Are they still there?
他们还在那儿吗?

Yang Yang: I think so. I just ran inside the building. Please come quickly.
我想是的。我刚刚跑进大楼,请赶快来。

Officer: All right. Be sure to protect yourselves, and patrol cars will be right over there.
好的,注意保护你们自己,巡逻车马上就过去了。

Typical Sentences
典型句型

1) My phone has lots of static.
   我的电话有很多杂音。
2) The connection seems to be very bad.
   通话质量似乎很不好。
3) The lines seem to be mixed up.
   好像是串线了。
4) The wiring in your phone may have gotten rusty.
   可能电话机里的电线生锈了。
5) My phone doesn't work right.
   我家电话工作不正常。
6) My phone is out of order.
   我家电话出故障了。
7) What seems to be the problem?
   可能是什么样的故障呢?
8) Okay, we'll take care of that. Have a try after six this evening.
   好的,我们会帮您处理的,今晚6点之后再试一下。
9) 911 Emergency. May I help you?
   911报警台,需要协助吗?
10) Someone has broken into our house.
    有人闯入我们家了。

11) Be sure to protect yourselves, and patrol cars will be right over there.

注意保护你们自己,巡逻车马上就过去了。

背景知识

电话服务种类(二):

(4)国际长途:中国人虽然打美国国内长途不多,但打回中国的国际长途却很多。可以要求电话公司开通国际长途,但费用非常昂贵。中国人一般选择购买电话卡的方式。电话卡也有两种,一种是有形卡,可以在商店、售卡机等处购买;一种是虚拟卡,在网上购买,通过信用卡付账,如 First Phone Card 公司提供数十种电话卡。使用电话卡,要根据提示输入很多号码,先输入接入号,再输入密码,再输入国际代号和国内的区号及电话。

(5)免费电话:即集中付费的电话(Free Phone)。美国的免费电话通常有几个号码,如 1-800、1-888、1-877 等,使用这几个号码打电话可接通由被叫用户在申请时指定的电话。主叫用户免收通信费用,由被叫用户集中付费。这类电话号码一般是服务电话,是争取客户的一种方式。

(6)紧急电话:美国电话号码是七位数,但少数电话除外。遇到紧急的事情需要救助或者报告时,可以拨打911,包括抢劫、强暴、火灾、疾病、骚扰、殴斗等。如果接听电话的人认为你所说的情况不够紧急,会建议你改用另一个电话叙述详细情况。

(7)其他问题:公用电话(pay phone)的资费标准比较高,打一次市话(3分钟内)一般50美分,如果用电话卡打国际长途,会多扣除50到75美分;大学校园电话(campus phone)在学校内部直接拨后面五位就可以了,如要打外线就要先拨9再拨外线号码,从外面打进校园电话,就要拨完整的七位号码,也要避免用校园电话打国际长途,因为也会多扣钱。

① What's wrong with ...? 往往用来询问某人或某物有什么问题或毛病。
② out of order 意为"状态不好,不整齐",如:
　Her stomach is out of order.(她胃不舒服。)

Mobile Phone Service
移动电话服务

Topic Introduction
话题导言

　　如果从中国的大城市去美国,比如北京、上海或者广州,你一定会发现美国人的移动电话(mobile phone,也称 cell phone)拥有率比中国大城市还要低。

　　我们的手机号码目前长达 11 位数字。美国人手机号码却只有七位数字,与固定电话无异。这也是西方人比较崇尚一个标准模式的缘故,全美的号码除极少数外都是七位数字。据知,美国提供移动电话服务的主要公司是 AT&T 和 SPRINT Nextel,也有几个小公司。

情景对话

　　丁唐(Ding Tang)新办一个移动电话时碰到了一些不太明白的问题,为此他要咨询一下移动电话服务公司。

Dialog 1

Ding Tang:　Hello, I'd like to know how to enroll in① your cell phone program.
　　　　　　您好,我想知道怎么注册你们的移动电话服务项目。

Clerk:	We have several plans. Please look through these posters first. 我们有几种方案,请您先看看这些招贴吧。
Ding Tang:	I know something of these plans. 我对这些方案有些了解。
Clerk:	Any questions? 有什么问题吗?
Ding Tang:	One question. What if I already have a cell phone, and don't need one you provide?[②] 一个问题。如果我已经有了一个手机,而不用你们提供的那个,该怎么做?
Clerk:	You can still use that one. But we don't give any discount. 您仍然可以用您的那个,但我们不提供话费折扣。
Ding Tang:	Do I still have to pay deposit? 我还要交纳押金吗?
Clerk:	No, sir. 不用交押金,先生。

Dialog 2

Clerk:	May I help you? 能帮您吗?
Ding Tang:	How can I go through[③] all the procedures to get cell phone service? 如果要得到移动电话服务,我有哪些手续要办呢?
Clerk:	You'd choose one of these plans, and look over the contract. If you agree, we can sign it. 您要从这些方案中选择一个,看看这个合同。如果您同意,我们就可以签字了。
Ding Tang:	How can I pay the bills? 我怎么付账呢?
Clerk:	There are many ways for you to pick up[④], by credit card, by personal check, by pre-paid account or by cash. 有很多方法可供选择,可以用信用卡、个人支票、预付账户或者付现金。

Mobile Phone Service 31

移动电话服务

Ding Tang: Must I pay deposit?
我必须交押金吗?

Clerk: You don't have to if you have a credit card. Otherwise, you have got to.
如果您用信用卡就不必。否则,就要交押金。

Ding Tang: All right. I see.
好的,我知道了。

Clerk: Please fill the form and sign here.
请填写这个表格并在这里签字。

Dialog 3

Clerk: Hello, Sprint Sulphur Store. May I help you?
您好,斯普林特·萨尔弗店。能帮您吗?

Ding Tang: I suspect your company has over-charged me last month. I was within my plan and didn't use one minute more.
我怀疑你们公司上个月多收了我的钱。我在方案范围内打电话,没有超过一分钟。

Clerk: Your phone number, please?
请问您的号码?

Ding Tang: 212-123-4567.
212-123-4567。

Clerk: That's a New York number. Just a second, and let me check... You phoned 4087 night and weekend minutes last month and 420 daylight minutes. But your plan only allowed you to phone 3500 night and weekend minutes.
那是纽约的号码。稍等,我来查一查,……上个月,您打了4087分钟的夜间和周末电话,打了420分钟的白天电话。但是,您的计划只允许您打3500分钟的夜间和周末电话。

Ding Tang: Did I?⑤ Perhaps my daughter did. I'll ask her. Thank you anyway.
是吗?也许是我女儿打的,我问问她。无论如何还是谢谢您。

Typical Sentences
典型句型

1) I'd like to know how to enroll in your cell phone program.
   我想知道怎么注册你们的移动电话服务项目。
2) I need to change my cell phone number.
   我想改变我的手机号码。
3) I know something of these plans.
   我对这些方案有些了解。
4) I cannot receive phones these days because of no ringing.
   因为不响铃,我这些天接不到电话。
5) What if I already have a cell phone, and don't need one you provide?
   如果我已经有了一个话机,而不用你们提供的那个,该怎么做?
6) How can I go through all the procedures to get cell phone service?
   如果要得到移动电话服务,我有哪些手续要办呢?
7) How can I pay the bills?
   我怎么付账呢?
8) Must I pay deposit?
   我必须交押金吗?
9) You don't have to if you have a credit card. Otherwise, you have to.
   如果您用信用卡就不必。否则,就要交押金。
10) If my prepaid account is out of money, will you cut off your service?
    如果我的预付账户中的钱用完了,你们会切断服务吗?
11) I suspect your company has over-charged me last month.
    我怀疑你们公司上个月多收了我的钱。

Mobile Phone Service 31

移动电话服务

Background 背景知识

移动电话服务：同固定电话一样，移动电话也推出多个方案供消费者选择。举个例子说，某公司的一个服务方案是：月费 24.99 美元，一个月总共可以通话 2400 分钟，不区分本地通话还是美国国内长途通话（夏威夷和阿拉斯加两个州除外），其中白天工作时间（星期一至五上午 7:00 至晚上 9:00）可以通话 500 分钟，其余 1900 分钟可以在晚上和周末使用，晚间和周末可以使用白天的时间，但白天不能超用晚间和周末的时间。通话时间包括主叫和被叫时间，超过时间限额以上的通话，收费相当高，达到每分钟 50 美分。

手机本身是免费赠送的，但要在该公司入网一年以上；若中途退出则要购买正在使用的这个手机，有的公司则实行押金制度。美国全国的时区有多个，在哪个时区入网就按那个时区的时间计算。

注 释

① enroll in 与 register 都是"注册"的意思，用于学生注册课程、病人入医院治疗、接受某种服务等。
② What if ...? 是"要是……，怎么办？"，如：
What if they can't come on time tomorrow morning? (他们要是明天早晨不能准时来,怎么办？)
③ go through 是"办理"的意思，指要经历的步骤、手续等，如：
You've to go through many formalities if you want to go abroad. (如果你要出国，得办理很多手续。)
④ pick up 这里是"选择"的意思，与 choose 相同。
⑤ Did I? 是 Did I phone so many minutes? 省略了后半部分的问句。

189

Network Service
网络服务

Topic Introduction
话题导言

美国的互联网服务非常发达,政府、学校、图书馆、银行、医院、公司等各种服务都是网络化的。居民在自己家里就可以轻松地通过互联网向政府提出意见、申请各种证照,更可以在家里实现个人银行账户的转存、支付、更改密码,此外还可以查阅图书馆的网上资料,选择网络课程接受高等教育,甚至获得博士学位。

要做到这些,有一点至关重要,就是你家里的电脑必须和网络连接起来。表面上看大部分普通居民都是通过电话线把电脑和互联网连接起来,其实这些服务是由专业的网络服务公司间接提供的。普通美国人多选择ADSL,它通过电话线加装一台ADSL终端设备就可以享受宽带数据服务了,并且打电话和上网互不干扰,速度也快。申请网络服务首先要选择一家网络服务商(internet service provider,简称ISP),并且注意其信誉、质量、收费标准和服务等,可以多向周围的人咨询。

Situational Dialogs
情景对话

刘杭(Liu Hang)想在家里开通宽带,因为互联网不仅可以提供很多资料,而且可以让她认识很多新朋友。

Network Service 32

Dialog 1

Liu Hang: I brought a laptop[①] from China, and I'd like my computer connected with Internet. Could you tell me how?
我从中国带了一台笔记本电脑来,我想把它连接到互联网上。能告诉我怎么做吗?

Clerk: Do you live on-campus or off-campus?
您住在校内还是校外?

Liu Hang: Off-campus.
校外。

Clerk: All right. You can apply for the broadband service.
好的。您可以申请宽带服务。

Liu Hang: I will have a try. But when I bring my laptop to a classroom or a conference room, how can I connect it with the campus network?
我会试一试的。但当我把电脑拿到教室或者会议室时,我怎么把电脑和校园网连接起来。

Clerk: You have to set up another connection. Better bring your computer here. Someone here may help you.
您要设置另外一个连接。最好把您的电脑拿到这儿来,有人会帮您的。

Liu Hang: Okay, I'm afraid to trouble you too much.
好的,我恐怕太麻烦你们了。

Clerk: No trouble, madam. That's our job.
不麻烦,女士,这是我们的工作。

Dialog 2

Liu Hang: It's really annoying that I don't have the Internet service at home.
我家没有连接互联网,真烦人。

Clerk: You may consider[②] using the ADSL.
您可以考虑使用 ADSL。

Liu Hang: Can I make a phone call while getting on the Internet?
上网时也能打电话?

Clerk:	Yes, of course. It'll provide wide band data business through a common phone line. All you need is to add③ an ADSL terminal device on your phone line. 当然可以，它通过普通电话线提供宽带数据业务，只要加装一台 ADSL 终端设备即可。
Liu Hang:	Is it very expensive? 是不是很贵？
Clerk:	No, it's cheap. You can browse the web page quickly with ADSL. 不，很便宜。您可以通过 ADSL 快速浏览网页。
Liu Hang:	That's good enough. 那够好。

Typical Sentences
典型句型

1) I'd like my computer connected with Internet. Could you tell me how?
   我想把电脑连接到互联网上。能告诉我怎么做吗？

2) I will have a try. But when I bring my laptop to a classroom or a conference room, how can I connect it with the campus network?
   我会试一试的。但我把电脑拿到教室或者会议室时，我怎么把电脑和校园网连接起来。

3) You may consider using the ADSL.
   您可以考虑使用 ADSL。

4) Can I make a phone call while getting on the Internet?
   上网时也能打电话？

5) It'll provide wide band data business through a common phone line.
   它通过普通电话线提供宽带数据业务。

6) All you need is to add an ADSL terminal device on your phone line.
   你只需要在电话线上加装一台 ADSL 终端设备即可。

Network Service 网络服务 32

7) You can browse web pages quickly with ADSL.
   您可以通过 ADSL 快速浏览网页。
8) It is said that a new technique to connect network has been developed, called Cable Modem,
   据说又开发出一个新的网络接入技术,叫线缆调制解调器。

背景知识

互联网的接入方式:

(1) 综合业务数字网(Integrated Service Digital Network,简称 ISDN):即一线通,是采用数字传输和交换技术,将电话、传真、数据、图像等多种业务综合在一个统一的数字网络中进行传输和处理的技术。有了 ISDN 用户线路,就可以同时上网、拨打电话、收发传真了;

(2) 数字数据网(Digital Data Network,简称 DDN):是随着数据通信业务的发展而迅速发展起来的新型网络,其传输的数据质量高、速度快、网络时延小等优点,尤其适合于大容量、多媒体、中高速通信的传输;

(3) 非对称数字用户环路(Asymmetrical Digital Subscriber Line,简称 ADSL):是通过普通电话线提供宽带数据业务的技术,具有下行速率高、频带宽、性能优、安装方便、不需交纳电话费等优点,目前在美国家庭和个人使用最为广泛的一种接入技术;

(4) 线缆调制解调器(Cable Modem):通过线缆调制解调器即 Cable Modem 和有线电视(Cable TV)网进行数据传输的技术。

E 化词语:最为常见的当然是 email 这个词,人们原来多写成 e-mail,但现在都写成 email。其中,E 化词语的 e 是 electronic(电子的)的缩写。还有如下一些词语,也是常见的一些 E 化的词:

e-bank 网上银行
e-business 电子商务
e-cash 电子现金
e-check 电子支票

e-commerce 电子商务
e-currency 电子货币
EFT(Electronic Fund Transfer)电子资金转账
e-management 电子管理
EOS (Electronic Ordering System)电子订货系统
e-payment 电子支付
e-purse 电子钱包
e-service 电子服务
e-world 电子世界

① 就像汉语一样，英语中对一个物品的称呼也会有多种，如汉语中的"手提电脑"、"笔记本电脑"、"便携式计算机"等几个词，对应的英语是"laptop"、"notebook"、"portable computer"等。

② 注意 consider 一些派生词的含义。如：considerable (相当大的，重要的), consideration (考虑，思考，体谅), considering (鉴于), considerate (关切的，体贴的)。

③ add 还可以构成短语，如：add fuel to the flame (火上浇油)。

Opening an Account
开设账户

Topic Introduction
话题导言

英美等西方国家的金融服务业非常发达,业务种类繁多,服务水平也很高。不管你是移民,还是学生,抑或是短期逗留,银行是不可能不去的,在那里你可以得到满意的服务。

开立账户是你到银行首先要做的事情,因为不管是现金还是支票都可以通过银行进行必要的周转,这样才能使你的日常生活更加方便和安全。

Situational Dialogs
情景对话

丁唐(Ding Tang)要存一些钱到银行,但是开设什么样的账户呢?这是一个需要好好思考的问题。

Dialog 1

Ding Tang: I would like to open a bank account.
我想开一个账户。

Banker: What kind of account do you want to open, sir?
先生,你想开什么样的账户?

Ding Tang:	I want to keep the money in the bank until I go back to China next spring. 我想将这笔钱存在银行里,直到我来年春季回中国。
Banker:	If you make a savings account, you can deposit or withdraw money anytime you want. If some money won't be needed for a certain period of time, you can make a certified deposit. 如果你开的是储蓄存款账户,你就可以随时存取。如果有些钱一段时间不使用的话,你可以采取保付存款方式。
Ding Tang:	Well then, I'd prefer the latter. What is the annual interest rate for a certified deposit account? 那么,我选择后者。保付存款的年利息率是多少?
Banker:	5.8%. Please fill out these forms. 5.8%,请您填这些表格。
Ding Tang:	I've finished it. Here you are. 我已经填写完了,给您。

Dialog 2

Banker:	Good morning. Can I help you? 早晨好,我能帮您的忙吗?
Ding Tang:	I'd like to open both a checking account and a savings account. 我想开支票账户和储蓄存款账户。
Banker:	Certainly, sir. Please fill in the forms. 当然可以,先生。请填这些表格。
Ding Tang:	All right. I've finished them. Here you are. 好的,我填完了,给您。
Banker:	I've to remind you that to open a savings account you'll need at least 500 dollars. 提醒您一句,要开储蓄存款账户,至少需要500美金。
Ding Tang:	What if the amount in my account falls below the minimum requirement? 账户上的存款低于最低要求时会怎样呢?
Banker:	In that case, you'll lose that month's interest. 那样的话,你会失去当月的利息。

Opening an Account 33

开设账户

Ding Tang: I see. Where should I sign my name?
我知道了,我在哪里签字呢?

Banker: At the bottom of the form. I would suggest you sign in English.①
在表格的底端,我建议你用英文签名。

Ding Tang: Finished.
签完了。

Banker: Thank you. The number printed here is your account number.
谢谢,印在这里的号码就是你的账号。

Ding Tang: How can I get my checks?
我怎样得到我的支票呢?

Banker: We'll mail the checkbooks to the address you have put down on this form. You'll receive the checkbooks.
我们按照你在表格上填好的地址把支票簿寄给你。你将收到这些支票簿。

Ding Tang: Thank you very much.
十分感谢。

Dialog 3

Ding Tang: What is the proper procedure to open a money market account, sir?
先生,开货币市场账户怎么办手续?

Banker: You should fill in the application firstly, and then we'll give you an account card②.
先填一张申请表。然后我们就给你一张账户卡。

Ding Tang: I have ten thousand US dollars. How much should I keep in the account?
我现在存一万美元,账户中我应该保持有多少钱?

Banker: At least three thousand and you have to deposit in the account for three months.
至少三千,而且你还要至少存够三个月。

Ding Tang: But I am wondering if there is any risk for my money.
但是,我不知道我的钱是否有风险。

Banker: No risk at all.
完全没有风险。

Ding Tang: By the way, what is the annual interest rate?
顺便问一下,年利多少?

Banker: It varies from time to time. At present it is 5.6%.
利率经常变动,现在的利率是 5.6%。

Typical Sentences
典型句型

1) I would like to open a bank account.
   我想开一个账户。

2) What kind of account do you want to open?
   你想开什么样的账户?

3) I want to keep the money in the bank until I go back to China next spring.
   我想这笔钱存在银行里,直到我来年春季回中国。

4) If you make a savings account, you can deposit or withdraw money anytime you want.
   如果你开的是储蓄存款账户,你就可以随时存取。

5) If some money won't be needed for a certain period of time, you can make a certified deposit.
   如果有些钱一段时间不使用的话,你可以采取保付存款方式。

6) To open a savings account you'll need at least 500 dollars.
   要开储蓄存款账户,至少需要 500 美金。

7) What if the amount in my account falls below the minimum requirement?
   账户上的存款低于最低要求时会怎样呢?

8) In that case, you'll lose that month's interest.
   那样的话,你会失去当月的利息。

9) What is the annual interest rate for a certified deposit account?
   保付存款的年利息率是多少?

10) I'd like to open both a checking account and a savings account.
    我想开支票账户和储蓄存款账户。

Opening an Account 开设账户 33

11) Here are the forms you need to fill out.
    这是你需要填的表格。
12) I would suggest you sign in English.
    我建议你用英文签名。
13) The number printed here is your account number.
    印在这里的号码就是你的账号。
14) We'll mail the checkbooks to the address you have put down on this form.
    我们按照你在表格上填好的地址把支票簿寄给你。
15) You'll receive the checkbooks.
    你将收到这些支票簿。

背景知识

银行营业服务：英美银行的营业时间(office hours)一般是上午9:30到下午4:30，中午没有午休时间，大多数银行实行五天工作制，也有少数银行是六天工作制。进入银行，不论人多人少照例是要排队的。等候时距离要离得远一些,当柜员(teller)叫到你(Next, please.)的时候，你才可以走到柜台前办理业务。你走到柜员面前时，她会主动向你打招呼：Hello, how are you today?（你好吗？），你也要回应她的问候：Pretty good, and how are you?（很好,你好！）。

开立户头：不同的银行,服务的程序可能会有不同。但大多数银行都有专门的人员负责开立新的户头，他们就是银行顾问(banker),他们和柜员不在同一个服务区域。关于开户的一些问题，都可以从他们那里得到解答,他们也会给你一些中肯的建议。银行户头的种类很多,有的有利息,有的没有；有的利息高一些,有的低一些；有的要求保持一定的存款额度才有利息；还有的要求存够一定的期限才会有利息；甚至有的有当场的现金或者礼品返还作为奖励。这不像国内银行都执行国家的统一规定存款利率。以 U.S. Bank 为例,可以选择的主要账户种类有：(1) Savings Account,即储蓄账户,有较低的利息；(2) Checking Account,即支票账户,要求保持一定的存款额度才有利息,银行向你发放印有你个人姓名地址的个人支票簿;(3) Money Market Account,即货币市场账户,利息较高,但要求存款有较高的余额(如 5000 美元)和较长的存期;等等。你可以根据个人的资金使用情况选择一种或几种开立户头。

银行卡:开立户头之后,工作人员会问你是否需要银行卡(统称 bank card),一张银行卡对应一个银行户头,你可以在柜员机(即 ATM[3])上存钱、查询和取钱。如果要求得到银行卡,请注意一定要填写正确的地址,因为该银行卡和支票簿都是通过邮局邮寄给你的。拿到卡之后,要打电话到银行激活,注意开户时提供的信息一定要真实可靠。特别是收到密码后要记住,并销毁该邮件,以防心怀不轨的人盗用你的银行卡。

① 在银行留签名的主要目的是以后当你使用支票或者银行卡时,可以核对持卡人是否就是本人。
② 这不同于银行卡,这只是一张类似于个人名片的小纸片,上面印有账号等信息。
③ ATM 是 automatic teller machine 的缩写。

Depositing and Cashing
存款和取款

Topic Introduction
话题导言

在像美国这样的西方国家,人们跟现金打交道的几率很小,一般都把钱存到银行的账户中,因为携带大量现金不但不方便,而且很危险。初到美国,把你的钱不管是现金还是旅行支票存入当地银行是非常重要的一件事情。而且,当你到银行存入大量现金时,银行职员会感到非常吃惊,可能会说,"You crazy guy, why take so much cash?"(简直是疯了,竟带这么多现金?)这句话没有贬义,只是说明他(她)大吃一惊。

虽说绝大多数西方人都不太使用现金,但平时身上带少量现金总是必要的,一是因为周末的农民市场(farmers' market)、庭院售卖(yard sale)等地方不使用银行卡或支票,你得使用现金;二是有很多服务是投币式的,如图书馆复印资料、从公共建筑物内的饮料机购买饮料和小吃、公共汽车购票、使用风景点的望远镜等等;三是据说在大城市遇到抢劫时可以用小钱"消财免灾"。当然,还有很多情况得使用现金。

情景对话

身上携带少量现金总是必要的,李康(Li Kang)需要去银行取一些钱。

Dialog 1

Teller: May I help you?
能为您服务吗?

Li Kang: I'd like to withdraw 1000 dollars.
我想取 1000 美元钱。

Teller: Please fill in the slip, state the exact amount you wish to withdraw.
请填这个单,写明您要取的确切数目。

Li Kang: Yes. And here is my passport. Is that all?
好的,这是我的护照。可以吗?

Teller: Please show me your bank account card.
请把您的银行开户卡给我。

Li Kang: Here it is.
给您。

Teller: Do you want large ones① or small ones?
您要大面额还是小面额?

Li Kang: Five hundreds, eight fifties, and ten tens②, please.
请给我 5 张 100 美元的、8 张 50 美元的、10 张 10 美元的。

Teller: Please wait a minute. I'll get the money from the cashier.
请等一会儿,我得从出纳那里取钱。

Dialog 2

Teller: What can I do for you?
要我帮忙吗?

Li Kang: Please deposit this check into my savings account.
请把这张支票存在我的储蓄存款账户中。

Teller: Would you please sign your name on the back of the check.
请在支票的背后签个名字,好吗?

Li Kang: By the way, can I have 200 dollars in cash?
顺便问一下,我可以拿 200 美元的现金吗?

Teller: Certainly. How would you like it?
当然可以。你想要多大面额的货币?

Li Kang: One hundred and ten tens, please.
请给我 1 张 100 美元的和 10 张 10 美元的。

Depositing and Cashing 34

存款和取款

Teller: All right. Here you are.
好的,给您。

Dialog 3

Li Kang: Excuse me. Can you cash these traveler's checks for me?
打搅了,你能为我将这些旅行支票兑换成现金吗?

Teller: Certainly, sir. How would you like to pay?
先生,当然可以。您要什么样的面额?

Li Kang: Some big notes and some small notes.
给些大面额的,给些小面额的。

Teller: All right, sir. Please sign your name here.
好的,先生。请在这儿签名。

Li Kang: By the way, can I have a card for the automatic teller machine?
我可以要一个自动取款卡吗?

Teller: I think you can as long as you have a bank account with us.
我认为,只要你有我们的银行账户,就可以申请自动取款卡。

Li Kang: Thank you very much.
非常感谢。

Typical Sentences
典型句型

1) What can I do for you?
   要我帮忙吗?
2) Please deposit this check into my savings account.
   请把这张支票存在我的储蓄存款账户中。
3) Can you cash these travelers' checks for me?
   你能为我将这些旅行支票兑换成现金吗?
4) I would like to cash this check.
   我想兑换这张支票。
5) I'd like to change 1000 dollars.
   我要兑换 1000 美元。

6) Would you please sign your name on the back of the check?
请在支票的背后签个名字,好吗?

7) By the way, can I have 200 dollars in cash?
顺便问一下,我可以拿200美元的现金吗?

8) How would you like it?
你想要多大面额的货币?

9) Can I have a card for the automatic teller machine?
我可以要一个自动取款卡吗?

10) I think you can as long as you have a bank account with us.
我认为,只要你有我们的银行账户,就可以申请自动取款卡。

取钱:大多数银行的服务都分为两个区域,一个是顾问区,实际上是有被称作"银行顾问(banker)"的专业人员指导客户如何开户;另一个是柜台服务区,主要办理存款、取款、转账和汇款等具体业务,这儿的工作人员叫做"柜员(teller)"。要想得到现金有两种方式,一种是直接到银行的柜台上去填单取现,与在国内到银行柜台取钱的区别不大,记住带上两种身份证件(如驾驶执照、护照、学生证、社会安全卡等,其中至少有一种上面要有照片),以及银行开户卡,不用输入密码;第二种是用银行发给你的银行卡直接到自动柜员机上(Automatic Teller Machine, ATM)取钱,要输入密码。

存钱:一般情况下,在美国,不管是你打工得到的工资,还是某些种类的奖学金,都是以普通转账支票的形式支付给你,你得先到银行去把支票存进你在银行的账户中至少一天,才能支取现金;而如果你得到是现金支票(cashier's check)或者是带去的旅行支票(traveler's check),你就可以要求银行直接付给你现金,或者存入账户中。把支票存入账户时,银行工作人员都要求你在支票背后签字。如果是把别人的支票存入你的账户中,一定要得让他先在支票背后签字表示同意该支票转让给你。

礼貌热情:美国的银行服务都非常热情,工作人员都会主动给

Depositing and Cashing 34

你打招呼。见面常说"How are you today?"你也要回答"Pretty good, and how are you?" 以示礼貌;办完业务工作人员也常向你道再见"Have a nice day!"你的回答也可以很简单"You, too!"如果碰到比较熟悉的人,还往往会和你聊一聊当前的社会新闻,如音乐会、体育赛事、违法案件等等。

有时,你存完钱或办完其他业务,柜员可能会问你 "Do you need your balance?"意思是说是否将你账户的余额打印在业务清单的背后,根据情况,你可以回答"Yes"或者"No",但记住说"Thank you"。

注 释

① one 在指代上文出现过的名词时可用复数 ones。
② 数词往往是不用复数形式的,这里加了复数词尾的数字实际上是用作了名词,如 ten tens 就是 ten pieces of ten-dollar notes,这属于日常简略的说法。

Remitting Money
汇款

Topic Introduction
话题导言

在境外生活或工作的中国人,还会遇到汇钱回中国的问题,但语言不通使他们不少人只得委托一些中介机构帮助他们汇款,多支付了一些手续费。实际上通过美国的银行转汇到国内银行的账户上,汇款1万美元以内的手续费也就是25美元左右。

其实,到银行办理汇款的语言很简单,如:send my money to China(把我的钱汇到中国)、wire some money to my account with Bank of China(电汇一些钱到我在中国银行的账户上)、remittance fee(汇款手续费)等。

Situational Dialogs
情景对话

叶丽敏(Limin)在美国工作了一段时间了,她需要汇款回中国,但是怎么汇呢?她先请教了有经验的朋友。

Remitting Money 35

Dialogue 1

Limin: Hello, this is Limin speaking. I'd like to ask for your advice①.
您好,我是丽敏,请教您些建议。

John: This is Johnson Smith. Please do as you like.
我是约翰,请随便问吧。

Limin: I want to send some money to China. How had I better send it, by postal order or by bank draft?
我想寄些钱到中国。最好该怎样汇,用邮政汇票还是银行汇票?

John: How much do you wish to remit?
你想寄多少?

Limin: The amount is twenty thousand dollars.
寄 20000 美元。

John: The best way to remit it is by bank draft.
最好的办法是银行汇票。

Limin: I wonder why people use postal orders.
我不知道人们为什么还用邮政汇票。

John: Postal orders are more convenient for small sums.
邮政汇票对于小数额汇款更方便。

Limin: Thank you for your advice.
谢谢您的建议。

Dialogue 2

Teller: Can I help you, madam?
女士,能为您效劳吗?

Limin: I'd like to remit some money to China. But I don't know how.
我想汇些钱到中国,但不知道怎么办理。

Teller: There are a lot of ways, such as bank drafts, electronic remittance, credit card, etc.
有很多方法,如银行汇票、电子汇款、信用卡等等。

Limin: Which one can get to China soonest?
哪种方法可以最快到达中国?

Teller: Electronic remittance. It can reach your specified account in China within twenty-four hours.
电子汇款。它能 24 小时之内到达您指定的中国帐户上。

Limin: That sounds fine. I'd prefer it.
听起来不错，我就用这种吧。

Dialogue 3

Limin: Good morning. I'd like to remit some money to Hong Kong. May I have an application form, please?
早上好，我想把钱汇到香港，能给我一张汇款申请单吗？

Teller: Yes, you'll find some on the desk over there.
可以，在那边的桌子上就有。

Limin: Thanks. ... Here is my application form. I'd like to send 2000 dollars to Hong Kong.
谢谢，…… 给您我的申请单，我想汇 2000 美元到香港去。

Teller: Very good, madam. Excuse me, but how do you spell the name of the payee②?
好的，女士。请问，收款人的名字怎样拼法？

Limin: Leung Cheehwa. L-E-U-N-G, C-H-E-E-H-W-A.
梁建华，L-E-U-N-G, C-H-E-E-H-W-A。

Teller: That's all right.
好啦。

Limin: By the way, what is the rate of exchange today?
顺便问一下，今天的兑换率是多少？

Teller: It is 1 U. S. dollar to 7.68 Hong Kong dollars.
兑换率为 1 美元比 7.68 港元。

Limin: What time will the draft reach Hong Kong?
银行汇票什么时间到香港？

Teller: Within four days. You may remind the payee.
四天之内，您可以提醒收款人。

1) I want to send some money to China.
我想寄些钱到中国。

Remitting Money 35

汇款

2) I'd like to wire some money.
   我想电汇一些钱。
3) How had I better send it, by postal order or by bank draft?
   最好该怎样汇,用邮政汇票还是银行汇票?
4) How much do you wish to remit?
   你想寄多少?
5) The amount is two thousand dollars.
   寄 2000 美元。
6) How much will it be to wire two thousand dollars?
   电汇 2000 美元要多少手续费?
7) The best way to remit it is by bank draft.
   最好的办法是银行汇票。
8) Postal orders are more convenient for small sums.
   邮政汇票对于小数额汇款更方便。
9) How do you spell the name of the payee?
   收款人的名字怎样拼法?
10) What is the rate of exchange today?
    今天的兑换率是多少?
11) It is 1 U. S. dollar to 6.80 RMB yuan.
    兑换率为 1 美元比 6.80 人民币元。
12) What time will the draft reach Guangzhou?
    银行汇票什么时间到广州?

背景知识

美元纸币:美元纸钞的纸张、大小、颜色完全一样,很容易混淆,主要的区别是面值和人像有不同,如 George Washington(1元), Thomas Jefferson(2元), Abraham Lincoln(5元), Alexander Hamilton(10元), Andrew Jackson(20元), Ulysses Grant(50元), Benjamin Franklin(100元)等。美钞背面是绿色,所以我们对美钞总称为 greenback(绿色背面);正面颜色要淡一些,主体为奶白色,上方

印有"UNITED STATES OF AMERICA"字样。

美元硬币：共有6种，即1分、5分、1角、2角5分、5角和1元。硬币上都铸有拉丁文"motto"(众多之一)的字样。1分是铜币，正面是林肯的像，还铸有"IN GOD WE TRUST"(我们信仰上帝)及"LIBERTY"(自由)的字样，另外还铸有发行的年号。背面有 ONE CENT 以及"UNITED STATES OF AMERICA"字样。5分是铬、镍币，故称 nickel，正面是第三届美国总统杰弗逊的头像及其在他的家乡弗吉尼亚州夏洛茨维尔市的邸宅蒙蒂瑟洛（Monticello）的图景。1角是银币，正面为富兰克林·罗斯福总统的侧面头像。背面铸有火炬和树，以及"ONE DIME"的字样，通称 dime。2角5分也是银币，上面铸有华盛顿总统像和鹰(eagle)，又有 QUARTER DOLLAR 的字样，所以通称为 quarter，近年发行了以每州标志物为图案的银币，按照加入美国的顺序发行，成为少年儿童收集的新宠。5角也是银币，一面有女人立像，印有"我们信仰上帝"(IN GOD WE TRUST)，一面有 HALF DOLLAR 的字样，通称为 half dollar。1元硬币通称 silver dollar，现在流通比较少了。

注释

① advice 在指"忠告，建议"时为不可数名词，如要表示几项建议，可加上适当的量词，如：a piece of advice（一项建议）。

② 动词 +-ee 变成名词，表示"受动者"；而 +-er 为"施动者"，如：employee（雇员），employer（雇主）。

Credit Card and Checks
信用卡与支票

Topic Introduction
话题导言

出门在外,信用卡(credit card)是最实用的消费工具,是可以在信用额度内先消费、后还款的,使用起来非常便利。信用卡由于大多数是用塑胶制成,也称作"塑胶货币(plastic money)"。美国发行的信用卡主要有 Visa(维萨)、MasterCard(万事达)、American Express(美国运通)、Discover(发现)等系列,前两种发行最广泛。发卡机构不仅仅只有银行,许多专门从事信贷服务和大型的销售公司也发行信用卡,如福特(Ford)公司就联合银行发行了以"Ford"冠名的信用卡。

由于信贷市场的激烈竞争,各信用卡公司经常会推销他们的信用产品,如打电话到你家、开学时到大学现场受理申请、推出优惠期和优惠利率等。了解并学会一些常用的有关英文词语非常有用。

个人支票是美国生活中又一个不可缺少的消费工具,支付房租、购买食品、外出旅行等都可以使用个人支票付账,而不用携带现金。消费完毕,大名一签,抬腿就可以走人了。

Situational Dialogs
情景对话

丁唐(Ding Tang)准备申请信用卡,出门在外,拥有信用卡和个人支票总是比较方便些,但是也要警惕收到空头支票。

Dialog 1

Clerk: May I help you?
我可以帮您忙吗?

Ding Tang: Yes. I'd like to apply for a credit card.
可以。我想申请信用卡。

Clerk: All right. Please fill this application and sign your name at the bottom of the form.
好的,请填写这张申请表并在底端签名。

Ding Tang: But I have a couple of questions. What's your APR[①]?
但我两个问题,年利率是多少?

Clerk: For the first six months, it's 5.9%. After that it will be 19.80%.
头六个月,是5.9%;以后就是19.80%。

Ding Tang: How long is the grace period[②]?
还款期限是多长?

Clerk: Twenty nine days.
29天。

Ding Tang: Does that mean I don't need to pay interest for 29 days after the last clearing day?
那就是说,从上个结算日起我有29天不用支付消费款项利息?

Clerk: Yes, quite right.
对,没错。

Ding Tang: How about the annual fee?
年费是多少?

Clerk: Twenty five dollars.
25美元。

Ding Tang: I see. Thank you very much.
我知道了,非常感谢。

Dialog 2

Clerk: This is American Century Credit Service. May I speak to Mr. Ding?
美国世纪信用公司,能和丁先生通话吗?

Credit Card and Checks 36

信用卡与支票

Ding Tang:	Yes, speaking. 请讲,我就是。
Clerk:	You have submitted an application for credit card, right? 您递交了申请信用卡的申请,对吗?
Ding Tang:	Yes. What happened? 对,什么事?
Clerk:	Your application has been approved. I'd like to verify some of your personal information. 您的申请已经获得批准,我想核对一下您的个人资料。
Ding Tang:	OK. But is your credit card a Visa or MasterCard or American Express? 好的,不过,你们发的是维萨卡、万事达卡还是美国运通卡?
Clerk:	None of these, sir. Yours is a Gold Purchase Card. 都不是,先生。发给您的是购物金卡。
Ding Tang:	What does that mean? 什么意思?
Clerk:	When you buy things from us, you just need to pay 25% of the whole payment in advance and the grace period is 29 days. There is no annual fee and the APR is just 7.8%. 当您从我们这里买东西时,您只需要先付总购物款的 25%,还款的宽限期是 29 天。没有年费,年利率只有 7.8%。
Ding Tang:	But can I buy things from other company with this card, for example, Wal-Mart or Target? 但是,我可以用这卡在沃尔马或者塔吉特购物吗?
Clerk:	No, sir. You can buy anything you like from us online and the shipment is free. 不能,先生。您可以从我们网上买到您想要得到的一切,运送免费。
Ding Tang:	So, I see. I don't think I need this kind of credit card. 这样,我明白了。我想我不需要这样的信用卡。

Dialog 3

Clerk:	Bank of America Customer Service. Can I help you? 美洲银行客户服务部,能为您服务吗?

213

Ding Tang:	I got a check from one of your customers. Could you please help me to check if the check is good? 我从你们的一个客户那里得到一张支票，您能帮我查一下这张支票是否有效吗?
Clerk:	Sure. What's the account number? 当然可以,账号是多少?
Ding Tang:	12345 67890. 12345 67890。
Clerk:	What's the amount? 数额是多少?
Ding Tang:	$700.00. 700 美元。
Clerk:	I'm really sorry, sir. No sufficient funds in this account now. 先生,我真是抱歉得很,现在账上没有足够的资金。
Ding Tang:	Really? It's a rubber check③ again. Thank you anyway. 真的吗? 又是一张空头支票。还是谢谢您了。

典型句型

1) I'd like to apply for a credit card.
   我要申请信用卡。
2) I'd like to apply for a student credit card.
   我要申请学生信用卡。
3) How long can I have the grace period?
   还款期限是多长?
4) How about the interest rate?
   利率是多少?
5) What's your annual fee?
   年费是多少?
6) Why don't you issue a credit card to me?
   你们为什么不给我发信用卡?
7) You spend plastic money like water.
   你刷卡刷得太凶了。

8) Your credit card is maxed out.
您的信用卡超支了。
9) I'm sorry you are over your credit limit.
对不起,您的信用卡超支了。
10) Don't deposit this check until next Monday.
到下个星期一再存这张支票。
11) I guarantee this is not a rubber check.
我保证这不是空头支票。
12) Otherwise, you'll have to pay more than this.
否则,你将付得更多。

背景知识

信用卡(Credit Card):信用卡可向银行或信用卡公司申请,如你有一份较稳定的职业和收入,一般都较容易获得;如果你在大学读本科或研究生,有些银行发行一种专门给学生的信用卡。一般信用卡上都有持卡人的姓名、卡号、有效日期和签名,有的还加印有持卡人的相片。这样使信用卡更具有个人证件的特征,同时,也可避免万一遗失后被人盗用而遭受损失。在美国,信用卡也是一种很重要的个人证件。

对账单(Bank Statement):银行每个月寄给你的关于你账户收支状况的报告。不管你在银行开了什么户头,还是在使用信用卡,每个月都会按时收到收支明细清单。如果你发现其中有一笔钱不是你开支的,你可申请更正或者拒绝支付该项开支。

借记卡与信用卡 (Debit Card 与 Credit Card):Credit Card 是一种先消费后还钱的赊购卡;而 Debit Card 是银行发行的借记卡,与你在银行开设的户头相对应,使用的金额一般不能超过账户中的余额,由于账户种类的不同而分为 Checking Card、Savings Card、ATM Card 等。消费的时候使用 Credit Card 直接划卡,然后签字即可。使用 Debit Card 时可以像 Credit Card 一样直接划卡,然后签字(要告诉收款人使用 credit);也可以输入密码扣账,还可以同时向收款人说:Could you give me some cash?（能给我一些现金吗？）并告诉他多少，然后和你消费的数额一同扣账。

现金支票(Cashier's Check)：可以直接从银行支取现金的一种支票。这种支票指明了收款人是谁，别人不能代为兑现，只有在你账户中确实有这笔钱时，才能要求银行开具这种支票。因为它和现金一样，收票人不会担心该支票是空头支票(rubber check)，也不会被退回(bounce back)。所以，有人担心收到空头支票时，就要求付款人付 Cashier's Check，而不收个人支票(Personal Check)。

个人支票(Personal Check)：在银行开立了户头就可以申领的一种支票。你在银行开户之后，银行可能会发给一张银行卡、几本支票和账户卡。开始给你的支票是临时的，需要你自己写上地址和姓名，几天之后，印好姓名和地址的几本支票和一个塑料封面就会寄给你。支票被心怀叵测的人盗用虽然可以追回经济方面的损失，但麻烦也是一大堆。另外，如果开出了空头支票，也会给自己带来麻烦和损失，因为收款人一旦请求追债公司上门讨债，将会损失更多的钱财，个人声誉也会一落千丈。

注释

① **APR** 是 **Annual Percentage Rate** 的缩写，指的是当你过了还款日期还没有还齐所欠款项的时候，信用卡机构向你收取利息的百分比。如果你每次都还清了欠款，信用卡公司就赚不到这笔利息了，而只得到你的年费。

② **grace period** 指的是你还钱的宽限期，如你在 4 月 10 日刷卡消费，而每月 20 日是结算日 **(clearing day)**，从 4 月 20 日起你有 29 天（即 **grace period**）的时间是不用支付刷卡消费款项利息的，就是说，你最迟可在 5 月 19 日还清消费款项。

③ 本来账户中只有 500 元却开出了 700 元的支票，这就是 **rubber check**（空头支票），空头支票如果存入银行，就会打回来 **(return, bounce back)**，而且还要扣手续费 25 元，所以收到不可靠人士的支票时要先打电话到银行查问清楚。指"空头支票"类似的英语还有：**bad check**、**bum check**、**hot check** 等。

Renting a Car
租车

Topic Introduction
话题导言

在西方发达国家，私人汽车是人们交通的主要工具之一，特别是在美国，没有汽车就好像没有了腿，将会给你带来诸多不便。由于国土广阔，经济发展水平高，高速公路密如蛛网，使得美国号称是"汽车轮子上的国度"。据统计，全美国人均拥有汽车的数量为0.6辆，是全世界最高的，甚至有些人一个人就拥有数部汽车。

因为汽车拥有量高，所以在城市之间的交通距离不太远的情况下，人们都选择自己开车。作为一个初到美国的"外人"，解决交通问题的方法之一就是去租一辆自己喜欢的车。

Situational Dialogs
情景对话

高卫平(Weiping)去美国从事商务活动，为了解决交通问题，租车是个不错的办法。

Dialog 1

Weiping: Hello, is that the Rent-A-Car Company?
您好，是租车公司吗？

Clerk:	Yes, what can I do for you?
	是的,我能为您服务吗?
Weiping:	I'd like to rent a van for three days. Could you tell me the charge?
	我想租用一辆旅行车用三天。能告诉我你们怎么收费?
Clerk:	It depends on the model and make you prefer. For example, a Plymouth with seven seats will be 28 dollars per 24 hours.
	这要看您租什么牌子和型号的车,比方说,七座的普利茅斯是每24小时28美元。
Weiping:	That sounds great. I'd like to rent the van one way. Do you have any drop-off charge①?
	听起来不错,我想租单程,是否有另外收费?
Clerk:	No, sir.
	没有,先生。
Weiping:	Thank you very much.
	非常感谢。

Dialog 2

Clerk:	Family Rent-A-Car. May I help you?
	这里是家庭租车公司,能为您服务吗?
Weiping:	I need to rent a car one way to Chicago. Could you reserve me a car for next week?
	我想租车单程去芝加哥,能给我预留一辆车下周使用吗?
Clerk:	Yes, sir. When and where would you like to pick up the car?
	好的,先生。您什么时间什么地方要车?
Weiping:	At St. Louis International Airport on July 22 around 10 am.
	7月22日上午10点左右在圣路易国际机场。
Clerk:	When and where are you going to return the car?
	您什么时候什么地方还车?
Weiping:	At Chinatown of Chicago on July 24 around 5 pm.
	7月24日下午5点左右在芝加哥唐人街还车。
Clerk:	Hold on please, and let me check.
	请您稍等,我来查一下。
	……

Renting a Car 37

租车

Clerk: OK, sir. What kind of car would you like?
好的，先生，您喜欢什么样的车呢？

Weiping: I'd like a two-door Honda Accord with an air bag, or any other similar one②.
我想要一辆两门的本田雅阁，附有安全气囊，或者类似的车辆都行。

Clerk: Let me check ... we have a new two-door Buick available at St. Louis International Airport.
我来查一下…… 我们有一辆两门别克车在圣路易国际机场。

Weiping: Good. What's your rate, please?
可以，请问出租费如何算？

Clerk: $39.90 per day and free unlimited mileage.
每天 39.90 美元，不限里程。

Weiping: That's just fine. Anything else?
还行，别的呢？

Clerk: Would you like to purchase loss and damage insurance?
您要买遗失或损坏保险吗？

Weiping: Yes, of course.
是的，当然要买保险。

Typical Sentences
典型句型

1) I'd like to rent a van for one day.
我要租一辆旅行车用一天。

2) I will move to Bowling Green, Kentucky. Do you have a pick-up truck for two days?
我要搬家到肯塔基州鲍灵格林，你们有没有小卡车可以租用两天？

3) My friends and my family are planning to go to Yellow Stone Park. We need a van with seven seats.
我家和我朋友计划到黄石公园去，我们需要一辆七座的旅行车。

4) Could you tell me the models and makes of your cars?
你能否告诉我你们汽车的牌子和型号?

5) I'd like to reserve a Toyota Corolla for next Monday morning.
我想预订一辆丰田卡罗拉下周一早晨用。

6) I'd like to rent a car one way.
我想租车单程使用。

7) What's your rate, please?
请问,租车的费率是多少?

8) How much is a two-door Buick for three days?
租一辆两门的别克用三天多少钱?

9) How do you charge me, by day or by hour?
你们怎么收费,是按天还是按小时?

10) Can I leave the car at another agency?
我可以在别的车行还车吗?

11) $25 a day or $150 a week, unlimited mileage.
我们的收费是25美元一天,或者150美元一周,不限里程数。

12) $18 per 12 hours plus tax and insurance.
我们的收费是每12小时18美元,外加税钱和保险。

13) Would you like to purchase loss and damage insurance?
您要买遗失和损坏保险吗?

14) You may return the car at any of our divisions.
你可以在我们的任何分支机构还车。

租车公司:美国各大租车公司(Car Rental Company)在机场、酒店、市区等地都设有租车服务中心,并备有各种车型供顾客挑选。当你走出机场的时候,抬头就可以看到诸如 Rent-A-Car, Rent-Me, Rent-&-Run 等广告招牌,那就是汽车租赁公司了。如果想租车,可以先打个电话咨询一下,搞清楚他们有些什么车型和租车费用的计算方法。由于竞争的加剧,许多公司取消了按里程收费的方法。现在一般来说,租车费用的计算是根据使用车的时间来计算的,如

Renting a Car 37

租车

每 24 小时多少钱,而不管你跑了多少英里。当然,油钱是要自己负担的。不同的公司有时候价格相差很大,一定要价比三家。你可以租到小汽车,也可以租到货车。如果是搬家,可以考虑租一辆搬家专用的车辆。

租车方法:由于绝大多数的汽车租赁公司在各个城市都设有服务中心,你在一个地方租到了汽车,使用完以后,可以在全美任何别的城市归还,而没有必要再开回到原来租车的那个城市去。比方说,当你要离开一个地方的时候,就租一辆汽车开到目的地或开到机场,然后还给该公司当地的服务中心就可以了。这就是单程出租(One-way Rental)。你新到一个地方可以租车,你需要出去旅行时也可以租车,任何时候只要需要都可以租车。但最好提前一个星期用电话预约。

租车手续:要想租车,你必须持有合法的驾驶执照(Driver's License)和信用卡(通常要求是 Visa, MasterCard 或 American Express 中的一种),即使有再多的现金,租车公司也不可能把车租给你,因为不需要你提前支付租车费用,而是到你还车的时候再从你的信用卡中扣付你实际的租金。如果你使用无效证件或是无效信用卡,你的社会信用程度将受到极大的损害,以后办事情就会相当困难了。

注 释

① **drop-off charge** 指的是租车时不把车送回原处,而是停在其他地方加收的费用。对于这项费用,各公司有所不同,也有公司不收取 **drop-off charge** 的。
② 这是为了不把话说得太绝对的一种说法,以给别人更大的余地。类似的还有 **something like that** 等。

Laundry Service
洗衣服务

Topic Introduction
话题导言

洗衣服(washing clothes)是一件日常生活中极其平常的事情,就是这么一件极其平常的事情,中国和西方国家的差异也是非常大。在我国人们习惯于在阳台上、窗户外或庭院中的晾衣绳上或晾衣架上晒晾衣服。在美国这样的西方国家,你在一般情况下是看不到这样的景致的。这是因为他们所洗的衣物在洗后是需要用烘干机烘干的。

尽管大多数家庭都有洗衣设备,洗衣服务(laundry service)在英美国家仍然非常发达,每个城市的每个居民区都有方便、经济的洗衣服务设施。光临洗衣店的主要是单身男女、学生、家中没有洗衣机的人们,因为在这里可以得到非常好的洗衣服务,而且也不是很贵。酒店和旅馆也都有洗衣服务,有免费服务的,也有要另外收钱的。洗衣服务属于日常生活中十分普遍的行为,不需要使用过分严谨、正规的语言,只要用一般的礼貌语言就可以了,如 Can I get my clothes washed here?

Situational Dialogs
情景对话

脏衣服总是让丁唐(Ding Tang)和刘杭(Liu Hang)头痛,幸好美国的洗衣服务很发达,很容易找到洗衣店。

Laundry Service 38

Dialog 1

Attendant: May I help you?
能为您服务吗？

Ding Tang: I'd like to get my clothes washed[①] here.
我想在这里把我的衣服洗一下。

Attendant: All right, sir. Do you like your shirts starched?
好的，先生。您的衬衫要上浆吗？

Ding Tang: Yes, please. I'm leaving here tomorrow evening. Can I get these stuffs by tomorrow afternoon?
请上浆。我明天晚上要离开这里，明天下午之前能拿到吗？

Attendant: No, sir. But you can get them tomorrow morning if you choose our express service.
不能，先生。但如果您选择我们的特快服务的话，明天上午您就可以拿到。

Ding Tang: Any difference in price?
价格上有什么差别吗？

Attendant: Yes, sir. We charge 50% more for express, but it only takes 5 hours.
有的，先生。我们对加急服务增收50%的服务费，但只要5个小时就可以取衣。

Ding Tang: Okay. Thanks a lot.
好的，多谢了。

Attendant: You're welcome.
不客气。

Dialog 2

Liu Hang: Excuse me, sir?
打搅一下，先生。

Stranger: Yes?
什么事？

Liu Hang: Could you show me how to use the machine?
您能告诉我如何使用这洗衣机吗？

Stranger:	No problem. Just choose the right kind of water you need by turning this switch, say, stop it at "HOT" for hot water, and then put two quarters here and push the drawer inside, and then press the button "START". 没问题。转动这个旋钮选择您所需要的水，比方说，需要热水就停留在"HOT"的位置上，然后把两个25美分的硬币放在这里，把这个硬币盒推进去，然后按一下"START"这个键。
Liu Hang:	Thank you very much. ... But the coin drawer can't be pushed inside now. 非常感谢。……可这硬币盒现在推不进去了。
Stranger:	Oh, damn! The coin holder is full, I'm afraid. You may use another machine. 哦,该死的! 恐怕硬币箱满了。您可以用另外的机器。
Liu Hang:	Thank you so much. 非常感谢。
Stranger:	It's OK. 不客气。

Dialog 3

Attendant:	Good morning, sir. Your clothes are ready. Will you see if they are all right? 早晨好,先生。您的衣服都洗好了。请您查看一下是否满意?
Ding Tang:	Good. 很好。
Attendant:	Here they are, a shirt with medium starch, a suit of pajamas, and a man's suit. 都在这里,一件浆得适中的衬衫,一套睡衣,一套西服。
Ding Tang:	Oh, thanks. Just leave them here. 哦,谢谢。就放这里吧。
Attendant:	By the way, your suit has come unstitched. It might have torn even further in the wash. So we just stitched the suit before wash. But we are sorry to say we cannot get the thread of exactly the same color.

Laundry Service 38

洗衣服务

顺便说一句,您的衣服衬里已经脱线了。在洗涤时可能会撕裂得更严重。所以我们在洗涤前先用线缝了一下。但遗憾的是,我们找不到颜色正好相同的线。

Ding Tang: Yes. I notice that. Never mind.② You are very considerate. Thank you so much.

是的,我注意到了。没关系。你们考虑得真周到,太谢谢了。

Attendant: My pleasure, sir. Have a nice trip.③

乐于为您服务,先生。祝您旅途愉快。

1) I'd like to get my clothes washed here.
   我想在这里把我的衣服洗一下。
2) Do you like your shirts starched?
   您的衬衫要上浆吗?
3) You can get them tomorrow morning if you choose our express service.
   如果您选择我们的特快服务的话,明天上午您就可以拿到。
4) We charge 50% more for express, but it only takes 5 hours.
   我们对加急服务增收 50%的服务费,但只要 5 个小时就可以取衣。
5) Could you show me how to use the machine?
   您能告诉我如何使用这洗衣机吗?
6) Please tell us what time you want to get them back.
   请告诉我们你要求什么时候将衣服送回?
7) Is your dress colorfast?
   你的裙子不褪色的吗?
8) Don't worry. We'll stitch it before washing.
   别着急,我们会缝好以后再洗。
9) We have express service.
   我们有快洗服务。
10) There is a stain on my coat. Can you remove it?
    我的外套上有个污点,能去掉吗?

11) We'll do our best, but we can't guarantee anything.
我们将尽力,但不能保证一切。

Background 背景知识

美国的洗衣服务：我们可以从以下几个方面了解美国的洗衣服务：

(1) 洗衣店类型：普通洗衣店(laundry)，有专门的工作人员提供服务，只需要将衣服送到那里登记，支付规定的费用，按照约定的时间前往取回就可以了。自助洗衣店(launderette/coin laundry)，有一名工作人员或者根本就没有工作人员，要自我服务，不过也很简单，投入要洗的衣服后，塞进规定的硬币（多为50或75美分），按下开始键(START)就开始了；洗完之后，再取出衣服投入到干衣机(drier)里烘干，也要塞入硬币（也为50或75美分）。干洗店(dry-cleaner)，通常收费比较贵，负责洗净和熨烫，并有上门取送服务，人们只将高档的衣服如西装外套、纯毛衣物等送到干洗店去洗，很多干洗店都有 Don't dress up without us.这样的标语。

(2) 服务质量问题：一是衣服没有洗干净，可以礼貌地提出来，请求店员重新洗一次，如果不是因为有些污渍确实难以洗干净，你的要求通常会得到满足。二是衣服破损，由于洗衣店的原因而导致衣服破损，可以提出赔偿请求，索赔金额依据衣服本身的价格、破损程度、新旧程度来确定。三是衣服丢失，发现送到自己手上的衣服不是自己的衣服，应该立即要求店方追回自己的衣服，若能追回，当属无碍，若无法追回，可以向店方索赔。

(3) 其他问题：美国的洗衣机特别大，一次可以洗很多衣服，所以很多人，尤其是学生都是一个星期才洗一次衣服。根据所洗衣服的情况，可以选择冷水、温水、热水，洗衣粉的用量也要根据衣服的多少和脏的程度确定。烘干机也有多个温度控制可以选择，一定要根据衣服的质地选择恰当的温度，否则会造成缩水、变短、变粗、烧焦等问题。

Laundry Service 38

洗衣服务

注 释

① get my clothes washed 的字面意思是"让我的衣服被某人洗",意指洗衣服不是自己做的,这一句型同 have something done,意思是"把什么事情做了",如:
I'd like to have my shoes mended. (我想把鞋子补一补。)(鞋子不是自己补的,而是让别人补)

② Never mind.用于回答他人的道歉,意思是"不要介意,没有关系",与 That's all right.相同。

③ Have a nice trip. (祝您旅途愉快。)具有结束交谈的功能,相当于说了声"Good-bye",类似的说法还有:
上午说:Have a nice day! (祝您愉快!)
下午说:Have a happy evening! (祝您晚上愉快!)
周五说:Have a nice weekend! (祝您周末愉快!)
旅行前:Have a good journey! (旅途愉快!)
分手说:Good luck! (祝您好运!)

Making Appointments with Doctors
预约看病

Topic Introduction
话题导言

跟医院预约看病时间在英美等西方国家是天经地义的,因为他们倾向于线性思维,比较崇尚一个时段办好一件事,而特别忌讳一心顾几头的作风。而医生诊治的时候也都特别仔细,所需的时间也比较长,因而医生看病的时间也是排得满满的,临时去的病人很难插进去。所以,不预约看病往往会耽搁自己病的诊治,或者要等很长的时间。

电话预约是常用的约诊方式,接通后要自报家门,特别是中国人的姓名如果照读音说出去,他们很少知道是怎么拼写的,所以要告诉他们拼写方法。然后说:I'd like to make an appointment with Doc. Smith.(我想和史密斯医生约个时间看病。)或者 May I make an appointment?(我可以约个时间吗?)。有时,这次看完病后可以预约下次复诊的时间。

Situational Dialogs
情景对话

人难免会有点小病痛,杨洋(Yang Yang)这两天一直感觉不舒服,需要去看医生。丁唐(Ding Tang)也曾经看过医生。

Making Appointments with Doctors 39

预约看病

Dialog 1

Nurse: Hello, this is Carlton Hospital. May I help you?
您好,卡尔顿医院。能帮您吗?

Yang Yang: Hello, this is Yang Yang. I'd like to make an appointment.
您好,我是杨洋,我想预约看医生。

Nurse: OK. How do you spell your name, sir?
好的,怎么拼写您的姓名,先生?

Yang Yang: My family name is Y-A-N-G. My given name is Y-A-N-G, too.
我的姓是 Y-A-N-G,我的名也是 Y-A-N-G。

Nurse: Yes, sir. Mr. Yang, when is available for you?
写下了,先生。杨先生,什么时间对您比较好?

Yang Yang: How about four o'clock tomorrow afternoon?
明天下午 4 点如何?

Nurse: But could you come a little earlier, shall we say①, three thirty?
但,您能否早一点儿,比方说,3 点 30 分?

Yang Yang: It's OK for me.
我可以的。

Nurse: Let's make it three thirty.
那我们就定在 3 点 30 分吧。

Yang Yang: All right. Thank you very much.
好的,非常感谢。

Dialog 2

Nurse: Good afternoon, Doc. Cook's Surgery.
下午好,库克医生诊所。

Ding Tang: I wonder whether I could make an appointment to see the doctor.
我不知道能否预约来看医生。

Nurse: Of course. Is it urgent?
当然可以,紧急吗?

Ding Tang: Not very urgent. But I'd like to see him sometime these two days.
不太紧急,但我想这两天的某个时间来看。

229

Nurse:	Let me see ... He's almost booked solid these two days, except for tomorrow afternoon between 5:00 to 5:15, I'm afraid. 让我瞧瞧，……他这两天几乎预订满了，恐怕只有明天下午 5:00 至 5:15 分之间是空的。
Ding Tang:	Oh dear! I have a date that time, but I'll bring it forward or put it off② and manage to come to see the doctor then. 哦，天啦！那个时间我约了朋友，但我会把它提前或推迟，尽力那个时间来看医生。
Nurse:	That'll be fine. May I know your name, sir? 那很好，能告诉我您的姓名吗，先生？
Ding Tang:	Ding Tang. 丁唐。
Nurse:	All right, Mr. Ding, please come to see the doctor at 5:00 tomorrow afternoon. 好的，丁先生，请明天下午 5 点来看医生。
Ding Tang:	Okay, thank you and good-bye. 好的，谢谢，再见。

Dialog 3

Ding Tang:	When must I have a follow-up examination, doctor? 医生，我什么时候要复查？
Doctor:	Let me see, how about next Tuesday afternoon? 我想想看，下个星期二如何？
Ding Tang:	I'm sorry I have to work then. 不好意思，那时我要工作。
Doctor:	Is it all right for you next Wednesday morning? 下个星期三上午您行吗？
Ding Tang:	I'll be available from ten to twelve next Wednesday morning. 下个星期三上午 10 点到 12 点我可以来。
Doctor:	That's OK. 好的。
Ding Tang:	So I'll be here again ten o'clock next Wednesday morning, June 18. 这样的话，我就下星期三上午，就是 6 月 18 日，再来这里。

39 Making Appointments with Doctors

预约看病

Doctor: Yes, all right. See you then.
好的。到时再见。

Typical Sentences 典型句型

1) I'd like to make an appointment.
   我想预约看医生。
2) How about four o'clock tomorrow afternoon?
   明天下午4点如何？
3) But could you come a little earlier, shall we say, three thirty?
   但，您能否早一点儿，比方说，3点30分？
4) Let's make it three thirty.
   那我们就定在3点30分吧。
5) But I'd like to see him sometime these two days.
   但我想这两天的某个时间来看。
6) When must I have a follow-up examination, doctor?
   医生，我什么时候要复查？
7) Is it all right for you next Wednesday morning?
   下个星期三上午您行吗？
8) So I'll be here again ten o'clock next Wednesday morning, June 18.
   这样的话，我就下星期三上午，就是6月18日，再来这里。

Background 背景知识

美国医院门诊：与中国医院门诊最大的不同在于美国医生走动于各个诊室之间，而病人到指定的诊室后就不用动了，且往往是一个病人一间诊室。一些简单的机器也是检验人员推进诊室对病人进行检查的，所以进了诊室之后就看着医生们忙碌了。就诊的程序是：预约时间→准时到达后在接待处登记等候→听到护士叫名字后跟随护士到诊室去→护士询问病情并作记录（多用电脑记载病情，所以病历也是电子版的）→医生检查诊断→开处方→取药（或凭处方买药）→付账。

医学分科：internal medicine（内科）、surgery（外科）、dermatology（皮肤科）、psychiatrics（精神科）、ophthalmology（眼科）、cardiology（心血管）、obstetrics（产科）、gynecology（妇科）、andrology（男性科）、gastroenterology（胃肠科）、otolaryngology（耳鼻喉科）等。

注 释

① 这里（shall we say）是个插入语，意思是"我们不妨说，比方说"。类似的说法还有：I think（我想）、I believe（我认为）、I guess（我猜想）、by the way（顺便说一句，顺便问一下）、in fact（其实）、actually（实际上）、in my opinion（在我看来）、I don't know（我不知道）、I mean（我是说）等等，主要用以表示委婉、缓和语气、改变说法等。有时是一个人的说话习惯，并没有什么实际意思，正如中国人有时候总是带上一句"说句良心话"或者"说句不好听的话"。

② 短语 bring forward 和 put off 的意思分别是"提前"和"推迟"。例如：We have to put off the meeting till next Monday.（我们必须把会议推迟到下个星期一。）

A Narrative of Sickness
叙述病情

Topic Introduction
话题导言

按照预约的时间到了医院之后,护士会首先接待你,她会向你询问关于生病的问题,比如:When did it begin?(什么时候开始的?)How long does it continue every time?(病症每次持续多久?)Very serious or just slight?(厉害还是轻微?)Does any of your family member have the same symptom?(家庭成员是否也有这种情况?)Have you ever seen a doctor?(以前看过医生没有?)What medicine have you taken?(吃过什么药?)How do you feel the effects of the medicines?(感觉到这些药的效果如何?)……

对于英语口语不过关的人来说,要想向医生或护士叙述病情确实不是一件容易的事情,但掌握一些关于病症的词汇的话就简单多了。其实,护士或者医生了解到你是"老外"的时候,也会挑简单的词语和你交谈。不过,在美国这样的西方国家,到医院去就得由医生来决定你是不是病了,得的是什么病。作为病人,不能要求医生开哪种药,而只能叙述病情。

Situational Dialogs
情景对话

丁唐(Ding Tang)如约来到了诊所，先接受了护士的询问，然后是医生的诊断。刘杭(Liu Hang)也感到不舒服，去了医院接受诊治。

Dialog 1

Nurse: What brought you here, sir?
先生，您怎么到这儿来？

Ding Tang: I beg your pardon?[①]
请您再说一遍。

Nurse: I mean what is bothering you or why you are here.
我是说您哪里不舒服或者说您为什么到医院来。

Ding Tang: I am feeling chest pain these days, sometimes very bad but sometimes slight.
这些天我感觉到胸部疼痛，有时候很严重，有时候较轻微。

Nurse: Do you always have the chest pain or occasionally?
胸部是一直在疼痛还是偶尔疼痛？

Ding Tang: Not always. I felt the pain last Friday morning and it lasted about forty minutes on my way to work. And I thought it had been no more, but I felt the pain again yesterday evening.
不是一直疼痛，我上个星期五去上班的路上感到疼痛并持续了大约40分钟。我想不会再有了吧，但昨天傍晚我又感到疼痛。

Nurse: Do you feel the pain very sharp?
您是否感到疼痛非常厉害？

Ding Tang: Not always, it was very sharp for a few seconds, and then it became slight.
不总是，很厉害地疼几秒钟，然后就变得轻微了。

A Narrative of Sickness

叙述病情

Nurse:	Does any of your family members, like your father, mother or your brothers, sisters, have the same pain? 您家里人，像您的父母兄弟姐妹中，有没有同样的疼痛？
Ding Tang:	Actually I don't know. 说实话，我不知道。
Nurse:	Did any of them die very young? 他们当中有没有人死得比较早？
Ding Tang:	My father died when he was only 34. 我父亲 34 岁时就死了。
Nurse:	I'm sorry to hear that②. Do you know why? 听到这个我很难过。您知道为什么吗？
Ding Tang:	It is said to be cerebral hemorrhage, but I don't know exactly. 据说是脑出血，但我并不太确定。
Nurse:	Thank you. The doctor will be here to see you. Please wait here. 谢谢，医生会到这儿来看您，请在此等候。

Dialog 2

Doctor:	I have read what you just told about your chest pain. Are you suffering from③ the pain now? 我看到了您刚才说的胸部疼痛的情况，您现在痛吗？
Ding Tang:	No, doctor. No more pain now. 不痛，医生，现在不痛了。
Doctor:	When did you feel the pain the first time? 您什么时候第一次感到疼痛的？
Ding Tang:	Six months ago, I guess. That is last November. 我想是 6 个月以前，就是去年 11 月。
Doctor:	Did you take any medicine that time? 那次您吃了什么药没有？
Ding Tang:	Yes. I took some traditional Chinese medicine and it did work. 吃了，我吃些中药，也确实有效。
Doctor:	It worked! What kind of medicine? 有效！什么药？

Ding Tang:	Something to cure heart trouble, I think. 我想是些治疗心脏病的药。
Doctor:	Would you please lie down on the bed? 您躺在床上,好吗?
Ding Tang:	Sure. Must I take off my clothes? 好的,我要脱下衣服吗?
Doctor:	You don't have to. Just untie the buttons of your shirt. Please tell me where the pain was. 不必,只要解开衬衫扣子,请告诉我哪里疼。
Ding Tang:	Just here, it is inside here. 就是这儿,在里面。
Doctor:	Besides the chest pain, do you feel something uncomfortable in your stomach or nearby? 除了胸部疼痛,您还感到胃部或周围不舒服吗?
Ding Tang:	No, doctor. 没有,医生。
Doctor:	We need to have an ECG. Please wait here. I'll be back soon. 我们需要做一个心电图,等着,我马上就回来。

Dialog 3

Doctor:	Good morning, Ms. Liu. Please sit here. What seems to be bothering you? 早晨好,刘女士。请坐在这儿,您哪里不舒服?
Liu Hang:	I have a bad cold. I have been a bit under the weather[④] for the last few days. 我得了重感冒了,我最近几天有点不舒服。
Doctor:	Have you taken any medicine? 您吃过什么药了没有?
Liu Hang:	Yes, I took some aspirins. 吃了,我吃了些阿司匹林。
Doctor:	How are you feeling today? 您今天感觉怎么样?

A Narrative of Sickness 40

叙述病情

Liu Hang: I now feel a little bit feverish. I have a sore throat, and my nose is stopped up.
现在我觉得有点发烧。我喉咙痛,鼻子塞。

Doctor: Let me have a look at your throat first. Open your mouth and say "Ah".
我先检查一下您的咽喉,张开嘴,说"啊"。

Liu Hang: Ah ...
啊……

Doctor: Your throat is congested. Let me take your temperature. Please put the thermometer under your armpit.
你的喉咙充血。让我给你量一下温度,请把体温计夹在腋下。

Liu Hang: Do I have a fever now?
我现在发烧吗?

Doctor: Yes, a little. I'll give you an injection to bring it down⑤, and I'll prescribe⑥ some medicine for you.
是的,有一点儿。我给您打一针退烧,再给您开点药。

Liu Hang: Thank you for your treatment.
谢谢您的治疗。

Doctor: Don't mention it. I'm sure you will be all right in a couple of days.
别客气,我想你一二天后就会好的。

Typical Sentences 典型句型

1) I feel dizzy and I've got no appetite.
   我觉得头晕,没有胃口。

2) It was very sharp for a few seconds, and then it became slight.
   很厉害地疼几秒钟,然后就变得轻微了。

3) It started bothering me yesterday afternoon.
   我是昨天下午开始觉得不舒服的。

4) I have been a bit under the weather for the last few days.
   我最近几天有点不舒服。

5) I now feel a little bit feverish.
   现在我觉得有点发烧。
6) I have a sore throat, and my nose is stopped up.
   我喉咙痛，鼻子塞。
7) You look pale today.
   你今天看上去有些苍白。
8) Your throat is congested.
   你的喉咙充血。
9) What do you complain of?
   你哪里不舒服？
10) Sometimes it's difficult to shake off a cold.
    有时感冒不容易治好。
11) I'm sorry to hear that.
    听到这个我很难过。
12) I have alternately been shivering with cold and burning with heat.
    我时而冷得发抖，时而又热得像火烧。
13) Must I come again?
    我还得来吗？

背景知识

医院候诊：一般来说，只要你按时到达了医院，就不会等很久。到了医院，第一步要到接待处登记说明你已经到了，如果是第一次到这个医院就诊，你还要填写一个表格，医院好给你建立医疗档案。这种表格以前填在纸上，现在直接输入电脑系统，主要内容是就诊者的基本情况，特别要写明你拥有什么样的医疗保险，并出示你的保险卡给工作人员登记。登记之后，你会被要求到候诊室等候。候诊室备有饮用水、书籍、杂志、报纸等。听到护士叫到你的名字，就跟着护士到诊室去。有一点要注意，我们用汉语拼音写下的名字对于他们来说很不好发音，如 zhou、zhi、chang 等，护士叫你的

A Narrative of Sickness 40 叙述病情

名字时你可能浑然不觉,这时护士可能会读出名字的字母,所以一定要小心听。

美国的医疗保险:在美国这样医疗费用特别高的国家,人们为了防备因为生病而导致经济困难,绝大多数人都选择购买医疗保险(health insurance)。美国的保险业非常发达,购买之前一定多多比较各个保险公司的保单(policy)内容和缴费的费率(rate)。有时候,保障内容一样的保单,不同的公司费率差异很大。如某公司要求一年缴费240美元,负担普通门诊医疗的最高额为50,000美元;而另一家公司可能要求一年缴费248美元,除个人负担医疗费用200美元以外,其余全部由保险公司负担。所以,一定要找英语很好的朋友认真研究保单内容,结合自己的身体状况选择不同的公司和险种投保。

常用疾病与检查词汇:有些关于疾病的词汇,对于把英语作为外语的人们来说确实比较生疏,记住也比较困难。现将常见的词语列在下面供临时使用。

a burning pain 火辣辣的疼	diarrhea 腹泻
abdominal colic 腹部绞痛	dizziness 头昏,眼花
allergy 过敏症	fever 发烧
appendicitis 阑尾炎	flu 流感
asthma 哮喘、气喘	gastric distension 腹胀
bronchitis 支气管炎	gastric ulcer 胃溃疡
bruise / wound 伤痕	gastritis 胃炎
burn 烧伤	headache 头痛
cerebral hemorrhage 脑出血	fluoroscopy 透视
chest pain 胸部疼痛	follow-up examination 复查
chill 受凉	frozen section 冰冻切片
cold 感冒	have an ECG 做心电图
constipation 便秘	have an EEG 做脑电图
continuous pain 持续疼痛	heart trouble 心脏病
cough up blood 咳出血	hepatitis 肝炎
cough 咳嗽	hoarse voice 声音沙哑
cramp 抽筋	hypertension 高血压
indigestion 消化不良	rheumatism 关节炎
infection 传染	routine urinalysis 常规尿检

insomnia 失眠	short of breath 气喘
itch 痒	sore throat 喉咙痛
nausea 恶心	sputum 唾液
negative reaction 阴性反应	stomachache 胃痛
nervous breakdown 神经衰弱	suffocation 憋闷
painful urination 小便疼痛	ulcer 溃疡
pneumonia 肺炎	vomit 呕吐
positive reaction 阳性反应	whooping cough 百日咳
rabies 狂犬病	X-ray examination 做 X 光检查

注释

① 没有听懂对方说的话，怎么办？那就要求对方再讲一次，用英语表达这个意思有多种方式，如：I beg your pardon? Pardon me? Excuse me? Sorry? Come again? What was that again?等，注意用升调才是"您说什么？"的意思。用了降调，有的意思就变了，如 Excuse me.或 Pardon me.或 Sorry.就成了"对不起，失礼了"的意思。也可以直接说：Please say it again.（请再说一遍。）

② sorry 除了表示"对不起"以外，这里是"难过"的意思，听到不好的消息要表示同情，就可以说：
I'm sorry to hear that.（听到这点我很难过。）

③ 短语 suffer from 本义是"遭受某种痛苦"，这里表示"患某种病"，如：She is suffering from lung cancer.（她在患肺癌。）

④ 短语 under the weather 的意思是"身体状况不好"，和 ill、sick 意思相同。来源于船员用语，大海航行使船员身体不适，转义指普通的生病。

⑤ bring down 意思 "降低或减少某事物"，如：bring down the cost of living(降低生活费用)。

⑥ 要注意区别 prescribe 和它的同根词 describe(描述)的区别。

With a Dentist
看牙科医生

Topic Introduction
话题导言

　　看病贵,看牙科更贵。西方国家的医院有综合性的,也有分科设立的,牙科诊所显得格外突出。美国比较大的机构为其雇员购买的医疗保险通常是包括牙科的,但留学生的医疗保险则不一定有此项保险。因此需要注意的是,你的保险中有没有包括牙科在内。

　　去看牙医,一般都是起因于牙痛(toothache),要说痛得很厉害,就是:I've got a terrible toothache. 补牙(fill a tooth)、洗牙(tooth cleaning)、拔牙(pull out a decayed tooth)等都是常常用到的词语。

Situational Dialogs
情景对话

牙痛不是病,痛起来真要命。李康(Li Kang)牙又痛了。

Dialog 1

Nurse:	Good morning, this is Dr. Smith's office.
	早晨好,这里是史密斯医生诊所。
Li Kang:	Good morning. I have a bad toothache. I want to see the dentist.
	早晨好,我牙痛得厉害,我要看医生。

Nurse:	Do you have an appointment? 您预约了吗？
Li Kang:	Sorry, I do not. 对不起，还没有。
Nurse:	Is it very urgent? 是不是很严重？
Li Kang:	Yes. It is very urgent. I feel a terrible pain in one tooth that has a cavity. I could not sleep a wink last night. 是的，痛得厉害。一只牙有个洞，非常痛。我昨晚整夜都未合过眼。
Nurse:	But you haven't made an appointment. Could you come tomorrow afternoon? 但是您没有预约。您可以明天下午来吗？
Li Kang:	No, I have to see the dentist now. I can't wait. 不行，我必须现在就看医生，我等不了。
Nurse:	Wait a moment. ... Could you come this afternoon, at 4:00? 等一会儿，…… 您可以今天下午 4:00 来吗？
Li Kang:	That's too late! Can't the dentist see me now? 那太晚了，难道医生现在不能看我吗？
Nurse:	I'm sorry he can't. Can't you wait till this afternoon? 对不起，他不能。难道您不能等到今天下午吗？
Li Kang:	I can wait, but my toothache can't! 我可以等，但我的牙痛却不能等！

Dialog 2

Dr. Smith:	What's troubling you, sir? 先生，哪里不舒服吗？
Li Kang:	One of my teeth is playing up[①] again. 我的一颗牙齿又麻烦起来了。
Dr. Smith:	Sit on the chair, please. Good. Now which tooth is troubling you? 请坐在椅子上。好的，是哪只牙齿让您不舒服了？
Li Kang:	The one on the left of the upper jaw. 是左边上颚的那只。

With a Dentist 41

看牙科医生

Dr. Smith: Yes, the gums are swollen around it. You seem to have had② a filling in the tooth, and it's got some inflammation again.
是的,周围的齿龈肿胀了。您好像以前补过这只牙,而现在又发炎了。

Li Kang: That's right. I once had that decayed tooth cleaned and filled.
对的,我原来清洗过这只坏牙并补了。

Dr. Smith: I'm afraid that the only way is to extract the tooth. Please relax and we'll finish it soon enough.
恐怕唯一的办法就是拔掉这只牙。请放松,我们很快就完事了。
……

Li Kang: How much is the fee?
多少钱?

Dr. Smith: Here's the bill. Please settle it at the cashier's desk.
这是账单,请到收款台结账。

Dialog 3

Dr. Smith: What's the matter with you, sir?
先生,您怎么了?

Li Kang: Everything is normally all right. But when I bite something too hot or too cold, it really gives me great pain.
平常都还好,但当我吃太热或太凉的东西时,就疼得不得了。

Dr. Smith: Let me have a look. Open your mouth. There the second left lower molar ... there is a big cavity in it.
我瞧瞧,张开嘴巴,左下第二颗臼齿,有一个很大的洞。

Li Kang: Can I have it filled?
可以把洞填起来吗?

Dr. Smith: I'm afraid not. The cavity is too big. I'll have to have it out.
恐怕不行,洞太大,得拔掉。

Li Kang: Now?
现在?

Dr. Smith: Not now. Your gums are is swollen and inflamed. You'll have to take some antibiotics first.
不是现在,您的牙龈肿了,发炎了。您要先吃些抗生素。

Li Kang: All right. Thank you.
好的，谢谢。

Typical Sentences 典型句型

1) I have a toothache.
   我牙齿痛。
2) I couldn't sleep a wink with pain last night.
   昨天晚上我痛得一夜没有合眼。
3) You have a rather swollen cheek.
   你的脸都肿了。
4) I know you must have suffered very much.
   我知道你一定痛得很厉害。
5) Please examine my mouth.
   请检查我的口腔吧！
6) You have two decayed teeth.
   你有两只蛀牙。
7) Could you have them out?
   你能把它们拔掉吗？
8) I will plug them, if you want to.
   如果你要拔的话，我可照办。

Background 背景知识

牙科常用词汇：我们的牙齿及其周围组织都有自己的名称，我们去看牙医也要用到一些不常用的词汇，如：

cavity 蛀牙的洞　　　　　　gargle 漱口
compound 复合物　　　　　 inflammation 发炎
decay 蛀蚀，腐烂　　　　　 sour 酸的

With a Dentist 41

看牙科医生

floss 牙线
molar 白齿
plastic 合成树脂
toothache 牙痛

wisdom tooth 智齿
mouthwash 漱口水
gum 牙龈
stain 斑点,污渍

注 释

① play (somebody) up 意思是"给(某人)带来麻烦、痛苦或者困难",如:
My injured shoulder is playing (me) up today. (我受伤的肩膀今天很痛。)
play something up 则指"欲使某物显得比实际重要"。如:
She played up her achievement just to impress us. (她炫耀她的成绩就是为了让我们觉得她了不起。)

② 不定式的完成式用来表达过去的事情,如:
She regrets to have sold her house. (她后悔卖了她的房子。)
此例句中说的是"房子是以前卖掉的"。

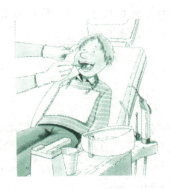

With an Oculist
看眼科医生

Topic Introduction
话题导言

和牙科一样,眼科诊所往往也是单独设立的。眼科或眼科学叫做 ophthalmology,眼科医生称作 ophthalmologist 或 oculist。

Situational Dialogs
情景对话

杨洋(Yang Yang)感到眼睛不舒服,就预约去眼科诊所诊治;丁唐(Ding Tang)游泳后也感染了眼病。

Dialogue 1

Nurse: Good morning, this is Dr. Phillip's Clinic.
早晨好,这里是菲利普医生诊所。

Yang Yang: I'd like to make an appointment. My eyes have become red and I feel very unhappy.
我想预约,我的眼睛变红了,感到非常难受。

Nurse: Is it serious?
严重吗?

With an Oculist 42

看眼科医生

Yang Yang: Very serious. I can't open my eyes normally and they are always tearful.
非常严重,我不能正常地睁开眼睛,眼睛总是流泪。

Nurse: Well then, please come at① 2:30 this afternoon.
那好,请今天下午两点半来吧。

Yang Yang: All right, thank you.
好的,谢谢。

Dialogue 2

Dr. Phillip: Good afternoon. Is there anything that bothers you?
下午好,您哪里不舒服?

Ding Tang: Yes, I feel pain and itch in my eyes.
是的,我感到眼睛发疼发痒。

Dr. Phillip: When did this begin?
什么时候开始的?

Ding Tang: Yesterday afternoon, I began to feel something wrong with my eyes when I came back from the school swimming-pool.
昨天下午,我从学校游泳池回家,就感到眼睛有些不对劲。

Dr. Phillip: Ah, let me have a look. Did you get something sticky② on your eyelids when you waked up this morning?
啊,我来看看。您早晨醒来时眼睑上有粘糊糊的东西吗?

Ding Tang: Yes, doctor.
是的,医生。

Dr. Phillip: You may get conjunctivitis.
您可能得了结膜炎。

Ding Tang: Is it serious?
严重吗?

Dr. Phillip: It is an infectious disease. Be careful not to infect it to your family members or others.
这是一种传染病。注意别传染给家里人以及其他人。

Ding Tang: Certainly I will.
我当然会的。

Dr. Phillip: I'll write a prescription for you. Take the medicine and use the collyrium to wash your eyes.
我开张处方给您,服药并用洗眼剂清洗眼睛。

生活流畅美语

Ding Tang: Thank you.
谢谢。

Typical Sentences
典型句型

1) I am suffering from trachoma.
   我得沙眼了。
2) Trachoma is a very dangerous eye-affliction.
   沙眼是很危险的眼病。
3) It is an infectious disease.
   这是一种传染病。
4) I have the doctor examined my eyes.
   我让医生检查了眼睛。
5) Is there anything else that bothers you?
   还有什么别的不舒服的吗?
6) By the way, what's the degree of your spectacles?
   顺便问一下,你眼镜多少度?
7) My eyesight suddenly got worse last year.
   我的视力去年突然变差了。
8) Let me see your eyes.
   让我看看你的眼睛。
9) Now show me your eyes.
   现在给我看看你的眼睛。
10) We'd better take a complete check and find out what's wrong.
    我们最好进行一次全面的检查,看看究竟怎么回事。

With an Oculist 42

Background 背景知识

看眼科医生

  眼睛不舒服就要去看眼科医生(Ophthalmologist)了。医生助手会首先询问病情并做初步的眼睛健康检查(Eye Examination)，接着医生会根据情况做一些处理，如开药、进一步的检查等。

  如果要配眼镜，就得先验光(Vision Test)，然后医生给你开验光单(Glass Prescription)，再去眼镜店配眼镜。在美国配眼镜是比较昂贵的，最普通的近视眼镜也要花费200美元以上。

配眼镜常用词汇：

glass optical lenses 玻璃镜片
plastic optical lenses 塑胶镜片
photochromic lenses 变色镜片
spectacle cases 眼镜盒
spectacle frames 眼镜架
stainless steel 不锈钢
pure titanium 纯钛
titanium alloy 钛合金
contact lens 隐形眼镜
round frames 圆形眼镜架
oval frames 椭圆形眼镜架
rectangular frames 长方形眼镜架
optometrist 验光师
sunglasses 太阳镜
sports spectacles 运动眼镜
kid's eyewear 儿童眼镜
reading glasses 老花镜

看眼科常用词汇：

achromatopsia/color blindness 色盲
hyperopia 远视
iritis 虹膜炎
keratitis 角膜炎
blepharitis 睑缘炎
cataract 白内障
mydriatic 散瞳剂
conjunctivitis 结膜炎
cyclitis 睫状体炎
dacryoadenitis 泪腺炎
amblyopia 弱视
asthenopia/eye strain 视力疲劳
astigmatism 散光
lacrimation 流泪
muscae volitantes 飞蚊症
mydriasis 瞳孔放大
myopia 近视
nyctalopia/night-blindness 夜盲
ophthalmia 眼炎
ectropion 外翻，睑外翻

249

生活流畅美语

retinitis 视网膜炎　　　　scleritis 巩膜炎
trachoma 沙眼　　　　　　fundus 眼底
uveitis 葡萄膜炎　　　　　glaucoma 青光眼
xerosis 干燥病　　　　　　heterotropia 斜视

注 释

① 注意 at, in, on 表示时间时的区别。
at 表示确切时间。如：
I have to get up at five tomorrow.（我明天5点必须起床。）
in 表示一天中某段时间。如：in the morning。
on 表示某一天或星期几。如：
Usually I am free on Sunday.（通常我星期天有空。）

② 当不定代词 something, someone, somebody 被形容词修饰时，形容词通常置于不定代词之后，如：someone important（重要的人），something urgent（紧急的事情）。

In Hospital
生病住院

Topic Introduction
话题导言

当生病比较严重或者医生对病情没有把握的情况下,医生可能会要求你住院治疗,这时就要和医生、护士、其他病人打交道。你若及时掌握自己的病情,这对于尽早康复很有帮助。同时,亲朋好友的探视,也会给病人的康复带来信心和勇气。

医院通常分为几个具体部门:Registration Desk(挂号处)、Out-patient Department(OPD,门诊部)、In-patient Department(IPD,住院部)、Nursing Department(护理部),病房又根据不同病情分为 Medical Ward(内科病房)、Surgical Ward(外科病房)、Isolation Ward(隔离病房)等等。

Situational Dialogs
情景对话

很多人都可能因病住院,刘杭(Liu Hang)和叶丽敏(Limin)就因病而在不同时间住院了。

Dialog 1

Doctor: We've taken a complete check and find out what's wrong.
我们进行了一次全面的检查,弄清楚了是怎么回事。

Liu Hang: Is it serious?
严重吗?

Doctor: I'm sorry, madam. You have got pneumonia and have to be hospitalized for a few days.
很抱歉,女士。您得了肺炎,要在医院住上几天。

Liu Hang: Is it really that bad?
真有那么严重吗?

Doctor: The in-patient nursing supervisor will arrange everything for you. Just relax. It's not that bad.
住院部护士长会为您安排好所有的事情。别紧张,没有那么严重。

Liu Hang: All right. Thank you very much.
好的,非常感谢。

Dialog 2

Doctor: Hello, Ms. Ye, how do you feel today?
您好,叶女士,今天感觉怎么样?

Limin: I'm feeling better now. I think the fever has already gone after taking the medicine.
现在好些了,我觉得吃药之后烧已经退了。

Doctor: That's fine, and you are looking much better today than yesterday. How is your appetite?
那就好,您看上去今天比昨天好多了。您的胃口怎么样?

Limin: I feel hungry again and eat with great relish.
我又觉得饿了,吃得津津有味呢。

Doctor: Do you care for fruit?
你喜欢吃水果吗?

Limin: Yes, I usually have some fruit after lunch or supper.
吃,我通常在午餐或晚餐后吃些水果。

In Hospital 43

生病住院

Doctor: I think you've heard the popular saying: "An apple a day keeps the doctor away".
我想您听说过这样一个流传很广的谚语:"一天一个苹果,医生远离我"。

Limin: Yes. Fruits are good for our health. Oh, doctor, when shall I be well enough to be discharged① from hospital?
是的,水果对健康是有益处的。哦,医生,我什么时候可以出医院?

Doctor: Don't worry. Stay in hospital for a few more days to get recovered. You can leave the hospital when you have completely recovered from your illness.
别担心。要在医院多呆些时日,以便康复。当你完全康复时,就可出院了。

Limin: Thank you, doctor.
医生,谢谢您。

Dialog 3

Adam: I am sorry to hear that you are not well.
听到你身体欠安,我很难过。

Limin: It's not serious. It's very kind of you to see me.
不严重。谢谢你来看我。

Adam: You've been here not too long. I'm sure to see you on such occasions②.
你来这里时间不太长,我是一定要来看你的。

Limin: It's the very saying that goes "A friend in need is a friend indeed".
这就是那句谚语"患难见真情"。

Adam: How many times does the doctor call on you a day?
医生一天来看你几次?

Limin: He comes twice a day.
他一天来两次。

Adam: Stay in hospital for a few more days to get better. Never worry about anything else.
在医院多呆些时日以便康复。千万别担心别的事情。

生活流畅美语

Limin: Thank you. Please remember me to your family and explain my sickness to the boss.
谢谢你,请代我向你家人问好,向老板解释我的病情。

Adam: Certainly I will. I hope you will get recovered very soon.
我一定会的。祝你早日康复!

Typical Sentences
典型句型

1) I am sorry to hear that you are not well.
听到你身体欠安,我很难过。

2) How do you feel today?
你今天感觉怎么样?

3) You are looking much better today than yesterday.
你看上去今天比昨天好多了。

4) How is your appetite?
你的胃口怎么样?

5) My fever has gone down.
我烧退了。

6) I feel hungry again and eat with great relish.
我又觉得饿了,吃得津津有味呢。

7) Do you care for fruit?
你喜欢吃水果吗?

8) I usually have some fruit after lunch or supper.
我通常在午餐或晚餐后吃些水果。

9) How many times does the doctor call on you a day?
医生一天来看你几次?

10) He comes twice a day.
他一天来两次。

11) Stay in hospital for a few more days to recuperate.
在医院多呆些时日以便康复。

12) You can leave the hospital when you have completely recovered from your illness.
当你完全康复时,就可出院了。

13) I hope you will recover very soon.
    祝你早日康复!
14) Now I shall be off, and take care of yourself.
    我要走了,多保重。

背景知识

生病住院:因为生病了而住在医院接受治疗,目的是让医生能很好地观察病情,以便尽快康复。常常会用到下列词语:make a quick recovery(恢复很快)、recover without any aftereffect(病愈没有后遗症)、favorable prognosis(预后良好)、take a change for the better/worse(转好/转坏)、intensive care unit(即ICU,重症病房)、critical patient(病危病人)、postpartum care(产后护理)、postoperative convalescence(手术后恢复)、restriction on diet(饮食限制)、bland diet(不刺激的食物)、special regimen(专门规定的饮食)等。

探视病人:去医院里看望病人时送什么礼物,应考虑到病人的病情和住院时间的长短。对大多数病人来说,送些轻松有趣的读物或填字字谜(word puzzles)的书籍都是很受欢迎的礼物。如果病人住院时间较长,可以送晨衣(morning gowns)、睡衣(sleeping wears)或靠垫(cushions)。看望病人也可以送鲜花和食物。但送花时要注意花的禁忌;送食品时要事先征得医生或病患家人的同意。

注 释

① discharge 的意思是"允许离开",如:discharge a soldier(允许士兵退伍)。
② on such occasions 意思是"在这样的情况下"。

At the Pharmacy
在药店买药

Topic Introduction
话题导言

美国的医院不一定都有药房(dispensary)专门给你配药,很多时候要到大街上的药店(pharmacy 或 drugstore)去买药。pharmacy 只卖药,drugstore 卖药及杂货。

有些药随便都可以买到,如阿司匹林(aspirin)和维生素(vitamin);有些药则是不能随便卖给你的,而必须有医生的处方(prescription),药店的药剂师(pharmacist 或 druggist)才能配药给你。

Situational Dialogs
情景对话

医生开了处方,往往要自己去药店买药。非处方药也可以自己直接购买而不需处方。

Dialog 1

Clerk: How can I help you, sir?
先生,有事情吗?

At the Pharmacy 44

在药店买药

Yang Yang:	A friend of mine asked me to buy something called Medicream. I have been to a number of smaller drugstores, but none of them has it.
	我的朋友要我买些叫 Medicream 的药。我去过多家小药店，但没有一家有这种药。
Clerk:	What's it for?
	这药有什么用处？
Yang Yang:	I think it is for cuts and burns.
	我想是治割伤和烧伤的。
Clerk:	We don't seem to have it either. How about other substitutions?
	我们好像也没有这药。别的替代品行吗？
Yang Yang:	I'm afraid not, for I'm asked to get it.
	恐怕不行，我是受人之托。
Clerk:	You may go to a specialized drugstore.
	您可以去专业性的药店看看。
Yang Yang:	All right. Thank you anyway.
	好的，谢谢您了。

Dialog 2

Yang Yang:	I'd like to have this prescription filled.
	我想照这个药方买药。
Clerk:	All right, sir. Let me see if we have them in stock①. ... Oh, yes, we have all of them; please wait a while.
	好的，先生。我看看我们是否有些这药。……哦，有的，我们都有，请等一会儿。
Yang Yang:	Yes.
	好的。
Clerk:	Here you are, sir. It's eighteen dollars and twenty cents in all.
	给您，先生。总共是 18 美元 20 美分。
Yang Yang:	Here's twenty dollars. How should I take them?
	给您 20 美元，这药怎么用法？
Clerk:	Take one tablet every six hours for this white bottle, and three tablets every eight hours for the yellow bottle. There are detailed

directions attached on the bottles. Here's your change.
白瓶子每六小时服一片,黄瓶子每八小时服三片。瓶子上贴有详细说明。这是找您的钱。

Yang Yang: Thank you very much.
非常谢谢你。

Dialog 3

Clerk: What can I do for you, sir?
先生,您要买些什么?

Ding Tang: I'm afraid I have got conjunctivitis and it is an infectious disease. I'd like to buy something to cure it.
我恐怕得了结膜炎,是一种传染病。我想买些药治一下。

Clerk: You'd need an ointment and an eye-drop. But we can't sell them to you now?
您需要药膏和滴眼液,但我们不能卖给您。

Ding Tang: I don't understand. Why not?
我不懂,为什么不呢?

Clerk: You must go to see your oculist first and he will write a prescription for you. You can have the prescription[2] filled here.
您必须先看眼科医生,他会开个处方给您,您再来按处方买药。

Ding Tang: Please do me a favor[3]. I don't like to see a doctor.
请帮个忙吧,我不喜欢看医生。

Clerk: Sorry, I can't. Take my advice and go to see an oculist.
对不起,我帮不了。听我的劝告,去看看眼科医生吧!

Ding Tang: It's really a lot of trouble. Anyway, thank you very much for your advice.
真是很麻烦。无论怎样,我都要非常感谢你的忠告。

At the Pharmacy 44

Typical Sentences 典型句型

在药店买药

1) How can I help you, sir?
   先生，有事情吗？
2) A friend of mine asked me to buy something called Medicream.
   我的朋友要我买些叫 Medicream 的药。
3) I have been to a number of smaller drugstores, but none of them has it.
   我去过多家小药店，但没有一家有这种药。
4) What's it for?
   这药有什么用处？
5) I think it is for cuts and burns.
   我想是治割伤和烧伤的。
6) We don't seem to have it either.
   我们好像也没有这药。
7) Do you have aspirin for myself?
   你们有阿司匹林吗？
8) I am not allergic to aspirin.
   我对阿司匹林不过敏。
9) How should I take it?
   这药怎么用法？
10) Take one tablet every six hours.
    每六小时服一片。
11) How many tablets does this tin contain?
    每罐装多少片？
12) I think that will be quite enough.
    我认为，这已足够了。

Background
背景知识

普通药和牌子药：你到药房去按照医生给你的处方买药，药剂师可能会问你：Would you like a generic or a name brand drug? 这句话的意思是说"您要买普通的药还是有牌子的药？"但究竟何指，恐怕一时还明白不过来。其实，generic drug 指的是包装上只贴有药名而没有贴制药公司商标的药品，就像我们在中国医院里拿到的用纸袋包装给你的药一样，这样药厂减少了包装的成本，药价也就便宜了许多，而质量上是没有什么不同的。你要是问药剂师有什么不同时，他可能回答你：The difference is in the price, not in the quality.（只是价格不同，质量上没有差异）。generic drug（普通药）也是按照美国食品与药品管理局（即 FDA，Food and Drug Administration）的药品标准生产的，质量不会有问题。

注 释

① **in stock** 意思是"有库存，有现货"。

② "处方药"的英语是 **prescription drug**，医生开药的单子上的 **RX** 就是表示 **prescription** 的意思。没有处方也能买到的药称作 **over-the-counter drug**，即 **nonprescription drug**（非处方药）。如果你需要用的药不需要处方也能买到，护士或医生就可能会说：You may buy the drug over the counter.（你可以直接到药店的柜台上买到这药。）

③ **favor** 在这里的意思是"恩惠，善行"，常和 **ask**, **do** 等动词连用，如：May I ask a favor of you?（请您帮个忙行吗？）

Getting Directions
迷路问路

Topic Introduction
话题导言

我们住在熟悉的中国大城市里,有时都会迷路,何况去了外国,又不熟悉周围的环境,因此迷路和问路都是难免的。但是,问路也要讲究一些礼貌原则,如不要靠得太近,说话要用客气的表达方法,不要过分紧张。一般说来,英美人士都会很热情地解答你的问题,有人甚至亲自为你带路。

美国有些小镇的人们比大城市的人们更加朴实,非常乐意帮忙,即使如此,也一定要注意礼貌问题。如开口要说:Excuse me .../Would you please ... 等,问完了要说:Thank you for telling me./I appreciate your help. 等等以示礼貌。还要面带微笑并称呼对方为 Sir、Madam、Miss 等。

Situational Dialogs
情景对话

尽管手里握着地图,刘杭(Liu Hang)和李惠敏(Huimin)还是迷路了,还好人们都很热心地为她们指路。

Dialogue 1

Liu Hang: Excuse me, sir. Could you tell me how to get to the Metropolitan Museum of Art?
打搅了,先生。请问您能告诉我怎么到大都会艺术博物馆吗?

Passerby: You mean the Metropolitan Museum of Art. It's near here. You may walk there.
您说的是大都会艺术博物馆吧,就在附近,您可以步行到达。

Liu Hang: But which road shall I walk?
但我要走哪条路?

Passerby: Go straight ahead and turn right at the second crossroads. And then walk about ten minutes you may see a middle school, and the museum is opposite the school. You can't miss it.①
一直往前走,在第二个十字路口那里往右拐。走大约十分钟,您可以看到一所中学,博物馆就在学校对面,您不会看不到的。

Liu Hang: Thank you very much.
非常谢谢您。

Dialogue 2

Huimin: Excuse me, I can't find the subway entrance.
打搅了,我找不到地铁站入口了。

Passerby: Are you going uptown or downtown?
你去住宅区还是市中心区?

Huimin: I am a stranger here. I have no idea about uptown and downtown. I just want to go back to my university.
我是刚来到这里的陌生人,我不知道哪里是住宅区,哪里是中心区。我只想回到我的大学。

Passerby: Back to which university?②
回到哪个大学?

Huimin: I'm a student of the University of Chicago.
我是芝加哥大学的学生。

Passerby: OK. You are just near the right entrance. Look, over there, in the building, have you seen the sign?
好的,你就在你要找的入口附近。瞧,在那边,在这个建筑里,你看到标牌了吗?

Getting Directions

Huimin:	Oh, there it is! Thank you. 哦，在那里！谢谢。

Dialogue 3

Liu Hang:	I'm confused. Where are we now? 我糊涂了，我们在什么地方呢？
Ding Tang:	Oh, I don't know either. We are completely lost. 啊，我也不知道。我们真的迷路了。
Liu Hang:	Here comes a police officer. Let's ask him. 来了一个警官，我们去问问他。
Ding Tang:	Excuse me, sir, may I ask where we are now? 先生，劳驾您，请问我们现在在什么地方？
Police:	Yes, you're in the middle of the Washington Avenue. 你们在华盛顿大道的中段。
Liu Hang:	I've got a map. Could you show us on the map? 我有一张地图，您可以指给我们看看吗？
Police:	Of course. You're right here. Where would you like to go? 当然可以，你们就在这里。你们要到哪里去？
Liu Hang:	We are going to the Civic Square. 我们要去市民广场。
Police:	It is three blocks from here. Just go straight ahead. 离这儿有三个街区远，一直往前走。
Ding Tang:	Thank you very much. 非常感谢。

Typical Sentences 典型句型

1) Can I get some directions?
   能问一下路吗？
2) Would you please tell me how to get to the Zoo?
   您可以告诉我怎样到动物园吗？

3) Do you know which bus I should take to get to the Metropolitan Museum of Art?

你知道我乘哪一趟汽车到大都会艺术博物馆？

4) Could you show me the way to the nearest subway station?

您可以告诉我最近的地铁站该怎么去吗？

5) Could you direct me to the Bank of America?

可以告诉我到美洲银行怎么走吗？

6) Is there a Bank of America branch around here?

附近有美洲银行的分支机构吗？

7) Could you direct me to the eastbound freeway on-ramp, please?

可以告诉我往东走的高速公路入口在哪里吗？

8) Did I pass the Sixth Street?

我走过了第六街了吗？

9) If I go down this street, do I run into Telegraph Street?

如果我沿着这条街往前走，我能到电报大街吗？

10) It takes more than half an hour to get there on foot.

步行到那里要花半个多小时。

11) The bus stop is on the other side of this street.

汽车站在这条大街的另一边。

12) You should see a bus stop at the corner.

你在拐角处应该看到汽车站。

13) I can't find the subway entrance.

我找不到地铁站入口。

14) Are you going uptown or downtown?

你去住宅区还是市中心区？

背景知识

街道称呼：美国是近二百年发展起来的国家，城市建设都是按照规划进行的，街道显得比较规整。林荫大道叫做 Boulevard，通常

Getting Directions

缩写为 Blvd；宽大的马路为 Avenue，多为南北走向，缩写为 Ave；一般的街道称为 Street，缩写为 St.；Drive 是对通向某个学校或住户或机构的道路的称呼，沿途较少建筑物。尽管每条街道都有名称和编号，但是人们也有迷路的时候。地区或城市地图是个很好的帮手，每个城市的街区地图都非常详细，只要知道名称就都可以找到。美国门牌号码的编排也与我们不同，第一或前面的两个数字代表街区，后面的数字是该住户在本街区的排序，有时中间还间隔一些数字，供以后在这些地方盖房子的住户使用。例如：3022 Washington Blvd 表明该户位于"华盛顿大街的第 30 个街区的第 22 号"；若你看到 248 D Street，要找 511 D Street，方法就是再往数字大的方向走三个街区，进入 5 街区，很快就可找到了。

问路技巧：(1)选准对象，问路要选熟悉当地的人士，如警察、小贩、小店店主等，别担心什么，他们一定会回答你的。(2)称呼得当，见到成年男子称 Sir，Miss 是对未婚女子的称呼，Madam 用来称呼成年女性，不确定如何称呼就选用礼貌句式，如 Would you please tell me the way to Wal-Mart? 或者 Excuse me, could you show me how to drive to the Main Street? 等等。(3)问得具体，问路之前要搞清楚自己要去的地方在什么街、机构的确切名称等等。

注　释

① You can't miss it. 的意思是"您不会找不到的"，miss 是"错过"的意思。
② 英语口头交际中，实际上很多问句都是使用陈述句式表达，只是在句末使用问句语气。如：
You are from China?（您从中国来吗？）

Something Wrong at Home
家什故障

Topic Introduction 话题导言

家中的诸多物件总有出问题的时候,今天冰箱坏了,明天水龙头漏水,后天炉灶电路又断了,还有空调、洗衣机、洗碗机、电视机、屋顶、门窗、淋浴器、坐便器等等,真是麻烦一个接一个。

这些东西坏了或者出了问题,会影响我们的日常生活以至情绪和精神状态,所以就得修理。如果是自己的房子、自己的家什,就得自己负责修理,仍在保修期内的,要找售后服务部门维修;过了保修期的还要自己出钱。如果是租用别人的房子,房东该负责的就应该让房东负责,这包括房屋以及连同房屋一同租用的家什,如空调、冰箱、衣柜、炉灶、卫生间设施等。有一点可能观念不同,就是该房东负责的事务切莫越俎代庖,否则可能会闹出矛盾来的。

Situational Dialogs 情景对话

老房子总是容易出现问题,李康(Li Kang)租住的房子不仅空调坏了,房顶还开始漏水。

Something Wrong at Home 46

家什故障

Dialog 1

Clerk: Hello, this is Rainier Real Estate. May I help you?
您好,兰尼埃房产公司。能帮您吗?

Li Kang: Yes. I'm a tenant of 722 South Carlton Street in Pullman. There is something wrong with the air-conditioner.
是的,我是在普尔曼的南卡尔顿街722号的租户。空调有些问题。

Clerk: Which trailer are you referring to?
您说的是哪一家的?

Li Kang: Number 2.
第二家。

Clerk: What seems to be the problem?
可能是什么问题呢?

Li Kang: The machine doesn't work properly. It can't produce cold air. It's very hot these days.
机器运转不正常,没有冷空气出来,这几天很热。

Clerk: I'm sorry for that. There're two switches on the wall beside the middle window. One is for the heater and the other is for the air-conditioner. To operate the air-conditioner, which one do you switch?
对此我感到抱歉。中间窗户旁边的墙上有两个开关,一个是暖气开关,一个是空调开关。开空调您用的哪一个?

Li Kang: I switched the upper one.
我开的上头的那个。

Clerk: You've got the right one. Does the machine make very loud noise?
您开对了,机器有很大的噪音吗?

Li Kang: Yes, I think so.
我想是的。

Clerk: I'll have it repaired sometime Wednesday morning. Anybody at home then?①
我会安排人星期三上午来修理,那个时间有人在家吗?

Li Kang: Yes, I am free every Wednesday.
有,我每个星期三都有空。

Dialog 2

Mender: Hello, sir. I'm coming to repair the air-conditioner.
您好，先生。我是来修空调的。

Li Kang: Hello. I'm waiting for you every minute.
您好。我正在等您呢。

Mender: Would you please switch it to "ON"?
请把开关拨到"ON"的位置。

Li Kang: All right, sir. How long can you make it work properly?
好的，先生。您要多长时间能把它修理好？

Mender: It depends.②
这要看情况。
……

Mender: It's finished. Please turn it on and see if you get cold air.
修好了，请帮我开一下，看看是否有冷空气。

Li Kang: What was the matter?
什么问题？

Mender: It's too old. It's twenty-eight years old and no more freon.
太旧了，28年了，氟利昂也没有了。

Li Kang: Is it that old? No wonder.
那么旧了吗？难怪。

Mender: Yes, no wonder. I came at 9:30 and now it's 11:25. Would you please verify my working time here today?
是，难怪。我9:30来的，现在是11:25，请您证实一下我今天到这里工作的时间，好吗？

Li Kang: How?
怎么做？

Mender: Please sign here.
请在这儿签字。

Li Kang: All right.
好的。

Mender: Thank you very much. The machine is working properly now.
非常感谢，机器现在工作正常了。

Li Kang: Thank you for repairing the air-conditioner.
谢谢您来修理空调。

Something Wrong at Home

家什故障

Dialog 3

Clerk: Y & C Properties. May I help you?
Y & C 房产公司,能帮您忙吗?

Li Kang: It rained hard last night. Water came down through the leakage inside the closet. I think there is a leakage in the roof of the house.
昨晚下了大雨。水顺着衣柜里的裂缝流了下来,我想是屋顶有了裂缝。

Clerk: I feel upset to hear that. Did the rain bring any trouble to you?
听到这话我感到不安。这场雨给您带来麻烦了吗?

Li Kang: It's nothing, but just a few of my clothes have got wet.
没关系,但衣柜的衣服湿了几件。

Clerk: I'm sorry. The house is almost 100 years old. But believe me, I'm having the roof mended today.
不好意思。房子差不多100年了,但相信我,我这就安排人今天去维修房顶。

Li Kang: Okay. I'm waiting for your workers.
好的,我等着您的工人们。

典型句型

1) My TV set is out of order.
我的电视机出了问题。

2) There is something wrong with the air-conditioner.
空调有些问题。

3) The machine doesn't work properly. It can't produce cold air.
机器运转不正常,没有冷空气出来。

4) The faucet in the bathroom has something wrong.
卫生间的水龙头有问题。

5) How long can you make it work properly?
您要多长时间能把它修理好?

6) The machine is working properly now.
   机器现在工作正常了。

7) Thank you for repairing the air-conditioner.
   谢谢您来修理空调。

8) Water came down through the leakage inside the closet.
   水顺着衣柜里的裂缝流了下来。

9) I think there is a leakage in the roof of the house.
   我想是屋顶有了裂缝。

10) Does the machine make very loud noise?
    机器有很大的噪音吗?

11) What seems to be the problem?
    可能是什么问题呢?

背景知识

　　家用电器维修问题：在这一点上西方人与我们的做法有些不同,值得我们了解:(1)预约:与其他任何事情一样,家里有东西坏了,需要找人来修理。先打电话去约个时间,请求派人上门维修或者送到维修服务公司去。(2)收费标准:对于很多大件家电的维修,如冰箱、空调等都是派人上门服务,价钱是不能事先说好的,但可以了解收费办法,一般情况下是按照维修人员的工作时间计算劳动价格(labor),再加上更换的零部件的成本(cost of parts)。(3)交费方法:公司派人上门服务,工作人员不能直接收钱。作为顾客的你只需要在工作记录单上注明从几点工作到几点,并签名。然后公司再邮寄账单给你,你再把填好的支票邮寄到公司。

　　家用物品词语：因各家喜好和习惯不同,不同的家庭会拥有不同的家用物品,主要有:

air-conditioner 空调机　　　　　　bookcase 书架;书橱
answering machine 电话答录机　　　closet 衣柜
bathroom 浴室,厕所　　　　　　　 computer 电脑
bathtub 浴缸　　　　　　　　　　 cupboard 碗橱

46 Something Wrong at Home 家什故障

dish washer 洗碗机
dryer 吹风机
dust catcher 吸尘器
DVD player DVD 播放机
electric iron 电熨斗
flush toilet 抽水马桶
grill 烧烤架
hand shower 手握式淋浴器
heater 供暖器
ironing board 烫衣板
laptop 便携式电脑
laundry drier 干衣机
LCD TV set 液晶电视机
microwave oven 微波炉
mower 割草机
MP3 player MP3 播放器
oven 烤箱
pan 平底锅

printer 打印机
refrigerator 冰箱
rice cooker 电饭锅
shoe cabinet/storage 鞋柜
steam and dry iron 蒸汽电熨斗
stove 炉灶
tea table 茶几
television set 电视机
toaster 烤面包片器；烤面包炉
toilet 座便器
TV bench 电视柜
typewriter 打字机
VCD player VCD 播放机
VCR 录像机
wall cabinet 壁橱
wardrobe 衣柜
washing machine 洗衣机

注释 Notes

① 这是一个简略问句。口语中人们常常省略很多次要的句子成分，而直接说出主要部分，如 Anyone in?（有人在家吗？）就是 Is there anyone who is in? 的省略形式。

② It depends. 表示对某件事没有把握时说的，如同汉语的"看情况吧"、"到时候再说吧"等。

A Traffic Accident
交通意外

Topic Introduction
话题导言

月有阴晴圆缺，人有旦夕祸福。我们每天都在祈求平安，但我们仍然时常亲眼目睹或亲身经历我们都不愿见到的种种灾难。交通意外是现代社会中人类生命和财富的一大杀手。万一遇到交通事故，该怎么表达以及人们会说哪些话，也是我们应该关注的问题。

一旦出了意外，应立刻打911电话报告警察并叫来救护车，打电话时可说：There's been an accident on the highway.（高速公路上出了交通事故。）；如有人受伤，就说：Some people have been hurt in the accident.（有人在车祸中受伤。）；如有人死亡，就说：Some people have died in the accident.（有人在车祸中丧生。）注意看路边的标志，说出地点方位。如遇自己卷入交通事故，应迅速自救，包括拨打911。

Situational Dialogs
情景对话

高卫平(Weiping)可真够倒霉的，瞧他这天遇上的车祸。而刘杭(Liu Hang)则目睹了交通事故。

A Traffic Accident   47

Dialog 1

Weiping: It seems① my leg is broken?
我的腿好像断了。

Stranger: Do you have any pain? Is it serious?
痛吗？严重吗？

Weiping: Yes, I can't stand up. I feel acute pain in the left leg. It seems I had my shoulder hit, too.
是的，我站不起来。我感到左腿剧烈疼痛。我的肩膀似乎也撞伤了。

Stranger: Should I call for the police?
需要我去叫警察吗？

Weiping: Of course. Let's go to hospital first.
当然。我们先一起去医院吧！

Stranger: I carry automobile liability insurance. Would you offer it to the insurance company?
我有汽车责任保险。请你向保险公司提出赠偿要求，好吗？

Weiping: No, I don't know those such things. Will I have it paid by the insurance?
我不懂这些东西。我将会得到保险公司的赔偿吗？

Stranger: Yes. My insurance company will contact you.
是的。我的保险公司将和你联系。

Dialog 2

Stranger: Help, help!
救命，救命！

Liu Hang: Where's your hurt?
您伤到哪里了？

Stranger: I've lost my sense② in the left leg. It seems to me it is broken.
我左腿失去了知觉，好像断了。

Liu Hang: Don't worry; I can't see any cuts in your leg.
别担心，您的腿上看不到伤口。

Stranger: Please give me your hand because I can't stand up now.
请帮个忙，我站不起来。

生活流畅美语

Liu Hang:	You'd better be sent to hospital. Where is the telephone? 最好送您到医院去。哪里有电话？
Stranger:	Don't let the driver escape from here. I have a mobile telephone in my bag. 别让司机逃跑了，我包里有移动电话。
Liu Hang:	The policemen have been here and the driver is talking to them. 警察已经来了，司机正和他们说话。
Stranger:	Is the telephone through to the hospital? 电话打到医院去了吗？
Liu Hang:	Yes, the ambulance is coming right now. Anything else I can do for you? 是的，救护车马上就来。还要我帮别的忙吗？
Stranger:	Please call 789-7264 to ask for my friend Bill. 请打电话789-7264叫我的朋友比尔来。
Liu Hang:	Okay. 好的。

Typical Sentences
典型句型

1) Do you have any pain?
   你痛吗？
2) Where were you hit?
   你伤在哪里？
3) It seems I had my shoulder hit.
   我的肩膀似乎撞伤了。
4) Should I call for the police?
   需要我去叫警察吗？
5) Do you know where the nearest hospital is?
   您知道最近的医院在哪儿？
6) Let's go to hospital.
   我们一起去医院吧！

A Traffic Accident

7) Would you offer it to the insurance company?
请你向保险公司提出赔偿要求,好吗?

8) I carry automobile liability insurance.
我有汽车责任保险。

9) I will have it paid by the insurance.
我将会得到保险公司的赔偿。

10) What is the procedure?
我应该办什么手续?

11) My insurance company will contact you.
我的保险公司将和你联系。

12) Show me your driver's license please.
请出示您的驾驶执照。

背景知识

公路杀手:美国人喜欢在高速公路上驾车是很明显的。据说,在美国汽车可以到达任何地方,密如蛛网的公路是人们生活中天天都要打交道的。公路,特别是高速公路,限制了你的驾驶速度,包括最高速度限制和最低速度限制。也就是说,你既不能开得太快也不能开得太慢。开得太快,容易出问题是人人都知道的,而太慢又容易出现交通阻塞。要开好车,必须训练有素。美国公路交通的方便、快捷为世人所知,然而不幸的是,公路交通事故造成的死亡人数也占据了美国死亡人数的大部分。据说,死在公路上人数已经超过了美国自独立战争以来的在所有战争中的阵亡人数。美国人民为他们现代化的交通付出了最惨重的代价,交通事故就是夺去这些生命的杀手。

避免意外:人的生命只有一次,任何人都不会拿生命开玩笑。避免交通意外就是珍惜自己的生命。据统计,飙车是交通事故的主要原因。实际上,很多情况下我们事后想一想都可以避免事故的发生,只要:(1)严格遵守交通规则,听从交通警察的指挥;(2)确保汽车上路之前没有任何安全隐患;(3)遇到坏天气,宁可不出车。此

外,笔者发现,粗心大意在很大程度上是造成交通意外的祸首,如有个大巴司机仗着自己技术精湛,一边高速行车,一边看报纸,一不小心就把前面的小车撞飞了。

注 释

① seem 的句型比较灵活:It seems to sb. that ... (看起来……),如:
It seems to me that you have known the secret. (在我看来,你是知道了秘密。)
也可以说 sb seems to do ...,如:
He seems to need a wife. (他看来需要一个妻子。)
还有 sb. seems ...,如:
She seems (to be) very happy these days. (她这些天看来很高兴。)

② sense 在这里的意思是"知觉,感觉",另外它用作名词还可以表示"道理,识别力",如:
She talks a lot of good sense. (她讲的很有道理。)

Acknowledgements（致谢）

本系列能够以目前这种状态面世，得感谢很多人：德高望重的我国著名英语教育家、英语语法学界权威张道真教授，多年以来对笔者的教导和关心；广州乃至全国许多高校的前辈和同行，从他们身上笔者学到了很多东西，尤其值得一提的有恩师胡光忠教授、周力教授；美国爱达荷大学（the University of Idaho）的 Edwin Krumpe 博士、Steven Hollenhorst 博士和我的美国同学 Andrew Stratton、Natalie Meyer 以及路易斯安那州萨夫市 W. W. Lewis 中学校长 Oci McGuire 夫妇等都曾从不同方面给我以帮助；北京大学出版社外语编辑室的编辑们为本系列的选题、编校付出了辛勤的劳动；特别值得一提的是，本系列的部分前身是在广东语言音像出版社的有关领导及编辑的帮助下出版的，他们的约稿促使我编写了那个系列；还要提到的有广东涉外经济职业技术学院的刘乐老师，通读了全书初稿并提出了很多很好的意见和建议，还对人物的设计提出了独到的见解；更有其他许多朋友、领导和同事，对书稿的编写工作和出版从不同的侧面给我以支持和鼓励，如张婷婷女士、黄雨鸿先生、赵宁宁小姐、杜传贵先生、胡德奖先生、葛彬女士、何传春女士、王正飞先生等等，恕不一一枚举。

邱立志

2008 年 5 月 5 日